The Conquest of the Karankawas and the Tonkawas, 1821–1859

NUMBER TWENTY
Elma Dill Russell Spencer Series in the West and Southwest

The Conquest of the Karankawas and the Tonkawas

1821–1859

KELLY F. HIMMEL

TEXAS A&M UNIVERSITY PRESS
College Station

The paper used in this book meets the minimum requirements
of the American National Standard for Permanence
of Paper for Printed Library Materials, z39.48-1984.
Binding materials have been chosen for durability.
∞

LIBRARY OF CONGRESS CATALOGING-IN-PUBLICATION DATA

Himmel, Kelly F., 1950–
     The conquest of the Karankawas and the Tonkawas, 1821–1859 / Kelly F. Himmel.
     p.   cm. — (Elma Dill Russell Spencer series in the West and Southwest;
no. 20)
     Includes bibliographical references and index.
     ISBN 0-89096-867-5
     1. Karankawa Indians — History — 19th century.   2. Karankawa Indians — Wars.
3. Karankawa Indians — Government relations.   4. Tonkawa Indians — History —
19th century.   5. Tonkawa Indians — Wars.   6. Tonkawa Indians — Government
relations.   7. Texas — History — 19th century.   8. Texas — Politics and government.   9. Texas — Social conditions.   I. Title.   II. Series.
E99.K23H53   1999
976.4'00497—dc21   98-33376
                                                                      CIP

People know what they do;
they frequently know why they do what they do;
but what they don't know is what they do does.

—MICHEL FOUCAULT

Contents

Preface

Nothing impresses thinking men so seriously as the contemplation of the social struggle, for its immorality offends their moral feelings deeply. Individuals can consider ethical requirements, they have consciences, but societies have none. They overfall their victims like avalanches with irresistible destroying power. All societies, large and small retain the character of wild hordes in considering every means good which succeeds.

— LUDWIG GUMPLOWICZ

The Anglo-Texan conquest of the Karankawas and Tonkawas in the nineteenth century exemplifies the destroying power of the social struggle. In 1821, American Indian groups occupied all of Texas. They supplemented subsistence economies by raiding and by trading captives, horses, and hides for firearms and other European goods in regional, continental, and intercontinental trade networks. Politically, Texas was nominally a part of the disintegrating colonial empire of Spain, but Spanish authority hardly extended beyond the small settlements of La Bahía, San Antonio, and Nacogdoches. By 1859, American Indian groups held only the plains of the northwest and the more isolated mountains and deserts of the far west. They tenuously survived by hunting and raiding. Anglo-Texan farmers, ranchers, and slaveholding planters controlled an agricultural economy that was increasingly linked to the growing world-economy that dominated the eastern two-thirds of the state. United States troops on its border with Mexico and in a chain of military posts from the Red River to the Rio Grande insured the political security of the Anglo-Texan colony. In addition, the Anglo-Texan state had quashed a serious attempt at rebellion among the Tejanos in the far south. Thus, it had cemented its political and economic authority over the contested region between the Nueces and the Rio Grande. Texas had become an integral part of a rapidly expanding, industrializing, and modernizing capitalist state. Evidence exists from world-system theory that incorporation into the modern world-system takes place very quickly, in a forty- to seventy-five-year period, in which there is a definite break in an area's history and extensive political and economic structural transformation.[1] Texas, during the period from 1821 to 1859, experienced such a rupture.

For the Karankawas and the Tonkawas, the period from 1821 to 1859 was particularly devastating. Both were thriving ethnic communities, with a long history in Texas and the southern plains, at the beginning of the period. By 1859, the Karankawas had been driven to extinction on the banks of the Rio Grande, and the remnant of the Tonkawas had been removed from Texas, across the Red River, into Indian Territory. However, because of limitations of space or interest, all of the previous ethnohistories of the Karankawas and the Tonkawas have treated the Anglo-Texan conquest in a perfunctory manner.[2]

In telling this story of conquest, I draw upon a long sociological tradition (see Appendix 1) stemming from Ludwig Gumplowicz's conquest hypothesis and John Hobson's analysis of imperialism at the turn of the century to the later development of world-system theory and the related internal colonialism model.[3] From this tradition one can discern two ideal types of conquest: conquest for expropriation and conquest for exploitation. As ideal types, they represent extreme forms. Therefore, one would expect intermediate forms of conquest to occur and to change over time as the cultural, political, and economic contexts of conquest are constructed and reconstructed by human actors within structural frameworks.[4] Consequently, an analysis of conquest demands a theoretical orientation that not only addresses process and is historically situated, but incorporates multiple levels of understanding social change and sees the conquered as well as the conquerors as social actors. However, the unique qualities of the case under examination, the Anglo-Texan conquest of the Karankawas and the Tonkawas in the nineteenth century, alter to some extent the questions that guide the explication of the sociological dimensions of conquest.

In general, at least four sociological approaches to understanding the processes and outcomes of conquest exist that are applicable to the Western conquest of American Indians: (1) a cultural-evolutionary approach; (2) an analysis of the cultural, economic, and political institutional organization of the conquered group and the conquering group; (3) an analysis of the political, economic, and cultural conditions surrounding conquest; and (4) an analysis of the specific choices made by particular human actors, from both the conquered group and the conquering group. The cultural-evolutionary approach to the study of social change has plagued sociology since the nineteenth century and offers little in the way of understanding the processes and outcomes of conquest. The limited number of categories in these cultural-evolutionary schemes obscures and discounts the variation in social organization among the conquered groups and conquering groups. The use of evolutionary, classificatory schemes to categorize social groups has at times been extremely damaging to the pursuit of knowledge in the case of the indigenous people of Texas. Anthropologist John Swanton carried the evolutionary model to an extreme with his depiction of Texas as a "cultural sink"—an area in which culture was "poorly" or "negatively" developed. However, as early as the 1950s, Andrée Sjoberg and William Newcomb launched a repudiation of the cultural sink hypothesis.[5] Also, the cultural-evolutionary approach neglects history, glosses over process, and leaves no space for human action.

Analysis of the specific cultural, economic, and political institutional organizations of the conquered and conquering groups offers more promise in aiding our understanding of conquest. Yet, I would argue that the circumstances surrounding the specific historical events of conquest assume greater significance in the understanding of conquest as they allow us to look at the processes of conquest. For example, one scholar, using an approach based on type of social organization and population size to explain the conquest of the Americas, collapses the tremendous variation in the processes of conquest into four categories based on outcomes.[6] Thus, reliance on the cultural, economic, and political organizations of the conquered and conquering groups in understanding conquest has many of the same limitations with regard to history, process, and human agency as the evolutionary approach.

Concerning the conditions surrounding conquest, one can identify four broad interactive arenas within which the processes of conquest occur: (1) the geopolitical environment, (2) world-economic or market relations, (3) the culture worlds of the conquerors and the conquered, and (4) the mutual constructions of the cultures of the conquered and conquering groups based on their historical experience with the other and with conquest. At least three distinct geopolitical environments existed in the Texas case. First, one must note the location of the indigenous group in relation to Western capitalist development. Next, one must understand the location of the indigenous group and the colonial group in relation to other competing indigenous groups and colonial groups in the region. The dominant presentation of nineteenth-century Texas history during the twentieth century has been that of a three-way conflict between Anglo-American settlers or the United States, Mexico, and the Comanches and their allies.[7]

Finally, one must take into account the degree of direct administrative and military control available to the colonial state in shaping the actions of the indigenous people and the settlers.[8] A lively debate exists among historians of the American West as to whether increased state control diminished violence between social groups or not. Certainly, increased state control changed the nature of social violence between Anglo-Americans and American Indians from mutual retaliatory raids by relatively unorganized groups with accompanying atrocities to large-scale military actions. At times they resulted in the massacre of large numbers of American Indians, and eventually led to the concentration of defeated Indians on reservations where they were subject to a more low-intensity violence in the form of poor sanitary conditions, inadequate shelter, starvation, and lack of protection from enemies. The geopolitical environment is crucial to understanding the processes and outcomes of conquest by its role in limiting or expanding the choices of action available to social actors.

Closely related to and overlapping the geopolitical environments of conquest are the world-economic or market relations existing during conquest. Incorporation into the market relations of the modern world-system had profound effects upon the indigenous people of North America, as well as those in the remainder of the non-Western world.[9] As a result of increased prosperity and competition engendered by entering into trading relationships with the West, many indigenous groups altered their cultural, economic, and political organizations and their economic and political relationships with other indigenous groups. Of course, the contact between Native America and the West introduced new diseases that played a major role in disrupting and altering American Indian cultures and lives.[10] In addition, deepening levels of incorporation from peripheral trading partners to direct competitors over resources with European-origin settlers led to even more dramatic, disruptive, and rapid changes for indigenous groups.[11] At the same time, European-origin settlers fell subject to the demands of deeper incorporation into the modern world-economy. The overlapping and interrelated geopolitical and world-economic aspects of incorporation into the modern world-system may be processes to some large degree beyond the control of indigenous people, as well as settlers. The idea of the lack of local control over regional and global political and economic conditions and events underpins many accounts of the European–American Indian encounter in Texas prior to the nineteenth century.[12] However, one must take both economic and political conditions into account in any analysis of conquest.

At the cultural level, the degree to which the conquered and conquering groups share, understand, and accept the cultures of the other shapes the processes and outcomes of conquest. The cultural arena includes the constellation of beliefs or ideology that supports what a group believes to be proper diet, dress, land and resource use, activity, institutions, and values. Many researchers see European American racism as central to the outcomes, as well as the processes, of the European American conquests of American Indian groups.[13] I would argue, while not denying the overpowering presence and importance of European American racism, that both conquered groups and conquering groups relied on the resources of their culture and their historical experience with the other to make decisions that guided the processes of conquest. In the Texas case, both settlers and indigenous people had experience with and knowledge of Indians and whites and acted upon that experience and knowledge.

As is clear from the above paragraphs, any theoretical line of inquiry that attempts to shed light on the processes and outcomes of conquest must be complex. The line of inquiry must take into account the changing geopolitical environments and world-economic relations during conquest. Against this backdrop of political and economic conditions, one must address the culture worlds of the conquered and the conquerors and the mutual constructions of those culture worlds. Since conquest takes place within a specific historical context, this line of inquiry would be incomplete without the addition of the fourth approach to understanding conquest—an analysis of the specific choices made by particular human actors, from both the conquered group and the conquering group. In Texas, as in other locations where state-organized people conquered nonstate people, the action of conquest took place in that fluid, ever-changing geographical and social space known as a frontier. Yet this frontier, like others, was an integral part of much larger processes with global connections. In addition to the sociological orientation, this work demands a commitment to history by exploring the range of possibilities available to human actors at any particular moment and by attempting to understand their social world as they did in order to preserve the situation and events as fully as possible.[14] In other words, this theoretical approach takes into account, as much as possible, the actions and motivations of the specific social actors engaged in the events associated with conquest and the manner in which the conditions of conquest noted above limit individual and collective choice and open up new choices.

At this point, I must explain that my conception of human agency is not that of isolated and discrete human actors striving to maximize self-interest. Rather, my conception of human agency derives from a more Meadian perspective that sees human actors as reflective beings, who exist, in a social form, as part of a "social mind" in conjunction with other humans and social structures created by humans. By being able to think about their situation, human actors make proactive decisions based upon their modes of reasoning, their assumptions about the world, and their shared social memories. Of course, I realize that the possibilities accessible to the human actor at the time limit human choice. In addition, I am also aware of the irony inherent in examining the decisions of human actors in a historical perspective, because we are largely unable to predict the outcome of our actions. I proceed from the premise that all people respond to dramatic social change in an understandable way. They seek to maintain the best possible living conditions for themselves as defined by their cultural orientation, and they try to avoid destruction at the hands of enemies.[15]

While both the reader and I would like to know more about what the Karankawas and the Tonkawas thought of their world and the crisis they faced, the lack of historical documents and an oral tradition reflecting the points-of-view of these people and our limited knowledge of their social organization, cultural practices, and social demography restricts such understanding.[16] Both the sources and the theoretical model dictate an Anglo-centric perspective. Yet, it is my hope that the experience of the Karankawas and the Tonkawas during this time emerges not only to help us understand the processes of conquest, but also to give us greater understanding of these earlier inhabitants of Texas.

In summary, the book elaborates the sociological dimensions of the Anglo-Texan conquest of the Karankawas and the Tonkawas. To do so it employs a theoretical approach centered around the conditions of conquest, taking into account human agency. At a more global level, the conditions of conquest include the interrelated and overlapping geopolitical environment and world-economic relations surrounding the conquest. Both conquered groups and conquering groups have limited control over these world-systemic processes. At a more local level, the conditions of conquest coalesce around the degree to which conquered and conquering groups share, understand, and accept the culture world of the other.[17] The mutual constructions of the culture worlds of the other are processes that are shaped by the interaction between the conquered group and the conquering group through the lens of unequal power relationships and each group's historical experience with the other. Finally, this theoretical approach takes into account the individual and collective decisions made by members of the conquered and conquering groups in a time of rapid social change and explores the limits and opportunities for decision and action within the changing conditions of conquest. As a result of this theoretical orientation, this telling of the story of the Anglo-Texan conquest places it within in a larger sociological context: Western imperialism and the expansion of the modern world-system. (For a discussion of the methodological problems associated with this effort, see Appendix 2.)

In addition, it may be useful to present a more detailed preview of the book for readers with diverse interests. Chapter 1 first presents an overview of conditions in Texas in 1821. Next it discusses the development of Anglo-American attitudes and actions toward American Indians during the two centuries of contact before 1821. Finally it focuses on the historical development of the Karankawas and the Tonkawas prior to 1821 and includes descriptions of Karankawa and Tonkawa culture in the nineteenth century. While Chapter 1 sets the stage, Chapter 2 begins the more detailed analysis of the Anglo-Texan conquest of the Karankawas and the Tonkawas. After presenting a brief overview of the economic and political environment of Mexican Texas, the chapter details the Anglo-Texan war with the Karankawas and the peace with the Tonkawas in Mexican Texas. Chapter 3 first summarizes the political and economic changes leading to and continuing during the Republic of Texas. It then shifts to the negotiation of conquest by the Karankawas and the Tonkawas during the era of the republic. Likewise, Chapter 4 begins with a summary of the political and economic environment surrounding the first period of Texas statehood, before shifting to the detailed narrative of the consolidation of the Anglo-Texan conquest of the Karankawas and the Tonkawas. The chapter also contains a brief description of the history of the Tonkawas after 1859. The book is divided into conventional categories for arranging nineteenth-century Texas history, but, I hope, not so rigidly as to obscure the rhythms and breaks of Karankawa and Tonkawa experience.[18] Chapter 5 returns to the more sociological orientation of the book by weaving together a general analysis of the Anglo-Texan conquest of the Karankawas and the Tonkawas centered around the theoretical orientation presented in the preface.

Finally, a note about the spelling of proper names. I have used contemporary names and spellings of geographical features—for example, the San Gabriel River instead of the Río San Xavier and San Saba River instead of Río San Sabá. For European American settlements, I have used the names and spellings current at the time of interest. For example, the reader may note the usage of La Bahía in the portions of the book that deal with the period before 1830 and Goliad in those portions that deal with the period after 1830. In one exception to this policy, San Antonio refers to the Spanish and Mexican religious, civil, and military complex that grew into the present-day city of San Antonio. For personal names, I have followed the spellings as they appeared in the documents or in standard reference works.[19]

Acknowledgments

The people who have commented upon some or all of the manuscript that preceded this book deserve my greatest thanks. First, I would like to dedicate this book to my wife, Mary, whose support and encouragement has been unflagging and indispensable to the completion of the project. I would next like to thank Gideon Sjoberg for his enthusiasm and availability as well as his insight. He guided an earlier version of this work as my doctoral dissertation, and he has been instrumental in the revisions that resulted in this book. I also appreciate the comments and suggestions offered by Andrée Sjoberg, Dale McLemore, Walter Firey, and Ronnelle Paulsen. In addition, the anonymous reviewers for Texas A&M Press not only saved me from several embarrassing errors when I ventured into fields distant from my academic training, but their critical support encouraged me to strive to produce a much better work. However, I take full responsibility for any time I have neglected to follow their advice.

In addition to this personal and academic support, I would also like to thank the staff at the Center for American History at the University of Texas at Austin, the Rio Grande Valley Historical Center at the University of Texas–Pan American, and the inter-library loan office at the University of Texas–Pan American for their courteous and professional help, without which I would have been unable to gather the data for the book. Also I would like to thank the department of sociology at the University of Texas–Pan American for its encouragement and material support.

The Conquest of the Karankawas
and the Tonkawas, 1821–1859

Texas in 1821:
Prelude to Conquest

Texas, in 1821, occupied approximately the eastern half of the present-day state. The Medina River separated it from Coahuila and the Nueces River from Nuevo Santander, while the Red River and the Sabine River separated Texas from the United States. To the north and west of the Balcones Escarpment, which divides the more humid, gently rolling coastal plains from the higher, drier, and, in places, more rugged Edwards Plateau and Rolling Plains, Comanchería sprawled across the southern Great Plains between Texas and New Mexico. The immediate coast of Texas was fringed by barren barrier islands of sand and shell. Within the barrier islands were shallow bays that merged by way of extensive marshes into flat, frequently waterlogged, prairies. In the interior of Texas, there were three main vegetational areas, reflecting changes in soil types and the increase in average annual rainfall from less than twenty-eight inches along the Nueces and Medina Rivers to more than fifty-six inches along the Sabine River. Immediately to the south and east of the Balcones Escarpment, the Blackland Prairies presented an undulating sea of tall grass. Farther east, the Post Oak Savannah contained a mosaic of oak woodlands, on the sandier soils, and tall-grass prairie on the deeper soils. East of the Post Oak Savannah, lay the Piney Woods, an area of dense forest dominated by pines on the uplands and towering hardwoods and patches of tangled undergrowth in the bottom lands.

One of the most striking geographical features of Texas in 1821 was its rivers. The rivers flowed generally from the northwest toward the Gulf of Mexico to the southeast. From west to east they were the Nueces, the Medina, the San Antonio, the Guadalupe, the San Marcos, the Lavaca, the Navidad, the Colorado, the San Gabriel, the Brazos, the Navasota, the San Jacinto, the Trinity, the Angelina, the Neches, and the Sabine. Seven of the first nine were either born in or rejuvenated by a series of remarkable springs that gushed forth at the base of the Balcones Escarpment.

Juan Antonio Padilla, an official of the government of New Spain, commented on the geography of Texas in 1820:

> In this region are seen the finest and most copious springs, rivers, lakes and lagoons, which water it and furnish life to a great number of wild but very useful products—to numerous herds of animals, cattle, buffalo, and other kinds of wild creatures, which furnish the greatest aid to subsistence, to a large number of wild horses, to countless animals of the chase, and to fish, woods, and other valuable products which promise the benefits of the best mineral ores ever seen.[1]

Yet, the rivers were far from an asset to European occupation. They were generally too shallow for navigation. Rather than supplying easy transportation, they served as formidable obstacles to land travel across Texas. Travelers on the Camino Real or San Antonio Road, the dimly marked track that linked Monclova in Coahuila with Nacogdoches in eastern Texas by way of San Juan Bautista on the Rio Grande in Coahuila and San Antonio in southwestern Texas, frequently faced long delays when confronted with the flooded rivers. Even when not in flood, steep, slippery banks and boggy approaches through extensive bottom lands slowed travel. At times the Spanish maintained small garrisons and ferries at the more difficult crossings. Yet, even when the boats were able to transport people across the rivers, horses and mules loaded with baggage still had to swim, at times with disastrous results.[2] Other tracks connected San Antonio with La Bahía, and an even more obscurely marked and difficult trail, the Atascosita Road, threaded its away across the coastal plain from La Bahía to Nacogdoches.

Not only was travel difficult within Texas, but Texas was difficult to reach from the outside world. Its shallow rivers prevented easy access from the Gulf. In addition, Texas had no ports, though the establishment of a port at Matagorda, at the mouth of the Colorado, had been ordered in 1808. Only a few landings existed where goods and people could be off-loaded by small vessels from ocean-going ships anchored offshore. A weekly mail service existed between San Antonio and Chihuahua by way of Monclova. This service provided a tenuous link to New Spain. Overland travel to the outside world, as it was inside Texas, was by way of poorly marked tracks through extensive areas of lands uninhabited by European-origin settlers. For example, despite attempts by José Mares in 1787 and 1788 and Francisco Almangual in 1808 to establish a direct route from San Antonio to Santa Fe, travel required a long and roundabout route from San Antonio to Monclova to Chihuahua to El Paso del Norte to Santa Fe. Even to the United States, overland travel was difficult. Although Nacogdoches was less than 130 miles from Natchitoches, Louisiana, at the head of navigation on the Red River, the journey took as long as five days along a poorly marked road in an area favored by bands of outlaws.[3]

Only a small European-origin population lived in Texas in 1821. Eminent Texas historian Eugene Barker eloquently described the situation:

> In this vast region there were only two villages, with a total population, according to the governor, of 2,516 souls. These were San Antonio and La Bahía, or Goliad. Nacogdoches had been, prior to the revolution and filibustering expeditions which began in 1812, a town of nearly a thousand people, but war and rapine scattered the inhabitants, and when Moses Austin passed through in the fall of 1820 it was entirely abandoned. A few stragglers and American squatters from the vicinity were collected by Seguin and given local organization, as we saw in the summer of 1821; and scattered here and there along the Sabine and Red Rivers were isolated families. Of the four missions near San Antonio, one was deserted, three were occupied and the land cultivated by families from the town, but all were in a state of dilapidation approaching ruin. The two missions near La Bahía were still maintained, but the priests had no real authority, and the Indians came and went at will. There were a few soldiers at La Bahía and a strong garrison at San Antonio, but the ayuntamiento complained that unmounted, unclothed, and without supplies they were useless in the field and a nuisance in the barracks, where they were compelled to eke out a meager subsistence by thieving from the citizens.[4]

However, Texas was not so empty as Barker suggests or so isolated from regional and global political and economic events as its geographical location would indicate. The year 1821 was a pivotal year for Texas in two respects. First, civil and military authority passed from Spain to a newly independent Mexico. Second, while the Anglo-American frontier of settlement reached the Sabine River and Anglo-Americans and American Indians from the United States began to settle informally along the Sabine and Red Rivers a few years earlier, the first formal Anglo-American colony began on the lower Brazos and Colorado Rivers.

The Anglo-Texan conquest of the Karankawas and the Tonkawas in the nineteenth century did not take place in historical isolation.

After the United States broke Native American power in the Trans-Appalachian West, population and economic activity exploded in the Old Southwest. By 1821, the frontier of Anglo-American settlement pushed to the border of Spanish Texas, which had been defined by the Adams-Onís Treaty of 1819 between Spain and the United States.

More directly important for Texas in 1821, the previous decade had been one of revolt and revolution. On September 16, 1810, Father Miguel Hidalgo issued his call for Mexican independence. During the War for Mexican Independence, Texas experienced several rebellions and expeditions led by outsiders to overthrow Spanish authority. These efforts had broad popular support in Spanish Texas, but the Spanish military brutally suppressed them in a campaign in 1813. Yet foreign adventurers, many of them from the United States, continued to attempt to wrest Texas from Spain in the name of Mexican independence.[5] Finally, four years after the apparent suppression of the revolt ignited by Father Hidalgo, Mexico gained its independence through a coalition of conservatives and former royalists, led by Colonel Augustín de Iturbide, who were unhappy over Emperor Ferdinand VII's acceptance of a liberal constitution, and Mexican *criollos*, native-born Mexicans of European descent, who were unhappy over the political domination by Spain and *peninsulares*, Spanish-born Mexicans. The coalition created the Plan de Iguala, which called for an imperial government concentrating power in the hands of the *criollo* elite and the Church, and Iturbide became Emperor Augustín I of the Mexican Empire.

In July of 1821, word of the new regime reached Governor Rafael Martínez in San Antonio. He was asked by Joaquin Arredondo, the military commander of the Internal Provinces, to mark the transfer of power in an impressive ceremony in which each military officer would swear on the hilt of his sword before a crucifix and a book of gospels to be obedient to the Catholic faith, to preserve the independence of the Mexican Empire, and to work for peace and harmony between Europeans and Indians. Then the civil officials, church officials, and the public would take the same oath en masse before an upraised crucifix.[6]

While the United States and Anglo-American settlement expanded toward Texas and Spanish authority evaporated over an economically depressed, demoralized, and, to some extent, depopulated Spanish Texas, pronounced shifts had taken place in Native Texas. Comanche power became firmly entrenched east of the Rockies between the Arkansas River and the Rio Grande, eastward into Texas. Comanche raids for horses and slaves extended to the coast of Texas and deep into Chihuahua, Coahuila, and Nuevo Santander. At the same time, they profitably traded captives, horses, bison meat, and robes to the Spanish and Puebloans in New Mexico.[7]

In Texas proper, the Wichita Confederacy (Tawakonis, Wacos, and Wichitas) abandoned their great trading center on the Red River after the ominous and sudden death of their influential leader Awakahei in 1811.[8] The Wichitas dispersed along the middle Red River, while the Wacos and Tawakonis located their stockaded villages with their distinctive "grass houses" along the middle Brazos, near the site of present-day Waco. The Tonkawas, retreating from the Comanches and immigrant Indians from the United States, hunted and camped in the Post Oak Savannah below the San Antonio Road. They reached the southwestern margin of the woodlands along the San Antonio River by 1820. The Lipans, having felt the full fury of Comanche expansion in the eighteenth century, scattered around the fringes of Comanchería from south-central Texas to the lower Rio Grande to the deserts and mountains of Coahuila and Chihuahua. The Karankawas held on to traditional lands between Galveston Bay and Corpus Christi Bay, but they too suffered from Comanche attacks when they ventured from their coastal marshes.

East of the Brazos, the Akokisas, Bidais, the Hasinai Confederacy, and the Keechis faced a somewhat different problem. They continued to occupy their traditional homeland, where they raised corn, beans, vegetables, and fruits and sold furs and hides to traders who came from Louisiana. Yet, they faced growing competition for land, game, and trading opportunities from Indians who had immigrated into Texas from the United States.[9]

After 1803, American Indians from Louisiana and the Old Southwest began to enter Texas in advance of Anglo-American settlement in search of new homes. At first they came in small groups with Spanish permission. For example, the Tensas requested permission to settle near the coast between the Trinity and the Sabine. The Spanish granted the request provided that they not move farther west, that they obey local officials, and that they inform the Spanish authorities of the activities of foreigners and other Indians in that sensitive area. In 1806 and 1807, 300 families of Attacapas, 104 families of Choctaws, and the remainder of the Coushattas, many of whom had entered Texas earlier, requested and received permission to enter eastern Texas. By 1820,

Padilla estimated the number of immigrant Indians at nearly 2,000, compared with 4,700 for the indigenous people of East Texas. This formal trickle would become an informal flood by the 1820s.[10]

In summary, the European-origin population of Spanish Texas declined substantially during the decade prior to 1821. Civil war and Comanche raids smashed the developing economy, which was already damaged by the loss of Louisiana and the United States Embargo Act of 1808. Expanding Comanche power and the arrival of Native American refugees from the United States threatened Native Texas economies oriented around trade patterns that had developed during the previous sixty years. As 1821 ended with the first settlers for Austin's colony encamped on the lower Brazos and lower Colorado Rivers, Texas was a distant province of the newly independent Mexican state. Its European-origin people struggled to overcome a decade of civil war and faced growing conflict with the Comanches.

Both the Karankawas and the Tonkawas of the nineteenth century were shaped by their interaction with the West and with other Native American social groups prior to the arrival of the Anglo-Texan colonists. This period of encounter led to the unique, historically shaped cultures of the two groups at the beginning of the nineteenth century. Anglo-Texans also developed their own distinctive cultural orientation on the Trans-Appalachian frontier, with distinct attitudes and beliefs about Indians, which the settlers carried with them to Texas.

ANGLO-AMERICANS AND INDIANS: THE CONTEST BETWEEN "SAVAGERY" AND "CIVILIZATION"

The Anglo-Americans who colonized Texas after 1821 were the products of a unique historical process that included two centuries of contact with Indians. This process and experience translated itself into attitudes and beliefs about American Indians that they carried with them to Texas. Anglo-Americans in the colonial period faced the "problem" of the Indian.[11] By necessity, they had to both live with Indians and come to have some understanding of Indians. Of course, Indians had to do the same with the European invaders and their descendants. By the time of the American Revolution, there was a general consensus among Anglo-Americans that Indians represented the past, the "savagery," from which all humankind had emerged or would emerge into "civilization."

However, the revolutionary generation could not assign American Indians to the rubbish heap of the past. In the middle of the eighteenth century, European evolutionary theory mounted an attack on the Americas in a theory of "American degeneration" that argued that the New World contained some combination of biological deficiencies that led to diminished capabilities for growth and development. The argument went so far as to propose that organisms that had flourished in a more favorable environment would be stunted or die if transported to America. As primary evidence for their theory, George Luis Leclerc, comte de Buffon and his followers cited the condition of the American Indian. They portrayed the Indian as feeble, sexually enervated, and lacking in sensation and feeling. For Anglo-Americans to rebut Buffon's theory they were forced to give the Indian the full qualities of humankind—vigor, intelligence, compassion, and, most of all, reason. Thomas Jefferson argued that all that was needed was instruction in the arts of "civilization" until the whites and Indians could live together, intermix, and become one people.[12]

A lively debate emerged in the new republic centered on the fate of the Indians and dominated by Jefferson's argument that Indians, while existing in "savagery," possessed the same rationality and human qualities as Europeans and could be "civilized" by them. During its first few decades, official policy of the United States toward American Indians focused on the basic assumption that Indians would cede land to the United States for use by Anglo-American settlers at low cost. A general expectation persisted that Anglo-American expansion would be a slow and orderly process; after all, it took 150 years for Anglo-American settlers to occupy lands between the Atlantic and the Appalachians. Also, the governing elite agreed that Indians held a surplus of land and that as rational human beings they would recognize this fact. Therefore, official opinion saw the planned fate for American Indians as ultimately humane and honorable, a policy of "expansion with honor," with three possible outcomes: (1) The Indians could withdraw westward and resume their migratory ways, because, in the view of the Anglo-Americans, all Indians were nomadic hunters; (2) They would die of disease or other natural causes as Anglo-American society and culture approached; or (3) They would become assimilated, "civilized," and transformed into white-approved, model Americans and eventually intermarry with and be absorbed into the dominant group.[13]

President Jefferson, in his message to the Miamis, Powtewatamies, and Weeauks of January 7, 1802, expressed the basic tenets of the expansion-with-honor program to the Indians:

> We shall . . . see your people become disposed to cultivate the earth, to raise herds of the useful animals, and to spin and weave, for their food and clothing. These resources are certain; they will never disappoint you: while those of hunting may fail, and expose your women and children to the miseries of hunger and cold. We will with pleasure furnish you with implements for the most necessary arts, and with persons who may instruct you how to make and use them.[14]

However, these gestures to aid Indians along the road to "civilization" also contained offers to buy their lands and dire warnings of the dangers in persisting in traditional lifestyles, as in the following message from Jefferson to Little Turtle, chief of the Miamis, regarding his people:

> We ask nothing of them but their peace and good will, and it is a sincere solicitude for their welfare which has induced us from time to time, to warn them of the decay of their nation by continuing to rely on the chase for food, after the deer and the buffalo are to become too scanty to subsist them, and to press them before they are reduced too low, to begin the culture of the earth and the raising of domestic animals. A little of their land in corn and cattle will feed them much better than the whole of it in deer and buffalo, in their present scarce state, and they will be scarcer every year. I have, therefore, always believed it an act of friendship to our red brethren whenever they wished to sell a portion of their lands to be ready to buy whether we wanted them or not, because the price enables them to improve the lands they retain, and turning their industry from hunting to agriculture, the same exertions will support them more plentifully.[15]

However, the westward expansion of the Anglo-American frontier proved to be much faster than expected. American Indian response proved to be less tractable than expected, and Anglo-American settlers showed little interest in intermixing on a scale that would have produced a peaceful amalgamation. The result was to be a deliberate policy of Indian removal. With the acquisition of Louisiana in 1803, the possibility of Indian removal became a greater reality for the leadership of the United States. President Jefferson went so far as to draft an amendment to the Constitution that would provide for Indian removal:

The legislature of the Union shall have the authority to exchange the right of occupancy in portion where the United States have full rights for lands possessed by Indians within the United States on the East side of the Mississippi: to exchange lands on the East side of the river for those . . . on the West side.[16]

In the Trans-Appalachian West between the end of the American Revolution and the War of 1812, the discourse of "savagery" versus "civilization" frequently took another turn. In the states on the Indian frontier in the last decades of the eighteenth century, the Indian was often regarded as an expendable, inferior savage. Jefferson's vision of civilization was not embraced by Anglo-American settlers. They wanted to expel Indians, not change them.

After 1789 American leaders turned to a policy that tried to combine expansion with permanent occupancy by "civilized" Indians. Yet, they were thwarted by an Anglo-American population greedy for land. They, along with Jefferson, believed that Indians should forfeit lands they did not use in a European manner. As the Indians desperately fought to preserve their lands, their "savage" actions were used to condemn them. The Anglo-Americans failed to temper their greed with morality, and they urged the government to remove or eliminate the "savage," "beast-like" Indians who resisted their advance.[17]

At this time the United States was in the beginnings of a transformation from an agrarian-mercantile capitalism to industrial capitalism characterized by highly specialized and complex interregional specialization supported by the expansion of cotton production in the American South. This transformation was characterized physically by rapid urbanization and development of improved internal transportation. The imperatives of industrial capitalism increasingly compelled Anglo-Americans to a possessiveness that equated morality with the accumulation of property and successful participation in the market economy. The market revolution had two profound impacts on Anglo-American and Indian relationships: (1) The demand for Indian lands grew, and (2) Indians who failed to acculturate assumed an even more degraded position in the eyes of Anglo-Americans. For example, Jefferson pointed to the example of some Cherokees who had sold their surplus of corn and cattle at the market in Knoxville and spent the proceeds on clothes, tools, and other consumer goods, rather than giving it away to their own "lazy" people as a model for "less civilized" Indians to make the transition to the market economy.[18]

By the outbreak of the War of 1812, Anglo-Americans and American Indians were living in close proximity to one another across all of the Old Southwest and west of the Mississippi in Louisiana and eastern Missouri, with a pocket of Anglo-American settlement on the Arkansas River, below present-day Little Rock. In the Old Northwest, the frontier of settlement reached Detroit, Fort Dearborn (Chicago), and the Mississippi River. A considerable American Indian population continued to live west of Ohio.[19]

General William Henry Harrison dealt organized American Indian resistance in the Old Northwest a severe blow with his defeat of Tecumseh's forces, under the leadership of the Shawnee Prophet, on the Tippecanoe in 1811. Nevertheless, the War of 1812 became an excuse for a massive assault on American Indian power beyond the Appalachians. General Harrison defeated the British and the remnants of Tecumseh's confederacy on the Thames.

More telling of Indian-white relations was General Andrew Jackson's slaughter of almost eight hundred Creeks at Horseshoe Bend. The campaign of 1813–14 was marked by the rhetoric of savagery versus civilization in which the Creeks were demonized as "savage dogs," "bloodthirsty barbarians," and "cannibals that reveled in . . . carnage." It culminated in an orgy of bloodletting. The soldiers cut strips of skin from the dead Indians for use as bridle reins. They looted the corpses for souvenirs, and in an eerie foreshadowing of later wars of American imperial embroilment, the soldiers cut off the tip of each dead Indian's nose to establish an official "body count." Interestingly enough, a young Sam Houston, who was to play such an important role in Indian-white relations in Texas, fought in Jackson's army at Horseshoe Bend and received a disfiguring arrow wound in his thigh.[20]

Horseshoe Bend was neither the first nor last such incident of extreme violence in the conquest of North America. Only forty-one years before, the Washington County, Pennsylvania, militia bound, hacked to death, scalped, and burned ninety-six peaceful, Christian Indians in Gnadenhutten, Ohio, in retaliation for "atrocities" committed by warlike Indians. Yet, Horseshoe Bend was used by Jackson to give violence against Indians a moral quality, a legitimacy, which was to have tragic consequences for the countless victims of American imperial expansion. In the aftermath of the carnage at Horseshoe Bend, General Jackson reassured his militia of frontiersmen: "How lamentable it is that the path to peace should lead through blood, and over the carcasses of the slain!!

But it is in the dispensation of that providence, which inflicts partial evil to produce general good."[21]

The Indian campaigns of the War of 1812 allowed the U.S. government to coerce massive land cessions from the Indians. Immediately after the war, millions of acres of land west of the Appalachians were transferred from Indian nations to the U.S. government. In particular, these years immediately after the War of 1812 saw the nation's first great cotton boom in response to the burgeoning demand for cotton to feed the textile mills of England—the beginning of modern industrial capitalism. The price of cotton reached thirty-five cents per pound in Charleston in January, 1818, before tumbling sharply after the Panic of 1819. The cotton boom put even more pressure on the Indians of the Old Southwest to yield their lands to the newcomers, and encouraged the southwestern push by Anglo-American settlers toward Texas. These events left American Indians between the Appalachians and the Mississippi at the mercy of Anglo-American settlers who saw Indians as another obstacle in their fight for survival and a government that saw Indian removal, to new homes beyond the Mississippi, as the only solution to the Indian "problem" in the United States.[22]

Even among Anglo-Americans who did not live on the frontier the image of the degraded, savage Indian became firmly entrenched during this period. The captive narrative had become a staple of popular American literature by 1800. The Indian was portrayed as the savage brute, the bloody savage, who terrorized the frontier. In lurid detail this literature described people tomahawked, the skulls of infants smashed against boulders and tree trunks, and women and children carried into the most degrading captivity. Even more sober accounts of Indians on the American frontier still presented a stereotype of the savage Indian—either living as noble hunters beyond the frontier or in degraded, diseased, debased drunkenness on the frontier.[23] These portrayals refused to recognize that many Indians were farmers, some were traders, and all maintained diverse and successful social orders in a world increasingly dominated by hostile Anglo-Americans.

Yet, other Anglo-Americans on the frontier saw American Indians in a different light. From shortly after their arrival in the New World, European settlers lived with and among American Indians. Some forsook their own world for years or a lifetime, and many came to respect the world of the other.[24]

It was this experience with Indians that the Anglo-Americans brought with them to Texas. The frontier nurtured both violence and tolerance. Indeed, during the long development of the Anglo-American and Spanish American frontiers in North America, European settler and Native American interests coincided at times, as in the development of the fur and hide trade. At the individual level some Europeans found life among Native Americans freer, and some Native Americans found life among the Europeans easier. However, this long period of mutual acculturation began to end in the first decades of the nineteenth century. A continent peopled by yeoman farmers as envisioned by Jefferson could not coexist with indigenous economies and cultures. Whetted by the greed and rapacity inherent in the market revolution, the discourse of "savagery" versus "civilization" had become a call for extermination.

THE KARANKAWAS

When Cabeza de Vaca and the other survivors of the disastrous Narvaez expedition washed ashore on the Texas coast in the late fall of 1528, they likely encountered the ancestors of the Karankawas. Betweeen the sixteenth century and the eighteenth century, at least five divisions of Karankawas lived along the Texas coast: the Capoque, also known as Cocos, in the vicinity of Galveston Island; the Cujanes, near the mouth of the Colorado; the Karankawas, in the vicinity of Matagorda and San Antonio Bays; the Coapites, around Aransas Bay; and the Copanos, between Copano Bay and Corpus Christi Bay. Each division contained at least four hundred people, and possibly more divisions were present at the time of European contact. During the spring and summer period of seasonal food scarcity along the bayshore, the divisions dispersed into smaller bands of thirty or forty individuals and moved to interior locations, where they possibly engaged in cooperative hunting ventures and traded with their interior neighbors. The larger divisions then recoalesced at bayshore locations during the fall and winter period of seasonal food abundance. The Karankawas remained within this well-defined geographical location through much of the historic period. In addition, archeologists have linked the Karankawas with coastal people who shared a similar lifeway for some five hundred years before contact and continued through the early historic period.[25]

For nearly two hundred years after Cabeza de Vaca left the Texas coast, the Karankawa-European encounter consisted of the occasional shipwrecked sailor who washed ashore on the Karankawa coast and left no record, with one notable exception. In 1685, a French expedition, led by René-Robert Cavelier, Sieur de La Salle, landed on the shores of Matagorda Bay, having missed its destination, the mouth of the Mississippi, by more than four hundred miles. With one of the three ships carrying the French colonists wrecked, La Salle made the decision to move inland. He ordered a log stockade and cabins built on the banks of Garcitas Creek, at a slight elevation about five miles above its mouth. After initial friendly relations, hostilities broke out between the French settlers and the neighboring Karankawas. Without their leader, who was murdered by one of his own men while searching for the mouth of the Mississippi, the French colony struggled with disease and strained relations with the Karankawas. When a Spanish expedition looking for the French colonists reached Fort St. Louis in April, 1689, they found the stockade plundered. Eventually, the Spaniards recovered five French settlers; two more preferred to remain with the Karankawas.[26]

More importantly for the Karankawas, the French intrusion galvanized Spanish will to occupy Texas. By 1722, Spanish settlement by way of Coahuila reached the Texas coast when an expedition led by Marqués San Miguel de Aguayo founded the mission Espíritu Santo de Zúñiga on Garcitas Creek, opposite and upstream from the ruins of Fort St. Louis, and a presidio, Nuestra Señora de Loreto, on the site of the ruins. The location proved as unhealthy for the Spanish as it had for the French. The Karankawas showed little interest in the mission. In 1726, the Spanish relocated the mission and the presidio to the Guadalupe River, above present-day Victoria, and, in 1749, to a site on the San Antonio River, which formed the nucleus of the Spanish settlement of La Bahía. In 1754, in order to separate the Karankawas from the Aranamas at La Bahía, the Spanish located a new mission for the Karankawas, Nuestra Señora del Rosario, some four miles to the west. From 1781 until 1789, the friars abandoned Mission Rosario due to Karankawa resistance. The Spanish opened a final mission for the Karankawas, Nuestra Señora del Refugio, at the confluence of the Guadalupe and San Antonio Rivers in 1793, at the request of two Karankawa headmen, Frejada Pinta and Llano Grande. In mid-summer of 1794, the Spanish removed the mission to Los Mosquitos, on the Guadalupe below its junction with the San Antonio. Finally, in January, 1795, the Spanish relocated the mission on Mission Creek, near the present site of Refugio. In December, 1806, the Spanish abandoned Mission Rosario and transferred the neophytes to Mission Refugio.[27]

The fifteen years prior to the reopening of Mission Rosario in 1789 were turbulent years for the Karankawas of the central coast. In 1778,

Karankawa headman José Maria led a band that allegedly attacked a stranded Spanish ship in Matagorda Bay. According to Spanish reports, they plundered the ship and murdered the captain, Louis Landrin, his twelve-year-old son, and all of the crew, except for one man of Indian descent from the Yucatan. The Landrin incident incited the fury of the Spaniards. As a result, the Spanish Indian agent and commandant at Natchitoches, Athanase de Mézèires, proposed an elaborate plan for a war of extermination and removal aimed at the Karankawas to Governor Croix in October, 1779.[28]

The Spanish authorities in San Antonio failed to carry out their plans because of a lack of funds for such a campaign and the need to use their limited military resources to protect San Antonio from the Lipans. However, hostilities prevailed between the Karankawas and the Spaniards for the next decade. During that time, the few Karankawas in the missions fled to their villages on the coast. By 1790, José Maria had died after a late conversion to Christianity, and the Lipan attacks had reached the Karankawas on the central coast. As a result, the Karankawas were ready to turn to the Spanish for help.[29]

The José Maria years marked an important turning point for the Karankawas of the central coast. First, a leader emerged that united elements of the heretofore autonomous divisions of the Karankawas. As a result, the Karankawas became a more cohesive political unit. Second, José Maria began a tradition of powerful and possibly hereditary band leaders that continued through the Anglo-Texan conquest. Third, the Karankawas, despite continued resistance and hostilities, came to look upon the Spanish, and later the Mexican, authorities at La Bahía as a source of protection when confronted with powerful outsiders. Fourth, the Karankawas became part of the larger pattern of smuggling, salvaging, and piracy that dominated the economy of coastal Texas during Spanish rule. Finally, as we shall see later, the European construction of the Karankawas as vicious cannibals came to dominate European thinking about Karankawas.

During the last fifteen years of Spanish rule, some Karankawas continued to use the mission established for them on an occasional basis as a part of their subsistence activities, but intensifying Comanche raids discouraged the Karankawas from using the mission. The priests and the Karankawas abandoned Mission Refugio in 1824 for the safety of La Bahía. At the time the Mexican government's order of secularization was executed on February 8, 1830, twelve Karankawas with their chief and eight Cocos remained attached to the mission.[30]

For the Karankawas around Galveston Island, the Spanish period had somewhat different consequences. The Spanish did not establish a mission for them on the upper coast. However, some Cocos relocated to the short-lived Mission Nuestra Señora de Candelaria on the San Gabriel during the middle of the eighteenth century. As a result, the Cocos became associated with some elements of the Tonkawas, particularly the Mayeyes. During the last three decades of the eighteenth century, the Cocos oriented themselves toward the other trading peoples of southeast and south-central Texas: the Akokisas, Attacapas, Bidais, Tonkawas, and some elements of the Lipans. The trading relationships between the Cocos and their neighbors certainly predated the last three decades of the eighteenth century.

At the time of Cabeza de Vaca, the Karankawas, or at least the Cocos of the upper coast, carried on a lively trade with their interior neighbors. Archeological evidence and the Cabeza de Vaca account indicate the following pattern of precontact Karankawa trade on the upper coast. The Karankawas supplied dried or smoked fish, seaweed, sea beans, shells, feathers, shark teeth, and oyster-shell knives and scrapers in return for maize, hides, sandstone, flint, ceramics, red ochre, deer-hair tassels, and stone beads.[31] The presence of European-origin goods would have made some of these commodities less valuable as glass and metal replaced shell and stone for ornaments and tools. Others, such as hides, became more valuable after European contact.

The salvage goods on the coast undoubtedly enhanced the trading position of the Karankawas in relation to their American Indian neighbors by providing them with access to European-origin goods outside of European-controlled trade channels. However, trade opportunities for the Karankawas of the middle coast were limited by the destruction of most of the American Indian people of the Rio Grande Plains. By 1790, disease, Lipan and Comanche raids, and missionization had virtually destroyed the indigenous people of the interior of South Texas. On the upper coast, by the last third of the eighteenth century, the Cocos were trading directly with Europeans, although European trade goods had certainly reached the Cocos earlier in the eighteenth century.[32]

In 1772, Captain Luis Cazorla, while traveling along the Atascosita Road from La Bahía to Orcoquisa, at the mouth of the Trinity, found the Cocos, with some Karankawas, Bidais, and apostate Aranamas, near the mouth of the Brazos River hunting deer for British traders. When Cazorla reached Orcoquisa, he met more Cocos, Akokisas, Attacapas, and Bidais, who were awaiting the arrival of British traders who came up the Trinity River from the Gulf by ship. Two years later in a letter to Governor-General Unzaga y Amezaga, de Mézèires reported that thirty families of apostate Cocos and Karankawas were living at the mouth of the Trinity River and selling horses and mules stolen from La Bahía to traders from Louisiana. Yet, during the first two decades of the nineteenth century, neither John Sibley, the U.S. Indian agent at Natchitoches, nor Juan Padilla considered the Cocos to be active in trade with either the Spanish or the Americans, though Padilla did include them among the "friendly tribes" of Texas in 1820.[33] However, they became among the first Karankawas to feel the impact of Anglo-American expansion.

After the United States expelled the self-styled buccaneer Jean Lafitte from his base, Barataria, in southeast Louisiana, he relocated on Galveston Island and built a new headquarters, Campeachy, in 1817. At first the Karankawas of the upper coast befriended the people of Lafitte's settlement. Soon disputes over alleged Karankawa thievery and abuse of Karankawa women by Lafitte's men led to violence that permanently removed the Karankawas from Galveston Island. In addition, the presence of the Lafitte enterprise greatly stimulated trading activities along the northwest Gulf Coast. The Lafitte settlement on Galveston Island found it more profitable to trade their booty to the Indians than to sell it to traders in New Orleans.[34]

The Karankawas did not cultivate crops but relied on hunting and gathering for their food. They geared their subsistence activities toward the marshes and bays, prairies and woodlands of the Gulf Coast. As such we would expect that they would orient their ceremonial life toward the hunting and fishing activities that sustained them. Unfortunately, we have limited knowledge of the Karankawas' ceremonial life world.

In 1839, Alice Oliver, who lived at Port Austin on the Texas coast, observed a Karankawa celebration after a successful fishing or hunting expedition. According to Oliver, they made a large fire inside a hut, drank a beverage they prepared from the leaves of the yaupon and chanted all night to the music of gourd rattles, reed whistles, and a fluted piece of wood over which they drew a stick to produce a droning sound. At the same time, a shaman, clothed in animal skins, danced around the fire. A few years earlier, Annie Harris had observed a similar ceremony that was performed in a tent at the full moon.[35]

There exists some evidence that the mythic world of the Karankawas centered around two forces, each with its own shamans, who also served as healers. The life force, which was called *Pichini* and represented by the colors white or red, ordered celebrations that affirmed the existence of the Karankawa. In these festive rituals, the Karankawas used turtle-shell or gourd rattles, reed whistles, and the *avacasele*, an unidentified musical instrument, which was perhaps the same as the fluted piece of wood and stick that Oliver and Harris described. In the funeral rituals, which were ordered by the death force *Mel* and represented by the colors black or blue, the Karankawas played the *cayman*, another unidentified musical instrument.[36]

By the 1830s, perhaps in response to the increased numbers of untimely deaths from disease and warfare, Karankawas practiced more simplified funeral rituals. After brief lamentations, the son and nephew of the dead leader Francisco "stretched him on the ground, broke his bows and arrows, and his rough musical instrument, and wrapped him in his blanket, first binding these articles in a rough bundle on his chest. Having obtained a rope they bound this around the body and literally dragged it off for burial."[37] The observers, Annie Harris's family, found the actions of the Karankawas unfeeling.

We know even less about other aspects of the social world of the Karankawas than we do about their ceremonial life. By the latter half of the eighteenth century, the Karankawa divisions had civil and military leaders, who tended to be hereditary.[38] As noted earlier, this pattern had become well entrenched, in conjunction with band consolidation and the uneasy alliance with the Spanish by the end of the eighteenth century.

In addition, the Karankawas had a third gender of biological males who had distinct social roles that resembled those of women. This third gender is known as the *berdache*. Among many American Indian peoples there was institutionalized acceptance of people taking on roles that were different from the normative roles for their biological sex. They may have performed special ceremonial roles. In work, behavior, and dress, male *berdache* took on some of the roles and characteristics assigned to women. Sexually, they may have been asexual or the passive sexual partners of men. They were neither men nor women. They were an alternative gender whose role consisted of a mixture of diverse elements.[39]

In the Karankawa world, the *berdache*, according to Cabeza de Vaca, "dressed like women and perform the office of women, but use the bow and carry big loads." In the eighteenth century, the *berdache*, or *monanquias*, as Fray Gaspar José de Solís rendered their name, went on campaigns with the warriors to be their sexual partners and to drive off the horses and mules during the raids. Apparently, they were quite strong, did much of the burdensome work, and served as sexual partners to the men who were men. As the Karankawa world disintegrated in the middle-nineteenth century, the *monanquias* lost some of their earlier status. However, this may reflect the intense disdain many Western observers felt when confronted with "men who were not men" or changes in the Karankawa world view after more than a century of close contact with the West.[40]

Physically, the Karankawa men were taller than most American Indians, and they were considered handsome by European standards. The women were short and stocky. All Karankawas wore little or no clothing. However, they did wrap themselves in skins and blankets to protect themselves from the winter cold. They also adorned themselves with paint and tattoos and wore ornaments made of shells, rattlesnake rattles, beads, buttons, cloth, feathers and hammered metal. On their heads were often wreaths made of grass or palm.[41]

In the early nineteenth century, the Karankawas continued to make extensive use of the natural resources of their marshy homeland for food. The bays yielded rich harvests of fish and shellfish, waterfowl and bird eggs. Although the bison no longer visited the coastal prairies, deer were numerous in the wooded river bottoms, and the abundant cattle of the coastal plains furnished additional meat and hides. Alligators yielded food and oil that gave the Karankawas a distinct odor that the Spanish referred to as *amizle*. The Karankawas found the rich alligator meat a "great luxury," and they killed them underwater with a sharp knife.[42] Some of the foods eaten by the Karankawas seemed quite unpalatable to European observers, though they did use cornmeal, molasses, and whiskey obtained from the European world. In addition, the coastal plain yielded a variety of seasonably available vegetable foods, including an abundance of roots and tubers.

Because horses were of little use in the marshes and bays, the Karankawas continued to rely on their dugout canoes, hollowed out of large tree trunks, and old skiffs, obtained from settlers, for transportation. The Cocos and others who had a more inland orientation likely made greater use of horses. The shipwrecked French sailor Francois Simars de Bellisle, who lived one year with the Cocos in 1719–20, described a hunt for bison in which horses were used. However, dogs were their most important domesticated animals. They also used an elaborate system of smoke signals to facilitate communication in their marshy homeland.[43]

The Karankawas in the early nineteenth century lived in portable huts or windbreaks constructed of poles and covered with hides or sailcloth. They skillfully used their long bows for both hunting and fishing. The Karankawas made their bows from the wood of the red cedar and stout war clubs from ironwood. After the arrival of the Europeans, they turned away from shell, flint, and garfish scales as the raw material for their arrowheads in favor of glass and metal, even though the use of stone and shell tools continued through the Spanish period. Sibley described a Karankawa arrowhead that he removed from a Spaniard who had traveled the long distance from La Bahía to Natchitoches for medical treatment: "It was made of a piece of an iron hoop, with wings like a fluke and an inche."[44] They also possessed lances, clubs, tomahawks, and long double-edged knives of European manufacture that they carried in deer-skin sheaths. In addition, the Karankawas built cane weirs to trap fish in the shallow bay waters. The Karankawas also made baskets and a distinctive pottery decorated with the tar (asphaltum) that naturally occurred along the Gulf Coast. However, they adopted iron kettles of European origin for cooking and playing as musical instruments.[45]

Finally, there can be no discussion of the culture of the Karankawas without a mention of cannibalism. Most contemporary anthropologists consider the Karankawas to have been ritual cannibals. However, Cabeza de Vaca did not mention cannibalism among the coast people of Texas. In fact, he reported that they were horrified by tales of the stranded Spanish sailors resorting to cannibalism in order to survive on the barren Texas coast. The first vague rumors of cannibalism among the Karankawas came from survivors of the La Salle colony. Later, the shipwrecked French sailor de Bellisle reported that he was an eyewitness to a particularly brutal incident of cannibalism. In de Bellisle's account, the Cocos he was accompanying on a bison hunt into the interior encountered an enemy people, the Toyals. In the ensuing fight, a Toyal man was killed. According to de Bellisle, ". . . one of them cut his head off and another cut the arms off, while they skinned him at the same time. Several of them ate the yellow fat which was still raw, and finally they devoured him completely."[46] De Bellisle's account was widely reported in Europe, and it followed a narrative style that had persisted for more than two hundred years that emphasized the viciousness and the strangeness of the Indian other. In this narrative style, the observer would claim to have witnessed the most depraved activities, cannibalism being a favorite.[47]

However, we can credit Fray de Solís, an official inspector of the Zacatecan college, for turning up the volume of Western accusations of

Karankawa cannibalism and depravity. In his account of his inspection of the mission to the Karankawas in 1768, he stated:

> They are cruel, inhuman, and ferocious. When one nation makes war with another, the one that conquers puts all of the old men and old women to the knife and carries off the little children for food on the way . . .
>
> These Indians are dirty, foul-smelling, and pestiferous, and throw off such a bad odor from their bodies that it makes one sick. They eat locusts, lice, and even human flesh. They relish foul-smelling things and spoiled food, and delight in the odor of the skunk, which they also eat.[48]

It is this sort of cultural construction, concerning cannibalism, food, and hygiene, as well as sexuality and work, that will be part of the focus in understanding the processes of the Anglo-Texan conquest of the Karankawas and the Tonkawas in the nineteenth century. From the earliest days of the European-Indian encounter, Europeans accused Indians of unnatural activities—cross-dressing, body piercing and tattooing, ritual cannibalism, male-to-male sex, and eating "spoiled" food. It was the "unnaturalness" of Indians that separated them from Europeans, and Europeans destroyed Indians to destroy unnaturalness.[49]

Even as late as 1805, John Sibley discounted reports of cannibalism among the Karankawas as a fabrication by the Spanish resulting from the persistent hostilities between Spanish authorities and the Karankawas. Yet, in his report to the U.S. government in 1807, Sibley enclosed an article from the Cincinnati *Gazette* on the Indians of Texas that described the Karankawas as a "treacherous and cruel" people who "invariably EAT their prisoners."[50]

THE TONKAWAS

The Tonkawas, or the Titskanwatits as they called themselves, of the nineteenth century reflect one of the outcomes of a complex set of events put into motion by the movement of Athabascan or Apache peoples into the southern Great Plains and further shaped by the expansion of Spanish, French, Comanche, and Anglo-American power into the region. Despite these massive changes over three centuries, the culture of the nineteenth-century Tonkawas remained anchored in the precontact traditions of the southern plains. At the end of the seventeenth century, the available evidence strongly suggests the presence of at least two culturally similar, Tonkawan-speaking groups in and near Texas: the Tonkawa and the Mayeye.[51]

The social structure and culture of these groups remains poorly known. However, the evidence suggests that they were primarily hunters who exploited the large herds of bison that ranged into the southern plains and that they had deep ties to the northern Caddoans—Wichitas, Keechis, and Pawnees. They were located by European explorers of the late seventeenth and early eighteenth centuries as living northwest of the Hasinai, in what is now central Texas and south-central Oklahoma. The Tonkawa were along and north of the Red River and the Mayeye farther south along the Brazos, Little, and Navasota Rivers. At the beginning of the seventeenth century the Tonkawa were living much farther to the north. Apparently the Oñate expedition in 1601 found the Tonkawas (Tancoa), also a hunting people, living between the Salt Fork of the Arkansas and the Medicine Lodge River, in what is now northwest Oklahoma or south-central Kansas.[52]

Besides the Tonkawan speakers, the Mayeye and the Tonkawas, other ethnic groups contributed to the development of the nineteenth-century Tonkawas. The Ervipiame were hunters and gatherers who lived in northeastern Coahuila at the end of the seventeenth century. They were most likely Coahuiltecan speakers. Another group of hunters and gatherers who lived along the lower Guadalupe and Colorado Rivers in the late seventeenth and early eighteenth centuries and known to the European world as the Cavas, Emet, Sana, Toho, and Tohaha were Sanan speakers. Farther north, a band of Wichita-speaking bison hunters, known to history as the Yojuane, were located by the Oñate expedition along the North Fork of the Canadian River in west-central Oklahoma. By the early eighteenth century, Yojuanes had reached as far south as the Colorado River in their pursuit of the bison.[53]

While the argument persists that the Tonkawas represent the historical cultural manifestation of the late prehistoric hunters and gatherers of central Texas, the ethnohistorical and current archeological data from the years immediately after contact are too sketchy to support this view. Yet, it is clear that the Tonkawas of the late eighteenth and nineteenth centuries had origins in a number of ethnic groups with roots among the nomadic peoples, who spoke several distinct languages, adopted a variety of subsistence strategies, and lived on the wide stretches of the southern plains between the middle Rio Grande and the middle Arkansas River. One of the cultural traits that distinguished the Tonkawas of the late eighteenth century and early nineteenth century from other historic peoples of the southern plains was their persistent use of hunting and gathering strategies, rather than such heavy reliance on the bison or agriculture in conjunction with seasonal bison hunts.[54]

The middle of the seventeenth century saw an acceleration of the Apache invasion from the northwest, southwestward Osage expansion fueled by firearms acquired from the French through the fur trade, and disorganization along and beyond the frontier of Spanish settlement as a result of epidemics and slave-raiding expeditions. These events reshuffled the location and altered the cultural, political, and economic lives of the indigenous people of the southern Great Plains.[55]

As early as 1698, formal contact between the Ervipiames and the West took place when the Spanish created a mission for them in northeastern Coahuila, between the Río Sabinas and the Rio Grande.[56] The Spanish founded new missions on the Rio Grande in Coahuila, between 1699 and 1702, and on the San Antonio River, between 1718 and 1722, which impacted many of the groups that would become Tonkawas later in the eighteenth century.

In the early eighteenth century, the Ervipiames became the nucleus of a Native American group known as the Ranchería Grande. Arising out of the chaotic conditions in Native Texas during the first half of the eighteenth century, the Ranchería Grande consisted of an amalgamation of disparate peoples. Besides the Ervipiames, the Ranchería Grande attracted the remnants of many groups shattered by the Apache and Osage onslaught, epidemics, Spanish slave raiding and missionization. During the first two decades of the eighteenth century, the Ranchería Grande numbered as many as two thousand people. They were frequently hostile to the Spanish. However, in 1722, the Spanish authorized the creation of a mission at San Antonio, San Francisco Xavier de Náxera, in response to the request of the Ervipiame chief of the Ranchería Grande, Juan Rodriquez.[57] The Spanish never built the mission, which was to have been located between San Antonio de Valero and San José.

During the next three decades, the Ranchería Grande, located on the San Gabriel and Little Rivers, became less hostile to the Spanish and an apparent haven for some Tonkawas. Under growing pressure from the Lipan Apaches, the leaders of the Mayeyes, the Ranchería Grande, and the Yojuanes requested that the Spanish authorities establish a mission for them. The Spanish responded by founding the Mission San Francisco Xavier de Horcasitas for the Ranchería Grande, the Mayeyes, and the Yojuanes in 1748. In 1749, the Spanish established Mission Nuestra Señora de Candelaria, for some Cocos and other Karankawas who wandered inland from the coast, and Mission San Ildefonso, for the Bidais, Akokisas, and related groups. The Tonkawa proper probably only came to the missions to trade, although a few Tonkawas may have briefly resided at the missions.[58] The Spanish situated the missions along the San Gabriel River west of its junction with the Little River. In addition, the Spanish located a presidio, San Xavier de Gigedo, in the vicinity of the missions, in 1751, in order to protect them from the Lipans.

The Lipans, under attack themselves from the Comanche-Wichita alliance to the north, harassed the missions. Besides facing the usual problems of desertions, disease, and drought, the missions on the San Gabriel seemed peculiarly ill fated. Strange phenomena frightened the Spanish and the Indians. The missionaries reported a terrifying ball of fire in the sky accompanied by the sound of a powerful explosion. Afterwards the river ceased to run and became polluted to drink. Even the air became toxic to breathe, and deep crevasses opened in the land. The mysterious murder of a priest and another Spaniard over an alleged adultery led to the dismissal of the commandant of the presidio, Don Felipe Rábago de Téran. Finally, in 1756, the Spanish abandoned the San Gabriel missions.[59]

The failure of the mission effort on the San Gabriel marked a turning point in the historical development of the Tonkawas. The Ranchería Grande and the Ervipiames disappeared from the historical record, and the Tonkawas became more prominent, as remnants of this amalgamation likely found shelter with the Mayeyes, Tonkawas, and Yojuanes. In addition, the abandonment of the missions on the San Gabriel led to a profound shift in Tonkawa-Spanish relations. The Tonkawas and their allies realized that the Spanish were unable to offer any meaningful protection from the Lipans. Thus, the Tonkawas turned northward to the Wichitas and eastward to the Hasinai Confederation and Bidais for support. This new alliance in turn linked them with the Comanches and the French and facilitated Tonkawa trade with the West. Soon, the Tonkawas were trading hides and captives to the French in return for firearms.[60]

This brief alliance proved to be formidable. The Tonkawas, joined by their allies, began attacking Spaniards traveling between San Antonio and the new Spanish mission for the Lipans on the San Saba River. The culmination of increasing Tonkawa hostilities toward the Spanish came with a remarkable show of force on March 16, 1757. Several hundred

American Indians—Tonkawas, Bidais, Hasinais, Wichitas, and Comanches—sacked the Mission Santa Cruz de San Sabá. However, the American Indian military alliance soon fragmented.

Spanish retaliation for the events on the San Saba led to the destruction of a Yojuane encampment. The Spanish-Lipan punitive expedition commanded by Colonel Don Diego Ortiz Parilla killed 55 Yojuanes and captured an additional 149 in their assault. Possibly another Yojuane ranchería on the Río de Fierro, likely the present-day Wichita River, was destroyed by the Lipans at this time.[61] The Lipans took 97 of the captives. The Spanish returned to San Antonio with 52, 25 of whom died of smallpox. They sold the remainder into slavery, in violation of Spanish law. The Lipans eventually traded many of their captives to the Spanish for horses and other goods.[62] Hostilities between the Tonkawas and the Spanish, focused on the new Spanish mission for the Lipans on the upper Nueces, continued through the 1760s. Many of the survivors of the assault on the Yojuanes likely found refuge with the Tonkawas. For example, in 1767, some Tonkawas, Mayeyes, Yojuanes, and Cocos were living together at the junction of the Little and Brazos Rivers.[63]

With the Spanish acquisition of Louisiana, Spanish authorities turned their attention to securing the northern frontier of New Spain from American Indians hostile to the Spanish. Initially, some Tonkawas led by Neques accepted Baron de Ripperdá's peace plan in 1773. The plan depended on an alliance between Spain, the Hasinai Confederacy, the Tonkawas, and the Wichita Confederacy for mutual protection and trade. Disappointed by the lack of protection and trade goods, the Tonkawas declined to participate in the alliance.[64] Interestingly, another element of the Spanish effort had been the failed war of extermination against the Karankawas, whose utility as a buffer against French expansion along the western Gulf Coast evaporated with the Spanish acquisition of Louisiana.

Although most of the remnants of the Ranchería Grande and the Yojuanes were consolidating into the Tonkawa tribe, some Mayeyes followed a somewhat different trajectory. After the abandonment of the missions on the San Gabriel, a portion of the Mayeyes followed the Spanish missionaries to the San Marcos River and later to the Guadalupe River and finally to the mission San Antonio de Valero. Other Mayeyes remained on the San Gabriel and continued to petition the Spanish to reopen the abandoned missions. Eventually, some of the Mayeyes migrated to the Texas coast with the Cocos and other Indians, who had been at the missions on the San Gabriel. Sibley reported that the Mayeyes were intermarried with the Cocos and living near the lower Guadalupe River in 1805.[65]

After the great epidemic of 1777–78 killed many Tonkawas, a Tonkawa leader by the name of El Mocho emerged. El Mocho, so called because of his one ear lost in battle with the Osages, was born a Lipan and had come to live among the Tonkawas. On October 8, 1779, Governor Domingo Cabello of Texas appointed El Mocho *capitan general* of the Tonkawas. In front of 400 Tonkawas, he decorated El Mocho with a medal of honor. Then he presented him a commission, a uniform, a baton, and a flag bearing the cross of Burgundy. El Mocho promised to the Spanish to obey their authority and settle his people in a permanent village. However, he had other plans. In 1782, he arranged to hold a "great fair" with the Lipans. In November and December of 1782, 4,000 Native Americans—600 Tonkawas, 2,000 Eastern Apaches (Lipans, Mescaleros, and Natagés), and 1,400 Akokisas, Bidais, Cocos, and Hasinais—gathered on the upper Guadalupe River to trade. The Apaches brought 3,000 horses, while the Tonkawas and their allies produced only 200 muskets with ammunition. In addition, El Mocho proposed that he should become the leader of an alliance between the Eastern Apaches and the Tonkawas to drive the Spanish from Texas. Disappointed with the ability of the Tonkawas to produce sufficient weapons, the Apaches rejected El Mocho's offer and left the "great fair" on Christmas Day with 2,000 of their trade horses. The Spanish Commandant-General Teodoro de Croix learned of El Mocho's plans from his agent, Andrés de Courbière, and ordered the execution of El Mocho. However, before the Spanish could carry out their plans, Captain Cazorla killed El Mocho in the plaza at La Bahía in July of 1784. At the same time, Croix made plans to cement relationships with the Indian alliance potentially loyal to Spain, including at least some elements of the Tonkawas, by distributing a wide variety of trade goods.[66]

A new Tonkawa leader, Yaculchen, led a delegation to the presidio at La Bahía and promised a return to cordial relations with the Spanish. In 1785, Yaculchen's Tonkawas agreed to Spanish demands that they have a permanent village on the Navasota and end the arms trade with the Lipans. In 1786, in order to cement these improved relations and deter further arms trading with the Lipans, the Spanish allowed a man by the name of Miguel Perez to return to the Tonkawas.

Miguel Perez's relatives were important Tonkawa leaders and his brother had become a chief after the death of El Mocho. The Lipans had captured Miguel Perez in the aftermath of the attack on the mission on the San Saba and had sold him into slavery in San Antonio, where he became a respected member of the community. Perez conveyed Governor Cabello's expression of displeasure with the Tonkawas for continuing the arms trade with the Lipans and easily convinced the Tonkawas that an alliance with the Spanish was in their best interests. Partially as a result, 150 Tonkawas joined a war party of about 200 Wichitas on their way to fight the Lipans. The Tonkawa-Wichita force encountered the Lipans on the Colorado, where they launched a surprise attack. The ensuing day-long battle forced the Lipans to retreat to the upper Nueces. The Lipans left behind 30 dead. The dead included 2 chiefs, Cuernitas and Panocho and the latter's son. More importantly for the Tonkawas, the raiders captured a large number of horses.[67]

During the next twenty-five years of Spanish rule in Texas, mostly peaceful but distant relations continued between the Tonkawas and the Spanish. However, political events on a broader scale took place that impacted the Tonkawas. In 1782, while El Mocho was planning his alliance with the Eastern Apaches, Benjamin Franklin, John Adams, and John Jay were negotiating the Treaty of Paris which would extend the territorial jurisdiction of the United States to the east bank of the Mississippi in 1783. As a result, Anglo-American traders increased the flow of arms to the Comanches in the western plains and the Osages in the eastern plains.[68]

These events had profound effects in Texas. The Comanches replaced the Lipans as the dominant Native American power in western Texas. In fact the Comanche invasion split the Lipans into two groups. The upper Lipans retreated into the rugged country of the lower Pecos southwestward across the Rio Grande deep into Coahuila. The lower Lipans went southeastward to the inner coastal plain of south-central Texas from the Colorado River southwestward to the Rio Grande. There they established trade relations with the Akokisas, Attacapas, Bidais, and their allies in southeast Texas. The Wichitas, no longer primary arms suppliers to the Comanches and under attack from the Osages, pushed southward into Texas and infringed on the hunting grounds of the Tonkawas. Finally, by 1815, Osage attacks, encroachment by the Choctaws and other displaced people from east of the Mississippi, and repeated epidemics weakened the Hasinai Confederation as an American Indian power in Texas.[69]

In the first two decades of the nineteenth century, Tonkawa political relationships with other American Indian groups reflected these changes. The Tonkawa alliance with the Comanches and the Wichitas withered.

Underscoring these altered ties, Tonkawas apparently did not participate in the Comanche and Wichita attack on the short-lived Spanish settlement of San Marcos de Nave in 1812, though in 1809 Spanish authorities sent an expedition of 190 men against the Tonkawas for harassing the new Spanish settlement. In 1812 and 1813, some Tonkawas joined Hasinais and Wichitas in the Magee-Gutierrez expedition to liberate Texas from Spanish control in the complicated struggles for Mexican independence.[70] A few years later, in 1817, several Tonkawas apparently joined the Arkansas Cherokees in their brutal military campaign against the Tonkawas' old enemy, the Osages.[71]

At the same time, renewed relationships with the Akokisas, Attacapas, Bidais, and lower Lipans in southeast and south-central Texas, centered around the hide trade, flourished. With the American acquisition of Louisiana in 1803 and the arrival of American traders in Natchitoches, the demand for hides exploded. A trader informed John Sibley that, in 1805, he had obtained from the Tonkawas as many as 5,000 deerskins in one year, in addition to tallow, bison "rugs," and tongues. This was at a time when deerskins sold for $40.00/100. Sibley also offered the following description of the Tonkawas: "They plant nothing, but live upon wild fruits and flesh: are strong, athletic people, and excellent horsemen."[72]

On the eve of the arrival of the Anglo-Texan colonists, the Tonkawas hunted for game along the inner coastal plain from the San Antonio River valley to the Navasota River valley. The Tonkawas lived in politically autonomous bands under the leadership of popularly supported chiefs. Judging from reports during the first half of the nineteenth century, the residential bands usually had a population of around forty families. Individual membership in clans that cut across residential band divisions cemented relations between the bands. Some of the clans reflected the diverse origins of the nineteenth-century Tonkawas as they were apparently vestiges of ethnic groups that had amalgamated with the Tonkawas during the difficult eighteenth century. Membership in the clans was passed through the mother's line and residence after marriage was with the wife's family.[73] Undoubtedly, the bands came together for ceremonial purposes and cooperated in times of war and in seasonal bison hunts on the plains.

Externally, the Tonkawas tolerated the presence of the Spanish colonial administrators and military in Texas and traded with Anglo-Americans in Louisiana. The Tonkawas experienced increasingly strained relations with the Comanches and the Wichitas and oriented themselves more toward the Akokisas, Attacapas, Bidais, and Lipans of southeast and south-central Texas, who also sold hides to the American traders in Louisiana. The centralization of the Tonkawas during the preceding 120 years developed in response to both the demands of the Spanish authorities and repeated losses of population due to epidemics and warfare that made the older ethnic divisions untenable. However, the centralization process had not been without difficulty. Some Tonkawas split off to join other groups, as did the Mayeyes.

At times, the emergence of strong leaders, such as El Mocho, pulled the Tonkawas away from the Spanish orbit. Nevertheless, political expediency, cultural association through the missions, and personal ties counteracted centrifugal forces. Yet, for most Tonkawas during the late eighteenth and early nineteenth centuries, the prosperity engendered by the hide trade with Louisiana was more salient to their existence than political relations with the Spanish. However, growing conflict with the Comanches and Wichitas threatened Tonkawa prosperity by denying them access to the herds of bison and mustangs on the Texas plains.

Even though the Tonkawas had been in close contact with the West since the middle eighteenth century, the Tonkawas maintained much of their traditional southern plains lifeways at the beginning of the nineteenth century. Before more fully exploring the culture of the early nineteenth-century Tonkawas, I will quote American explorer Zebulon Pike's description of the Tonkawas from his encounter with them on the Colorado River, at present-day Bastrop, in 1807.[74]

16th June, Tuesday—Marched early, and at eight o'clock arrived at Red river. Here was a small Spanish station and several lodges of Tancards, tall handsome men, but the most naked savages I ever saw yet without exception. They complained much of their situation. . . .

17th June, Wednesday—Came on by nine o'clock to a large encampment of Tancards, more than 40 lodges. Their poverty was as remarkable as their independence. Immense herds of horses, &c. I gave a Camanche [sic] and Tancard, each a silk handkerchief, and a recommendation to the commandant at Natchitoches. . . .

The Tancards are a nation of Indians who rove on the banks of Red river, and are 600 men strong. They follow the buffalo and wild horses, and carry on a trade with the Spaniards. They are armed with the bow, arrow, and lance. They are erratic and confined to no particular district: are a tall, handsome people, in conversation have a peculiar clucking, and express more by signs than any savages I ever visited: and in fact, language appears to have made less progress. They complained much of their situation and the treatment of the Spaniards: are extremely poor, and, except the Appaches [*sic*], were the most independent Indians we encountered in the Spanish territories. They possess large droves of horses.[75]

At the beginning of the nineteenth century, the Tonkawas continued to orient their culture world toward a nomadic lifestyle based on hunting deer and bison. The Tonkawas did not farm, although there are suggestions that the Tonkawas did raise crops at times in response to Spanish pressure to settle in villages and abandon their traditional nomadic lifeways.[76]

The rationale for this orientation toward hunting appeared in their mythic and ceremonial life world relating to the wolf, the most powerful and feared predator on the southern plains. In Tonkawa ideology, the Tonkawas emerged from the earth when a wolf smelled the Tonkawas buried in the earth and uncovered the first Tonkawas. The wolf consulted with the wisest wolves in the pack, and the pack agreed to let the Tonkawas survive if they would live only by hunting and stealing and never live in permanent dwellings. The Tonkawas were to respect the wolf as the chief of the game. In return, the wolf gave the Tonkawas fire, the bow and arrow, and the bison to feed and clothe themselves.[77]

With the wolf dance, the Tonkawas reenacted the emergence myth with Tonkawa men dressed in wolf skins. One of these wolf dances was witnessed by Robert S. Neighbors, superintendent of Indian Affairs for Texas, who was Indian agent to the Tonkawas during the first years of statehood. According to his account, there were about fifty adult men covered from head to foot in wolf skins. The men entered the ceremonial lodge in single file, moving about on all fours growling, snarling, and howling like wolves. Periodically, the "wolves" would put their noses to the ground and smell it. Suddenly, one of the participants detected something beneath the ground. He uttered a sharp cry and began scratching the ground at what was a predesignated spot. The others gathered around and joined in digging with their hands. Soon, they uncovered an Indian who had been buried there before the ceremony. The "wolves" ran about smelling him and examining him with intense interest. Next, some of the dancers, representing the older, more important wolves, met in a council to determine what should be done with this man. They advised the man to live as wolves did. They placed a bow and arrow in his hands, saying that he was to use this to provide himself with food and clothing. He was to wander about like the wolves, to kill and steal, and never to build a house or to farm. He was informed that to abandon this lifeway would result in his death.[78]

The remainder of the known Tonkawa ceremonial life from the nineteenth century centers around this orientation toward hunting and war. For example, the Tonkawas had a buffalo dance, a deer dance, a wild hog dance, a turkey dance, and a number of dances connected to warfare: a scalp dance, a scout dance, and a hold-shield dance. Some of these dances were for men only; others included both women and men. In addition, two of these ceremonies included the use of psychotropic drugs. In the deer dance the dancers apparently used the mescal bean, and in the wild hog dance they apparently used peyote.[79]

The material culture of the Tonkawas at the beginning of the nineteenth century remained largely traditional, with a few borrowings from the European world. The most notable were the gun, the horse, and metal tools. The horse played a particularly important role in the Tonkawa world. They were skilled at capturing wild horses. The horses not only served as efficient transportation, but were used in hunting and in war. In addition, horse hair was a particularly useful resource for a variety of Tonkawa crafts.

The Tonkawas made extensive use of the available food resources of their homeland in the Post Oak Savannah. The Post Oak Savannah covers more than 13,000 square miles of Texas between the Piney Woods and the Blackland Prairies. Southwest of the Navasota River, in the area occupied by the Tonkawas in the first decades of the nineteenth century, extensive areas of prairies exist on clay soils; the oak savannahs persist on sandy soils. Northeast of the Colorado River, near Bastrop, pines replaced the post oaks and blackjack oaks as the dominant overstory. While today the woodlands have a dense understory of yaupon, briers, and other brush, in the early nineteenth century, before the suppression of fires, the woodlands had a more parklike effect of widely spaced oaks over an understory of prairie grasses.[80] Dense brush or timber probably was confined to creek and river bottoms.

Tonkawas ate venison and bison meat, as well as a variety of native plant foods. They also caught and ate small mammals, birds, reptiles, fish, and shellfish. Some of the foods eaten by Tonkawas were highly unpalatable to people from the European world. Snakes seem to have been particularly favorite food items. Tonkawas were accused of eating dead and decomposing animals and other "spoiled" foods, so that some settlers called them "Carrion Indians." However, Tonkawas enjoyed a stew of browned venison or bison flavored with fruit of the chilipitin.[81] This dish is possibly the forerunner of the chile-flavored meat stew that is so familiar to present-day Texans.

In the Texas heat, Tonkawas went nearly naked. The men wore a long breechclout of deerskin or the leather armor that had been common among the peoples of the southern plains at the time of European contact. The women dressed in short deerskin skirts. To protect themselves from the biting cold of winter, the Tonkawas wore bison robes. Both genders painted and tattooed their bodies, though in a different manner. Men and women parted their hair in the middle and decorated themselves with necklaces and earrings of bones, shells, or feathers. The men wore more ornaments, including bracelets of iron or copper. By the 1840s, ethnic differences in dress among American Indian and other frontier residents became increasingly blurred by participation in the market economy.[82]

The Tonkawas lived in small, conical huts covered with brush or hides.[83] The primary weapons of the early nineteenth-century Tonkawas were the bow and arrow, the spear, the lance, and the gun. The Tonkawas created a potion from the mistletoe leaf that they placed on their weapons to assure success. The Tonkawas also made tack for their horses, horn eating utensils, baskets, rattles, and drums. They either made or traded for pipes in which they smoked tobacco or the tobacco-sumac mix popular on the southern plains.[84]

In addition, anthropologists ascribe another culture trait to the Tonkawas that would play an important role in the relations between them and the Anglo-American settlers—cannibalism. Today, most scholars contend that the Tonkawas were ritual cannibals, who consumed small portions of the flesh of enemies to gain strength or to exact revenge.[85] The Spanish did not report cannibalism among the Tonkawas. The only eighteenth-century report of Tonkawa cannibalism comes from the French explorer Sieur Du Rivage in 1719. Yet, overwhelming evidence of Tonkawa cannibalism exists for the nineteenth century.[86]

The people of Texas in 1821 faced a period of rapid social change unparalleled in their historical experience. Two of the ethnic communities of interest, the Karankawas and the Tonkawas, had deep roots in the region. At the global level, the European "discovery" of the New World at the end of the fifteenth century forever altered the possibilities for both groups by shattering old relationships and introducing new deadly diseases along with new technologies. At the regional level, the full impact of the European encounter became apparent by the middle of the seventeenth century. Apaches on horseback from the northwest and Spanish soldiers, missionaries, and settlers from the southwest converged on Texas. However, by the first decades of the eighteenth century, the American Indian–Spanish frontier had stabilized across Texas.

For the Karankawas, the Spanish period had the following political consequences. First, the five Karankawa bands or sub-tribes became more aware of their identity as Karankawas through their resistance to Spanish control. Second, Spanish demands that the Karankawas enter into political relationships with them led to the development of stronger band leaders that appealed to Karankawas beyond their own band in times of crisis. The stronger Karankawa identity and better-developed political structure, coupled with the Spanish presence, led to persistent tension between accepting the Spanish presence and its benefits and rejecting it because of its constraints. One hundred years of close relations with the Spanish and the West had equally profound consequences for the Karankawa economy. The destruction of the indigenous peoples of the interior of the Rio Grande Plains isolated the Karankawas on the middle coast from trade relations with other American Indians. The Cocos of the upper coast found traditional trade relationships with the people of the interior enhanced by the development of active European trade centers in Louisiana. The greatest changes in the material culture of the Karankawas came from the availability of glass and metal for tools and cattle for food.

The Tonkawas, living along the American Indian–Spanish frontier, experienced a more complex series of events in Spanish Texas. The combination and recombination of Indian communities shattered by disease; Spanish slave raiding, military action, and missionization; and the Apache invasion produced the Tonkawa "tribe" of 1821. The fascinating story of how these disparate groups became the Tonkawa remains poorly known. However, the following three factors played important parts in that process: (1) At least two of the American Indian peoples of the southern plains at the beginning of the seventeenth century (the Tonkawas and the Mayeyes) spoke Tonkawan languages; (2) The Tonkawas of the early seventeenth century likely had a cultural commitment to a nomadic hunting way of life. Thus, the Tonkawas could better resist the Apache and Spanish invasions than more sedentary people and provided a nucleus for other American Indian people who preferred to maintain a nomadic hunting way of life; and (3) A charismatic leader emerged among the Coahuiltecan-speaking Ervipiames at the beginning of the eighteenth century who united some of the shattered peoples into the Ranchería Grande, which then provided additional recruits for the Tonkawa tribe of the eighteenth century. Politically, during the period of Spanish influence, the Tonkawas dealt with powerful neighbors: the Spanish and a number of American Indian groups that took advantage of benefits conferred by possession of firearms and horses to expand at the expense of their neighbors. In response to the complex political situation, the Tonkawas placed a priority on independence and security. They entered into alliances with whatever group, Spanish or Indian, that furthered those goals. However, the shifting alliances on the frontier of Spanish Texas were to some extent based on personal considerations and not entirely the result of political and market demands beyond the control of social actors.

Eventually the Tonkawas located in the Post Oak Savannah of Texas, with three important economic consequences: (1) They had access to the bison and mustang herds on the prairies immediately to the west, while their residential locations hidden in the woodlands provided them with security from enemies; (2) They had control of a rich source of hides and pelts; and (3) They had access to the developing trade centers in Louisiana. At the material level the Tonkawas readily adopted the horse, metal tools, and firearms.

For both Karankawas and Tonkawas, the fluid ethnic boundaries prevailing at that time allowed individuals who wished to abandon their identity as Karankawas or Tonkawas to do so. The same fluidity allowed both groups to accept individuals dissatisfied with their own ethnic community. As a partial result, both groups maintained traditional beliefs in the face of active Spanish missionary efforts. Of course, our understanding of the ceremonial life of the Tonkawas, as well as that of the Karankawas, is limited by the loss of ritual that results from new economic orientations; loss of population, especially key personnel; and loss of confidence in traditional ways in the face of repeated disasters and demands for change.[87]

This development of tribal structures in Texas in response to state expansion was not unique to Texas. Everywhere, the expansion of states into areas occupied by kin-organized people tends to create tribes. States demand leaders of relatively stable, identifiable groups with which to trade and develop military alliances. In particular, the creation of tribes, such as the nineteenth-century Tonkawa, from disparate peoples is a common occurrence on the frontier of state expansion. New trade relations create new sets of connections, while war and disease accompanying state expansion reduce numbers, encourage alliances, force consolidation, and demand new group development.[88]

Meanwhile, the ethnic community that would come to dominate Texas after 1821 took shape in eastern North America. For the purposes of this analysis the most critical aspect of the Anglo-American experience lay in their two centuries of contact with American Indians. Despite incorporating American Indian cultural experience in the process of becoming Anglo-Americans and an official U.S. policy that American Indians were to be treated with humanitarian dignity, the mass of Anglo-Americans, after 150 years of frontier violence, saw American Indians as savages. Anglo-Americans constructed the Indians as the "dark" opposite of their "civilized" selves. Only two solutions existed for "savages." They could be "civilized," or they could be exterminated. Of course, conquerors always perceive their conquest as a "mission of civilization."[89]

Unfortunately, the cultural life of the Karankawas and the Tonkawas meshed with Anglo-American images of savagery. They hunted, fished, and gathered wild plants and invertebrate animals for their livelihood. They ate foods that Anglo-Americans found unpalatable. They wore few clothes and tattooed their bodies and ornamented them with feathers, shells, and bones. They held religious beliefs that were unknowable to Anglo-Americans and practiced religious rituals that were abhorrent to Anglo-Americans. For the Anglo-Americans, the conquest of the Karankawas and the Tonkawas would become the conquest of "savagery" by "civilization."

The Political Economy of Mexican Texas, 1821–35: Initiation of Conquest

❖
❖
❖
❖
❖
❖
❖
❖
CHAPTER 2
❖
❖
❖
❖

During the years from 1821 to 1835 a new political and economic environment emerged in Texas, which the Karankawas and the Tonkawas could not avoid and which shaped their encounter with the Anglo-Texans. First, the new Mexican state became the focus of renewed colonization efforts. Second, Texas became more firmly embedded in the expanding world-economy that arose after the end of the Napoleonic Wars. Finally, population growth and shifts, along with expanded trade opportunities reinvigorated the raiding and trading economy of the southern plains.

COLONIZATION AND IMMIGRATION

The newly independent Mexican state faced an enormous challenge in securing the sparsely populated north. Although Augustín I, following the policy of the Spanish viceroys, favored foreign colonization as a solution to the problem of underpopulation in the north, he did not proclaim a colonization law until February 18, 1823, a month before Republican interests toppled the empire.[1] While this law was in effect, Stephen F. Austin secured a charter for his effort to bring colonists from the United States to Texas.[2]

The Congress of the United States of Mexico passed the Colonization Law of August 18, 1824, which allowed the individual states to regulate colonization projects within their borders within certain broad guidelines. Coahuila y Texas did so in 1825. The federal law guaranteed foreign settlers title to their lands with few restrictions. No foreigner could claim lands within ten leagues of the coast or within twenty leagues of the international border. Also, no foreigner could own more than eleven square leagues of land. The law did not require foreign immigrants to become Mexican citizens or to adopt the Roman Catholic faith, though other laws prohibited any non-Catholic religious practice.

However, in 1828 a new law required citizenship for those who lived in Mexico for more than two years. By the time of the passage of the Law of 1824, 3,000 Anglo-Americans had entered Texas from the United States, most without permission from Mexican authorities.[3]

Under the laws of Coahuila y Texas, formal colonization took place under the oversight of empresarios. The empresario served as an agent for the Mexican government, and he had the authority to select colonists, allocate lands, and establish rules and regulations of conduct within his colony. For every 100 families settled by the empresario, he would receive one *sitio* of grazing land and five *labores* of arable land.[4] Between 1825 and 1830, the state government entered into contracts calling for the settlement of 8,000 families. These contracts covered almost all of Texas.

By 1830, when concern over Anglo-American immigration to Texas caused the Mexican government to prohibit further immigration from the United States, only three empresarios had been successful in attracting colonists. Stephen F. Austin's original colony, the most populous, lay between the San Jacinto and the Lavaca Rivers from the Gulf of Mexico to the San Antonio Road. With a charter under the 1823 colonization law that exempted his original colony from the requirement that foreigners could not occupy lands within ten leagues of the coast, Austin settled almost 1,200 families within his colony. To the west, Green De-Witt located another 100 families from the United States on the Guadalupe, Lavaca, and San Marcos Rivers around Gonzales. Finally, Martín de León brought in more than 100 families, mostly from Mexico, to his colony at Victoria on the lower Guadalupe River. Most of the settlers in de León's colony were also exempt from provisions of the colonization law prohibiting settlement within ten leagues of the coast because they were Mexican citizens. Other Anglo-Americans poured into Texas without the aid of empresarios. By 1830, more than 7,000 Anglo-Americans with their African American slaves lived in Texas.[5]

Mexico's president, Vicente Guerrero, emancipated all slaves in Mexico on the eve of the Mexican independence celebration in 1829. However, President Guerrero's actions emancipating the slaves of Mexico stemmed more from humanitarian concerns reflecting the growing, worldwide disapproval of slavery than from the desire to dam the flow of immigration from the United States into Texas.[6] Apparently, Mexican authorities did not attempt to enforce the emancipation laws in Coahuila y Texas. Six months later, the Law of April 6, 1830, prohibited immigration from the United States and ended empresario contracts with citizens of the United States, except Austin and DeWitt.

With Mexico unable to enforce either law in Texas because of a lack of troops and a lack of popular support among both Anglo-Texans and Tejanos, Texans of Mexican origin, the early 1830s saw a flood of illegal immigration from the United States into Texas. (In light of the perennial debate over "illegal" Mexican immigration into Texas and the United States, one must note the irony of the massive illegal immigration from the United States into Mexican Texas that led to the separation of Texas from Mexico.) At the same time, resident Anglo-Texans continued to bring in African American slaves as "contract laborers." By 1834, when the Mexican government repealed the immigration ban from the United States, there were probably 20,700 Anglo-Americans and their slaves in Texas. The immigrant flow continued, so that by the end of 1835, there may have been 35,000 Anglo-Americans with their African American slaves in Texas.[7]

In addition to the immigration from the United States, the Mexican authorities encouraged other foreign immigration. In Texas, only two small colonies of Irish immigrants took root. James McGloin and John McMullen founded San Patricio de Hibernia in 1830, northwest of Corpus Christi Bay. James Power and James Hewitson established Refugio in 1833, near the site of the recently abandoned mission for the Karankawas, Nuestra Señora de Refugio.[8]

While Anglo-Americans were pouring into Texas in search of cheap or free land and fleeing the economic depression in the United States following the Panic of 1819, other events in the United States sent a different stream of immigrants into Texas.[9] During the Monroe administration official support for the expansion-with-honor policy toward Native Americans continued to erode. Land cessions increased, and the federal government showed increased tolerance for state and individual harassment of Indians. Then, with the election of the frontiersman and Indian fighter Andrew Jackson in 1828, all pretense of equitable treatment toward Native Americans dissolved. The Indian Removal Act of 1830 allowed the president to forcibly remove American Indians to the new Indian Territory, west of Missouri and Arkansas Territory. As a result, Caddos, Cherokees, Choctaws, Creeks, Delawares, Kickapoos, Quapaws, and Shawnees moved into eastern Texas in search of new homes outside of the influence of an increasingly hostile U.S. government and even more hostile Anglo-American settlers.

In contrast, upon independence Mexico granted its Indians the possibility of citizenship, with the ability to secure the same rights and privileges as other Mexican citizens. For Indians who refused to accept the responsibilities of citizenship, the Mexican government continued the Spanish policy of annual gifts to maintain friendship. In addition they attempted to regulate trade with the Indian and use friendly groups to "pacify" groups more antagonistic to the Mexican state. In particular, the Mexican government found Anglo-American settler violence aimed at American Indians an embarrassment and an obstacle to successful implementation of its Indian policy.[10]

For the Karankawas and the Tonkawas, the most important consequence of colonization and immigration came from the location of the most successful empresario grants within or adjacent to their homelands. As a result, their lands became the focus of Anglo-American immigration. For the Karankawas, the exemption from or lack of enforcement of the provisions of the Colonization Law of August 18, 1824, which prohibited foreign settlement within ten leagues of the coast proved to be particularly harmful. Second, the right granted to the empresarios to govern their colonies within the framework of the laws of Mexico and Coahuila y Texas placed members of both groups under the nominal authority of the empresarios. However, unlike the American Indians in the United States, members of both groups possessed the possibility of claiming their rights as Mexican citizens in order to resist encroachment on their lands by outsiders. Growing American Indian immigration into eastern Texas, although outside of the areas occupied by the Karankawas and the Tonkawas, raised the possibility of new conflicts between the native people of Texas and the immigrant Indians.

INCORPORATION INTO THE WORLD-ECONOMY

Not only did Texas see a dramatic increase in population as a result of regional political events, but the period from 1821 to 1835 saw an equally dramatic increase in the degree of incorporation into the expanding world-economy. This period of economic integration contrasted sharply to the economic isolation and decline of the previous decade. Spanish authorities had attempted to prevent trade between Texas and Louisiana when the French had owned Louisiana and after the United States purchased Louisiana. Even during the period of Spanish control of Louisiana, authorities discouraged trade between the two provinces because Louisiana was not part of New Spain, but part of the Captaincy-General of Havana and had a different tax structure than Texas.[11]

Except for a thriving cattle trade between Texas and Coahuila and Texas and Louisiana in the 1780s and 1790s, much of the trade between

Texas and the outside world took place within informal channels during the Spanish period. American Indians, especially Wichitas, but also Cocos, Tonkawas, and their neighbors, exported hides, furs, horses, mules, and captives to French, Anglo-American, and sometimes English traders operating in Louisiana in return for guns, knives and other metal tools, and luxury goods. Not only did Indians participate in this trade, but so did Spanish and Tejano residents of Texas and a variety of foreign adventurers. Even the Spanish government attempted to profit from this trade by licensing a trading house, Barr and Davenport in Nacogdoches, under special rules to trade with the Indians. Barr and Davenport operated from 1798 to 1813. It ceased business when General Arredondo destroyed Nacogdoches in response to the Republican Magee-Gutierrez expedition in the Mexican Revolution.[12]

After 1821, the trade in hides, furs, horses, and mules continued. The official fur and hide trade through the Department of Nacogdoches amounted to $5,000 to $10,000 per year between 1828 and 1834. Trappers sold pelts of badgers, bears, beavers, jaguars, ocelots, otters, and pumas, in addition to the staples of the Texas fur and hide trade: bison robes and cattle and deer hides. The old American Indian trading groups had new competition from both Anglo-American trappers and traders that had begun to infiltrate the region as early as the 1780s and the newly arrived Indian groups in the southern plains. In 1832, Francis Smith was trading with "Métis," descendants of European-origin trappers and traders and American Indian peoples of the Red River of the North, who came to dominate the fur trade in the interior of North America during the first decades of the nineteenth century, as well as with immigrant Cherokees, Delawares, Kickapoos, and Shawnees, at his trading post at Tenochtitlan at the San Antonio Road crossing of the Brazos.[13] By 1834, Anglo-Americans had established large trading houses for the Comanches and other plains peoples on the Red River and on the Arkansas River. This action reduced the need for traders in Texas.[14] However, the elimination of the trading posts in Texas limited trade opportunities for Texas Indians, as the trading post was the nexus for trade.[15]

Not content to trap, hunt, and roundup wild cattle and horses, the Anglo-American colonists began to create a plantation economy paralleling the one developing in the Old Southwest. The rich, deep bottom land soils along the lower Brazos and Colorado were eminently suitable for cotton production. The explosive growth of the cotton textile industry in England and the organization of a profitable plantation system for cotton production, based on slave labor and the mechanized cotton gin in the United States, further encouraged settlers from the United States to push cotton production to its southwestern limits. By 1834, cotton exports from Texas to New Orleans totaled 7,000 bales per year worth approximately $315,000. Ranching also expanded. The Tejanos around Goliad and Victoria, drawing upon the ranching culture of coastal Mexico, supplied beef, hides, and tallow to both the Anglo-American newcomers and to more distant markets in New Orleans.[16]

Population growth and increased foreign trade demanded the development of ports along the Gulf Coast. By 1832, the fifty-year-old dream of Spanish and Mexican authorities had been realized. Matagorda, at the mouth of the Colorado River, with a population of 1,400, was the most populous port in the frontier states of northern Mexico.[17] For the Karankawas and ultimately for the Tonkawas, the intensive economic development surrounding the colonization between Galveston Bay and Corpus Christi Bay proved to be of critical importance.

While the center of population growth and economic development lay in lands adjacent to or held by the Karankawas, the lands of the Tonkawas lay along the fringes of the developing area. However, Anglo-American settlers founded Bastrop at the San Antonio Road crossing of the Colorado River in 1829. By 1834, the population of Bastrop had grown large enough for the creation of the municipality of Mina. In addition, Sterling Robertson located his colony on the Little River. By 1835, new Anglo-Texan settlements, Nashville and Sarahville de Viesca, grew up a few miles below the junction of the Little River and the Brazos and at the falls of the Brazos. So by the end of the period, the Tonkawas had begun to be squeezed between the expanding Anglo-American colonies and their enemies, the Comanches and Wichitas. It was in these radically changed political and economic conditions in Texas during the period from 1821 to 1835 that Anglo-Texans initiated their conquest of Karankawas and Tonkawas.

RAIDING AND TRADING ON THE TEXAS FRONTIER

The raiding and trading economy of the southern plains in the early nineteenth century had complex origins in regional interactions and even older cultural traditions. As early as the middle eighteenth century, the people of New Mexico, both Hispanos and Pueblos, were carrying on a lively trade with the Comanches who controlled the southern plains. This trade pattern continued an older tradition of trading between the agricultural people along the Rio Grande and the nomadic peoples of the plains that predated the Spanish conquest. Traders, known as Comancheros, carried corn, iron, and manufactured goods from New Mexico to the Comanches on the plains in return for bison robes and meat, guns, horses, and other livestock. By 1786, the trade proved to be so lucrative for both parties that the Comanches and the authorities in New Mexico signed a peace accord. However, because raids on Spanish settlements on the frontier of New Spain in Texas and southward into Nuevo Santander and Coahuila were the main Comanche sources for horses, mules, and cattle, the peace and trade between New Mexico and the Comanches only aggravated Comanche raiding into Texas. Comanche possession of the rich resources of the bison plains also led to their eventual control of the gun trade originating from French and later American traders in the Mississippi River valley.[18]

Paralleling the Comanche trade with New Mexico, the Indian peoples living east of the Comanches developed a lucrative trade with the United States based on bison robes, horses, and mules. By 1822, at least three well-developed trails for moving horses and mules existed between Texas and the United States. One route passed through Nacogdoches into Louisiana; a second route passed through Pecan Point on the Red River into Arkansas. Other horses were driven directly from Texas to the American settlements on the Missouri River.[19] Although many of the animals were rounded-up from the immense herds of wild horses that roamed the prairies of Texas, others were stolen from ranches of the settlers or from other Indians. It was sometimes easier to appropriate the work of others than to go through the arduous process of gathering one's own herd of horses.

Neither the Tonkawas nor the Karankawas embraced the Anglo-Texan concept of work—toiling in the fields—as a desirable goal, except in the most desperate situations. However, Tonkawa participation in the raiding and trading economy began to have an appeal, beyond supplying horses and fresh venison, to certain Anglo-Texans. During the first years of Austin's colony, the settlers had engaged the Wichitas only within the boundaries of the colony, but, in 1826, an expedition of the colonists went to the villages of the Wacos and Tawakonis. Since they felt they hadn't sufficient strength to attack the populous, well-defended towns, they returned home without engaging the Wichitas. Eventually, the twin enticements of raiding—booty and excitement—lured colonists into other expeditions. Hearing that "a party of Whacos and Towaconies had encamped at the mouth of the San Saba, for the purpose of raising a crop of corn" one hundred volunteers from Austin's colony, commanded by Abner Kuykendall and guided by "a Mexican and an Indian," went to the village.[20]

After losing the element of surprise through a chance encounter between the settlers' "spies" and the Indians, one of the settlers, William DeWees, described the raid: "We now received orders to ride in quickly and fire. We obeyed, but only succeeded in killing one man." The rest fled into the brush. In their pursuit of the men, the Anglo-Texans passed a great many women and children, but, as they "did not want to hunt these," they continued in pursuit of the Wichita men. DeWees explained: "As our frontiers are ever exposed to the fury of the Indians, we determined to set them an example of not injuring the women or children." The settlers rested in the abandoned village for three days, where they "found plenty of corn, meat, and beans." When they left, the settlers took with them all the pelts and hides they could carry, along with "brass kettles, saddles, beans, and seventy or eighty horses and mules."[21] The raids proved to be so successful, both in policy terms and for the participants that expeditions against the Comanches took place in 1832 and against the Wichitas in 1835 involving Anglo-Texans, Tejanos, and American Indians.

Would-be Anglo-Texan farmers became caught up in a pattern of raiding and associated trading that apparently flourished in the Southwest and southern plains at the time of European contact and became reinvigorated with the advent of the horse, the gun, and a European people who had their own tradition of a raiding and trading economy.[22] The Anglo-Texan settlers, in encountering a powerful and well-armed adversary, "played by the rules" of the raiding economy—they spared the women and children, limited their pursuit of the men, and did not burn the village—in sharp contrast to the "war of extermination" they carried out against the Karankawas for purposes of conquest.

Other times, the raids proved to be less than successful. In 1831, an expedition of nine men and two servant boys led by Rezin Bowie, ostensibly to search for the illusory "lost" silver mine near the abandoned Spanish mission on the San Saba River, encountered a large party of Wacos and Tawakonis, who recently had many of their horses taken by a band of Comanches. The encounter turned into a fight. The Bowie party lost one man killed and two others wounded, eight horses, and nearly all their blankets, pelts, and hides. For the Anglo-Texans who found raiding too "exciting," smuggling, particularly of coffee and tobacco, provided a tempting alternative.[23]

Trading facilitated the coming together of whites and Indians.

Traders had to know, understand, and tolerate multiple worlds. Yet, trade with the West profoundly changed Indian people. First, it broke down group loyalties and promoted individualism. Second, trade items went from being luxuries to being necessities. They supplanted old crafts and forced people into new divisions of labor to supply trade channels. While raiding and trading seem to be mutually exclusive strategies, they bound together the people of the southern plains in mutually advantageous ways. Raiding proved to be an effective means of redistributing resources in an economy in which many people lacked access to the poorly developed market. Finally, as long as the raids were limited in scope they did not preclude further trade relations and the potential for alliance-building associated with trade relations.[24]

The raiding and trading economy would reach its greatest development on the Texas frontier during the decade following the Texas Revolution. During the decade of the Republic of Texas, the raiding and trading economy would be a major factor in Anglo-Texan relations with the Tonkawas and, to a much lesser extent, the Karankawas. In Texas, however, raiding and violence would overshadow the trading aspects of the raiding and trading economy.

ANGLO-TEXANS, KARANKAWAS, AND TONKAWAS IN MEXICAN TEXAS

After the encounter between Austin and the Karankawas and the Tonkawas in Mexican Texas, the beginning phases of the conquest centered around the "war" with the Karankawas, the "peace" with the Tonkawas, and the Anglo-Texan–Tonkawa immersion in the raiding culture in Mexican Texas. All of these events, however, took place within the context of the attitudes and beliefs about Indians that the Anglo-American settlers brought with them to Texas. As one visitor to Austin's "upper colony" observed: "We soon perceived an unceremonious fashion which prevailed, of shooting down red men wherever they were found, was the order of the day."[25]

WAR WITH THE KARANKAWAS

Austin met both the Karankawas and the Tonkawas in his survey of Texas in the late summer of 1821, and he formed definite opinions about each group. After seeing abandoned campsites of the Karankawas and other signs that his men were not alone in the marshlands and prairies fringing the Texas coast, a group of Cocos made themselves known to Austin's party on September 17, near the mouth of the Colorado:

> Monday 17 started early and continued a S.E. course along the lake— at the lower end the Indian war whoop was raised from . . . and I immediately . . . descried an Indian coming towards me, who beckoned me to [stop] & made signs of Friendship [He] advanced towards me into [the] Prairie and was followed at a short distance by 14 warriors [I] advanced about 20 yds ahead of [my] company directing them to be prepared for battle if necessary . . . Chief asked me in Spanish [where I] was from and where going . . . he said they were Coacos . . . who I knew lived with the Karankawas . . . this induced me to watch them closely and refused to go to camp or to permit them to go up to the men, until one of the chiefs laid down his arms and five squaws and a Boy came up to me from their camp . . . they believed us too strong for them and therefore that they wd. not attack us (of their disposition to do so I had no doubt, if they thought they cd. have succeeded) some of the warriors then went up to the [men] and appeared friendly, I gave the chief some Tobacco and a frying Pan that we did not want and parted apparently good friends . . . the chief informed me that they were going to encamp on the road to trade with the Spaniards & Americans—he said we cd. not reach the mouth of the River with horses owing to the thickets he also said that there was a large body of Karanquas at the mouth.
>
> These Indians were well formed and apparently very active and athletic men, their Bows were about 5 ½ to 6 ft long, their arrows 2 to 3 well pointed with Iron or Steel [Some] of the young squaws were handsome & one of them quite pretty—they had Panther skins around their waist painted, which extended down to the knee & calf of the leg—above the waist tho. they were naked—their breasts were marked or tattooed in circles of black beginning with a small circle at the nipple and enlarging as the breast swelled.
>
> These Indians and the Karanquas may be called universal enemies to man— they killed of all nations that came into their power, and frequently feast on the bodies of their victims— the [approach of] an American population will be the signal of their extermination for their will be no way of subduing them but extermination.[26]

Austin constructed the Karankawas as violent savages and cannibals who could not live in proximity with Anglo-American settlers, despite the apparently peaceful encounter between his party and the band of

Cocos. Not surprisingly, conflict soon erupted between the Karankawas and the settlers from the United States. Austin's and the colonists' belief in Karankawa savagery contributed to the violence that would ensue along the lower Brazos and lower Colorado. However, other elements would intensify that violence. Not all the colonists were hardened by long experience on the frontier, many of them came from the more settled parts of the United States. Intending to carve plantations out of the coastal prairies, the settlers found themselves in a strange and sometimes terrifying new land.

For most settlers their first view of their new home was the barren Texas coast, and the first people they met were frequently Karankawas. Settler Noah Smithwick reacted in the following manner:

> They were the most savage looking human beings I ever saw. Many of the bucks were six feet in height, with bows and arrows in proportion. Their ugly faces were rendered hideous by the alligator grease and dirt with which they were besmeared from head to foot as a defense against mosquitoes.[27]

After landing at the mouth of the Brazos or the Colorado, the settlers moved inland to locate their lands. They led a "dreary" existence. They were desperate at times for want of food, shelter, and other basic amenities of life and terrified by the unbroken wilderness, with dangers real and imagined.[28] Moreover, they found themselves isolated from the United States by a three-day ocean voyage, had a regular service existed. The strangeness of their new homes, their isolation, and their sense of despair over their fate contributed to the potential for violence between themselves and the very different other who also occupied the same lands. At the same time, the Karankawas, used to exploiting their environment to the fullest, saw in the settlers a potential resource. They were attracted to the settlers as a source for gifts, trade goods, and food. Unfortunately, the Karankawas failed to distinguish the settlers' livestock from the feral cattle that they hunted and the provisions that the settlers stockpiled at the shoreline from salvage that they retrieved from the sea.

Tension and misunderstanding soon led to violence. In the summer of 1822, a party of settlers, after deciding to travel upriver because of the threat of illness, left four young men to guard their stores at the mouth of the Colorado. When the colonists returned in December to move their belongings upriver, the men and the provisions had vanished. The settlers assumed the loss to be the work of the Karankawas.[29] Tensions increased.

In February of 1823, the Karankawas, for the first time, killed two settlers, Mr. Loy and Mr. Alley, and injured two others, Mr. Clark and Mr. Brotherton. Since it is impossible to know if the deaths of Loy and Alley and the injuries to Clark and Brotherton were in any way provoked, this account reveals how the colonists responded to "depredations" on the part of the Karankawas. Within three days of the attack, Robert Kuykendall raised a small company of men to "chastise" the Karankawas for their actions. According to William DeWees, a participant in the settlers' reprisal, they soon located a Karankawa camp near the location of the Loy and Alley murders on Skull Creek in present-day Colorado County. They attacked the camp without warning and killed at least nineteen Karankawas. After scalping their victims, the men from the colony ate the food and stole the possessions of those they murdered or drove from their homes.[30] DeWees described the scalping:

> It was at this battle, and the only time in my life, that I undertook to scalp an Indian. These Indians had long beautiful plaits of hair. I recollected hearing my father tell of the manner in which the Indians used to treat their victims in the first settlements of the United States, and of their taking scalps from men, women, and children. Moved somewhat by a spirit of retaliation, I concluded that I would take a scalp of an Indian home, as a trophy from battle, but the skin of his head was so thick, and the sight so ghastly, that the thought of it almost makes the blood curdle in my veins.[31]

DeWees justified the actions of himself and his comrades by depicting the Karankawas as an "exceedingly fierce and warlike tribe, and also they are perfect cannibals."[32]

In Texas and the Southwest, by the nineteenth century, scalping was the norm among American Indians, as well as among Mexican and Anglo-American settlers. Most likely the practice of scalping enemies had its origins in precontact American Indian cultures. However on the frontier of conquest the custom of offering bounties for American Indian scalps spread the practice to both European Americans and Indians who would not ordinarily scalp their enemies. In addition, the bounty system ripped scalping from its moorings in the spiritual beliefs of American Indian people and transformed it into a lucrative economic activity.[33]

John H. Moore, another participant in the massacre on Skull Creek, offered the following explanation for the settlers actions:

The Carankawaes were a tribe of large, sluggish Indians, who fed mostly on fish and alligators, and occasionally, by way of feast, on human flesh. They went always without moccasins, striding through briars unharmed, making such tracks as would hardly be attributable to a human being. Each man was required to have a bow the length of himself. The fight was an entire surprise. We all felt it was an act of justice and self-preservation. We were too weak to furnish food for Carankawaes, and had to be let alone to get bread for ourselves. Ungainly and repugnant, their cannibalism being beyond question, they were obnoxious to whites, whose patience resisted with difficulty their frequent attacks upon the scanty population of the colonies, and when it passed endurance they went to their chastisement with alacrity.[34]

The DeWees and Moore accounts illustrate the power of cultural constructions in channeling behavior. Their knowledge that Indians in different times and places committed atrocities against whites and their convictions that the people they encountered were fierce, warlike, and savage cannibals, prepared them and other Anglo-Texan settlers to commit the very acts that so horrified them.[35]

During the year 1823, terror and desperation increased for both Anglo-Texans and Karankawas on the lower Brazos and lower Colorado. The settlers apparently instigated a massacre of a small party of Karankawas on the Brazos by the immigrant "Trinity" Indians. By the year's end, DeWees noted: "[O]ur prospects look very gloomy; if the Indians should attack us, I scarcely know what we should do."[36]

With the return of Austin from Mexico in 1823 and the arrival of more colonists, conditions improved greatly for the settlers by the end of 1824. Eugene Barker, taking an Anglo-centric view, summarized the conditions for the settlers in Austin's colony at the end of 1824 in the following sentence: "The conquest of the wilderness was well begun; the Indians were becoming respectful; food crops were abundant; comfortable cabins were building; and the tense anxious memories of 1822–1823, when the fate of the colony hung in the balance, were receding into the heroic past. . . ."[37]

However, conditions deteriorated for the Karankawas on the upper Texas coast. The colonists became more determined to remove the Karankawas from the lands the colonists coveted. The growing agitation to do something about the Karankawa "menace" led to a campaign against the Karankawas in the fall of 1824. The ferocity of the military action forced many Karankawas to abandon their traditional homes on the lower Brazos and lower Colorado. The colonists attacked the Karan-kawas at every meeting.[38] In November of that year the surviving Karankawa leaders from the upper coast sued for peace with Austin's colony through the offices of the military and the clergy at La Bahía. In return for an end to attacks by the colonists, the Karankawas agreed to abandon their use of the lower Brazos, lower Colorado, and lower Lavaca and remain west of the Guadalupe River.

This arrangement proved impracticable for the Karankawas. Other bands of Karankawas used the coastal lands west of the Guadalupe. To move to the interior would invite death by starvation or by attacks from the Comanches or the Lipans. For the remainder of 1824 and on into 1825, the colonists harried the Karankawas whenever they found them, as long as the colonists had superior numbers. If they saw Karankawas and felt unable to attack them, the settlers complained to Austin of the Karankawas' menacing behavior and asked for the militia to come to their aid.[39] Finally, in response to settler complaints, Austin informed Mexican official Mateo Ahumada in a letter dated September 10, 1825:

> In consequence of the continuous hostilities of the Carancahuase Indians, and considering the treaty of peace we made with them at La Bahía, in September last, which was broken by them without any cause whatever, and one of their parties having lately shown themselves between the Colorado and the Brazos, and in the vicinity of some of settlements making hostile manifestations, I have been compelled in view of the security of our people to give positive orders to the Lieu-tenant of the Militia in that section, to pursue and kill all those Indi-ans wherever they are found, with the exception of Prudencia's party, provided said Prudencia remains west of Buffalo Bayou, because it would be impossible to make a distinction between his people and the others, if they continue mixed together in our vicinity.[40]

With the report of the murder of members of the Cavinagh and Flowers family on the lower Colorado in early 1826, the colonists in-tensified their efforts to exterminate the Karankawas. Immediately after the Cavinagh and Flowers incident, a large party of Anglo-Texan set-tlers trapped a Karankawa band near the mouth of the Colorado River. Men, women, and children died by the score in a torrent of gunfire as they attempted to swim across the river and climb the steep bank oppo-site the pursuing settlers. According to eyewitnesses, the waters of the Colorado ran red with the blood of the Karankawas instead of with West

Texas mud. The location of the massacre came to be known to the settlers as Dressing Point, because the Karankawas received the "dressing" they so justly deserved in the eyes of the Anglo-Texans.[41]

The remainder of the "war" was less spectacular, but quite deadly, as parties of settlers murdered and broke up small bands of Karankawas that remained east of the Guadalupe River. Popular historian Ed Kilman, interpreting the remembrances of J. H. Kuykendall from that time, asserted that "Indian hunting," particularly "chasing squaws," became a "sport" in Austin's colony. In addition, it was not unusual for unmarried Anglo-Texan men to capture American Indian women to serve as "housekeepers." Apparently, the rape of American Indian women by Anglo-American men in the conquest of the American West took on an everyday quality.[42] At other times, the settlers took women and children captive and imprisoned them in San Felipe de Austin.

By the fall of 1826, the survivors, under the leadership of the mission-born Antoñito, sued for a new peace. The official campaign of extermination ended on May 13, 1827, in a meeting in the plaza at Guadalupe Victoria (Victoria). Empresarios Stephen F. Austin, Martín de León, and Green DeWitt; clerics Friar Miguel Muro and Brother José Antonio Valdéz; the commandant of La Bahía Jose Mariano Guerra; and Karankawa leaders Antoñito, Delgado, and Soldado attended. The participants forged a new treaty between Austin's colony and the Karankawas. Austin's colony agreed to end its hostilities against the Karankawas and return the captives imprisoned in San Felipe de Austin. The Karankawas agreed to remain west of the Lavaca River out of Austin's colony, to cease hostilities against both Americans and Mexicans, and to permit the free flow of people and goods through the lands they continued to occupy. Austin also gave the leaders of the Karankawas permission to return to Austin's colony to bring out any bands of Cocos that might remain.[43]

In order to better understand the ferocity and the sense of righteousness with which the Anglo-Texan settlers in Austin's colony wrested title to their lands from the Karankawas, one can examine a story told to John R. Fenn by his grandfather David Fitzgerald, a settler in Austin's colony:

> During the early settlement of the county a tribe of Coast Indians called Craankaways made a raid on some of the colonists below, killed some of the people, and carried off a little girl captive. After proceeding some distance, they camped, killed the child, and proceeded to eat

her, first splitting open the body, then quartering it, and placing the parts on sharp sticks and cooking them. They had just commenced this cannibal feast when a band of settlers dashed upon them, having been on their trail. The Indians were so completely absorbed in their diabolical and hellish orgie as to be oblivious to their surroundings and taken by surprise. In the fight which ensued all were killed except a squaw and two small children.[44]

According to Fenn, the Indian woman and her children came to the house of a settler. There she asked for food. Only the women were at home, and, being frightened, they gave the woman food. While the Indian woman and her children rested and ate, the settlers arrived and learned of her presence: "They consulted for a little while, and then decided it was best to exterminate such a race, and, proceeding to where they were, killed all three of them."[45] Fenn reported that their bones remained visible when he came to Fort Bend County as a boy in 1833.

The importance of this unsubstantiated tale lies in the mythic manner in which elements of truth rationalized the past. The settlers of Austin's colony intentionally dispossessed the Karankawas of their homes and land through a campaign of violence and terror. In order to justify such actions that violated their own moral code, it was necessary for the colonists to construct the other in such a manner as to legitimate their actions. In this story, the Karankawas were guilty of the most horrible crimes that removed them from the ranks of humanity. The settlers showed compassion, in the case of the farmwife, and judicious deliberation in their dealings with an other who did not deserve to exist among humankind.

In little more than five years, the colonists had pushed the Karankawas off their lands between Galveston Bay and the Lavaca River, with few voices raised among the Anglo-Texans in behalf of the Karankawas. Although Thomas Bell and six other settlers of Cedar Lake did petition Austin on October 3, 1825, to treat with a band of Karankawas, because "they say they are tired of war and the conduct of them induces us to believe they are in earnest for they have encamped in our stock range and disturbed nothing to our knowledge." Yet, the settlers' petition was not so much motivated by humanitarian concerns as fear: "also the upper settlement not having it in their power to aid us and we not being able to protect ourselves we think it proper to treat with them." There exists no evidence that Austin responded positively to this petition. Even the band of the friendly Prudencia, who Austin asked to remain out of the violence in his order of extermination, fled beyond the Lavaca.[46]

During the remainder of the Mexican period, the refugees from Austin's war attempted to rebuild their lives on the coastal plain between the Lavaca and the Nueces Rivers. They probably found it difficult to establish new hunting, fishing, and foraging rounds in unfamiliar locations. In addition, the disproportionate loss of men would have severely impacted the survival of a hunting and gathering society with a rigid gender division of labor. Finally, the disruption of the food supply made the Karankawas more susceptible to epidemics.[47] Some remnants undoubtedly joined other bands less affected by Austin's war. Others turned to the cattle of de León's colonists for survival. This action increased the potential for conflict between the Karankawas and the Tejanos of the central coast.

Between 1829 and 1835, the Tejano rancheros of coastal Texas made frequent appeals to the Mexican authorities in San Antonio for military aid to end the loss of cattle to the Karankawas. Lacking military support, the Tejano rancheros made renewed efforts to end the thefts through force. Unable to solve the problem through violence, prominent Victoria ranchero Placido Benavides suggested that the Karankawas, along with the local band of Tonkawas, be given title to the littoral lands, which were of marginal utility to the rancheros.[48] Nothing came of Placido Benavides's proposal in the tumultuous political climate of the middle 1830s.

Other displaced Karankawas found other solutions to the problem of survival. Prudencia's band apparently meshed traditional subsistence strategies with day labor for the Anglo-Texan ranchers along the lower Guadalupe River. According to Annie Teal, they worked for whiskey.[49] Others returned to their homeland. One band, apparently the survivors of the Dressing Point massacre, wandered for days without food or rest before reaching the Matagorda Peninsula, where they lived for a time. The limited resources of the relatively barren outer coast forced them to return to the mainland. There they found shelter and protection for several years at the Wightman plantation on Matagorda Bay in return for their labor. At the remote plantation, Mrs. Wightman found them agreeable companions, though "idle and dirty in the extreme":

> I felt no fear whatever from these neighbors, but would sleep with all our doors open, with twenty-five or thirty Indians within call. It was amusing to see them parade the streets of Matagorda with their long

plaid, red and blue garments, which I had made for them, the tails tipped with ornamental feathers. One of the young women learned to speak very good English; I dressed her in my clothes, and one day thought to have some fun with her, invited her to take tea with me. But the joke all turned to my own expense, for she not only used her knife and fork properly but her cup, saucer and plate like it was an everyday affair.

It took me a long time to become accustomed to their naked and hideous appearance, so that it did not shock me; I felt humiliated that I too was of the human species.[50]

The Karankawas eventually grew tired of plantation life. After several nights of "noise and dancing" accompanied by "rude instruments of music . . . importuning the Great Spirit to give them success . . . and to protect them," they left down the coast to steal from the "Mexicans."[51]

Other Karankawas who returned to their homeland were less lucky. Thirty-five or forty who returned were dispersed among the settlers of Austin's colony as slaves, prompting settler Mary Austin Holley to capture the harsh reality of the conquest in the romantic language of the time:

> Thus the shores and bays of this beautiful region, in which these fierce children of the woods once roamed, free as the lion of the desert, have been transferred to other hands. From being the rightful proprietors of the domain, they have become the hewers of wood and drawers of water to their invaders.[52]

Others who returned, refusing to yield their old hunting, fishing, and foraging territories, faced the wrath of the Anglo-Texan settlers who had appropriated their lands. In 1833, a band of Karankawas, "a lazy, shiftless tribe," went to the farm of Daniel Gilleland on the Colorado above Matagorda to beg for corn. Gilleland refused. The Karankawas argued and then withdrew. "Gilleland then collected a few of his neighbors, went to their camp, and attacked them at once. A pretty severe fight ensued in which several of the Carancahuas were killed and wounded . . . This taught the Carancahuas a good lesson. . . ."[53]

PEACE WITH THE TONKAWAS

Relations between the Tonkawas and the Anglo-Texans in Mexican Texas took a very different course. From his first meeting with the Tonkawas on the San Antonio River above La Bahía in August of 1821, Austin saw the Tonkawas in a much different light than he did the Karankawas. Austin dismissed the Tonkawas as "great beggars," and he perceived them as no threat to Anglo-American settlement. Although Austin was not hostile toward the Tonkawas, relationships between the Tonkawas and the colonists were unsteady at times during those first years of the Anglo-Texan colony. Early on, the Tonkawas began to investigate the new Anglo-American settlement. Blocked from trading with Anglo-Americans on the north by the Comanches and Wichitas and on the east by the recently arrived Indians from the United States, the Tonkawas apparently saw Austin's colony as a potential outlet for their hides and horses. As a result, Tonkawas began to enter the Anglo-Texan settlements in search of trade opportunities. During those first two trying years of Austin's colony, deerskins tanned by the Tonkawas clothed the settlers, and game killed by the Tonkawas fed the settlers. Yet, the settlers' friendship with and dependence on the Tonkawas failed to temper deep-rooted feelings of fear, distrust, and hostility toward Indians. When the colonists left on the expedition that ended in the Skull Creek massacre, they took along the local Tonkawa leader, Caritas, as both a guide and a hostage.[54] As the Anglo-Texan colony became better established, relations between members of the two groups deteriorated.

The murder of five Cocos, including one's Tonkawa wife, and the capture of the murdered couple's son by the "Trinity" Indians (probably immigrant Coushattas) at the apparent instigation of the Anglo-Texan settlers caused some Tonkawas to retaliate by stealing horses and corn and threatening some of the settlers. Instead of ordering a war of extermination against the Tonkawas, Austin marched after them, and he compelled Caritas to return the stolen animals and publicly whip the "marauders." In addition to public whipping at the hands of Caritas, Austin ordered the offending Tonkawas out of the colony and made it clear that in the future any Tonkawas caught stealing livestock would be shot. For the next three years, the Tonkawas continued to come into the colony to trade, and the settlers continued to complain about the loss of horses, cattle, hogs, and corn. In response to the settlers' complaints, Austin had the Tonkawas he deemed guilty of theft publicly flogged and their heads shaved by Tonkawa leaders and Anglo-Texan officials in an effort to keep the peace.[55]

Austin followed a well-developed strategy of using native leaders to enforce his rules. Thus he both incorporated the Tonkawas into his colony and strengthened the prestige and authority of Tonkawa leaders who were loyal to him. However the presence of race-hatred and an economy based on planting rather than trading precluded the full development of a search for accommodation and meaning in which the settlers and the Tonkawas could establish an order beneficial to both groups.[56]

However, only once did violence gravely threaten the developing policy of accommodation between the Tonkawas and the Anglo-Texan colony. In the spring of 1826, Gabriel Snyder lost six of his hogs. He blamed their disappearance on a Tonkawa hunting party camped nearby. Another settler complained that the same hunting party had frightened his wife, and yet another settler reported the loss of five bushels of corn, a few pounds of meat and a whet stone, along with the destruction of two gun rods and two straightedge ax blades. In response to these "depredations," the settlers organized a party of at least fifteen men to "chastise" the offenders. When the settlers found the nearest Tonkawa camp, they entered with guns drawn. They soon fired. In the ensuing fight, at least two Tonkawas and one settler died.[57] Austin, alarmed by the violence, demanded reports from all the settlers involved in the incident:

> . . . and, from my investigations, I felt satisfied that the presumed depredations of the Indians were not sufficiently established to justify the attack, although there were good reasons to suspect them. I lost no time in calling the Indians together; they arrived here on the 29th of April and remained four days. After having had a talk with them they declared themselves fully satisfied, and withdrew with the understanding that any of their tribe who should hereafter steal anything from our settlers, should be surrendered for punishment, and that, on their failing to do so, the party would be shot wherever he was found.[58]

The raiding and trading economy of the Tonkawas caused other difficulties between the Tonkawas and some members of the Anglo-Texan colony. Vital to the Tonkawa economy were raids on the Comanches and Wichitas for horses. In retaliation, they raided the Tonkawas. As the Anglo-Texans settled closer to the Tonkawa camps, parties of Comanches and Wichitas appeared in the Anglo-Texan settlements searching for Tonkawas. Soon the Anglo-Texan farms became their source of supply for horses, cattle, hogs, and corn. However, some Anglo-Texans took advantage of the Tonkawa raiding and trading economy by buying their stolen horses. William Rabb, a settler on the Colorado, complained in a letter to Austin:

The late visits of the Comanche must be ascribed to the misconduct and imprudence of some inhabitants themselves, who for the sake of dishonest self interest would sink the colony in irretrievable ruin— If some means could be devised to keep the Tonkaways and Lapans from coming among us, it is probable we should not be troubled with the Comanches.[59]

One of Austin's colonists, James J. Ross, established his plantation far up the Colorado in what is now Fayette County. Austin appointed him to head the militia for the upper Colorado settlements, and he led an expedition against a band of the Wichitas, which had come into the colony in pursuit of Tonkawas who had allegedly stolen horses from them. By 1828, Ross apparently became involved in buying stolen horses from the Tonkawas. Most likely, Ross was one of the persons referred to by Rabb in his letter to Austin.[60] In the 1840s, Colonel William Albert Pettus, who had lived in Austin's colony, recalled the following incident involving Ross, Rabb (who was also a member of the expedition against the Tonkawas in 1826), and other settlers:

> Capt. James J. Ross . . . was in the habit of fitting out and incouraging [sic] the Tonks in their thieving expeditions against the Upper tribes, and would purchase the property thus captured by the Tonks. This caused the Tonks to make his house a sort of rendezvous . . . [T]he people who had suffered so much from the conduct of the Tonks, resolved to expel them without delay, and assembling for that purpose they marched toward Ross' house where the Indians were. Ross . . . had been informed of the approach of the people and was determined to resist them. The people meditated no mischief against him, altho they greatly censured his course, but designed to operate alone against the Indians—when they had arrived near his house and was passing before his door on their way to the Tonk's camp, Col Ross hailed them, saying "halt, you are gone far enough" . . . Ross presented his gun, as they dismounted, and snapped it at them. Several guns were instantly discharged at him, and he fell dead. It was said he was killed by John Rabb's ball. John H. Moore was leader of the party, and was connected to Ross by marriage, both having married the Miss Cummings.[61]

This incident illustrates the divisions among the colonists arising out of the participation by some of the settlers in the raiding and trading economy of the Tonkawas and other American Indian peoples of the southern plains. Unfortunately, many of Colonel Pettus's other remembrances from Austin's colony lack substantiation and appear to be embellishments on the events recounted.

The politically astute Austin recognized that the Tonkawas were the only barrier between his colony and the Comanches and Wichitas of interior Texas. Therefore, he preferred to include the Tonkawas in the colony, rather than to exclude them and antagonize them. In addition, the Tonkawas lived along the western margin of the colony or outside its boundaries. As a result, the Tonkawas did not occupy potentially valuable agricultural lands. Austin accomplished his goal by using Tonkawa leaders to enforce his rules. This in turn enhanced the political strength of those leaders who found in Austin's colony not only a market for their goods, but also a potential ally in their struggle with the Comanches and the Wichitas. At the same time the Tonkawas along the Colorado and upper Lavaca Rivers were building an alliance with the Anglo-Texans, the Tonkawas along the San Antonio and Guadalupe Rivers were offering their aid to the Mexican government against the Comanches and Wichitas. In 1822, Tonkawa leader Joyoso visited the court of Emperor Augustín I to cement personally an alliance between Mexico and the Tonkawas. He not only offered military help but also guidance for Mexican officials to the "lost silver mines" on the San Saba.[62]

Austin's friend and neighboring empresario Green DeWitt reached a similar conclusion with regard to the Tonkawas from his colony at Gonzales, which was even more exposed to Comanche and Wichita raids than Austin's colony. After some of the settlers in DeWitt's colony accused the Tonkawas of stealing corn and livestock, DeWitt went to the Tonkawa camp nearest to Gonzales.

This was possibly the Tonkawa camp visited by the Swiss naturalist and early day ethnographer, Jean Louis Berlandier, between Gonzales and the Colorado River, just west of present-day Columbus, on April 21 and 22, 1828. Lieutenant José María Sánchez, another member of the Comisión de Límites, reporting on conditions in Texas to the Mexican government, described the Tonkawas and their camp as follows:

> . . . the *pueblo* or camp of the Tancahues was situated in the center of a thick grove at the entrance of which several horses were tied, apparently all very good . . . Their huts were small and barely numbered thirty, all conical in shape, made of light branches, covered with the same material, and an occasional buffalo skin. In the center of each is located the fireplace around which lie the male Indians in complete

inaction, while the women are in constant motion either curing the meat of the game, or tanning the skins, or preparing the food, which consists chiefly of roast meat, or perhaps making arms for their indolent husbands. The elder women work the hardest because the younger ones have a few moments of rest at the expense of the wretched elders. The men wear ear rings and other ornaments on their neck and hair, made of bone, shells, or showy feathers, while the women wear only black stripes on their mouth, nose, cheek, and breast. On the breast the stripes are painted in concentric circles from the nipple to the base of each breast. They wear nothing but a dirty piece of deerskin around their waist, leaving the rest of their bodies naked, and wearing their hair short.[63]

Realizing that the Comanches and Wichitas kept the Tonkawas from the buffalo prairies farther northwest, DeWitt concluded that if the Tonkawas were stealing, they were doing so to survive. DeWitt outlined his proposal to the Tonkawas to come to their aid:

I then laid before them the great benefits of going to work, and embracing the privileges of the laws of the land . . . and informed them at the same time that I was sent by you [Ramón Músguiz, political chief of the Department of Texas] to make them an offer of land where on to settle themselves, and that you had a great regard for them and wished them to become a great and good people.[64]

In addition, DeWitt offered to help raise money to buy the Tonkawas hoes and axes, to find someone to teach them to farm, and to help them secure title to lands to which they were entitled as citizens of Mexico and Coahuila y Texas. However, the Tonkawas remained committed to their cultural ideal of hunting and raiding as proper economic activities, but they did refrain from further thefts from the settlers in DeWitt's colony.

In 1821 two momentous changes occurred in Texas. Mexico secured its independence from Spain and official Anglo-American colonization began in Texas. First, in an effort to solve what they saw as a problem of underpopulation in the northern frontier states, Mexico continued to allow Anglo-American settlers to enter Texas legally throughout the remainder of the decade under the empresario system. Illegal Anglo-American immigration continued through the 1820s and grew after the Law of April 6, 1830, ended most legal immigration from the United States. The relentless westward push of Anglo-American settlement sent another stream of immigrants into Texas from the United States. American Indians displaced from their homes farther east began to enter Texas as early as the first decade of the nineteenth century. American Indians poured into Texas after the Indian Removal Act of 1830.

Second, the economy of Mexican Texas underwent massive changes as well. Cotton farming, cattle ranching, and a vigorous fur and hide trade arose on the rubble of the economy of Spanish Texas, which had been wrecked by a decade of revolutionary violence. The focus of economic growth shifted from the old Spanish settlements of San Antonio and La Bahía to the Anglo-American settlements on the lower Brazos and lower Colorado Rivers and the revitalized town of Nacogdoches at the overland gateway from the United States.

For the Karankawas, the establishment of Austin's colony led to a "war of extermination." The settlers forcibly dispossessed the Karankawas from the lands each group claimed. Only the intervention of Mexican political, military, and clerical authorities at La Bahía prevented the total destruction of the Karankawas on the upper coast. The Treaty of 1827 prohibited all Karankawas, even Prudencia's friendly band of Cocos, from living east of the Lavaca River. One or two Karankawa bands returned to the mouth of the Colorado, where they were sheltered by powerful local settlers in return for their labor. Others, most likely remnants of shattered bands, returned and became "servants" in Austin's colony. They found slavery better than starvation or death from settler violence. On the middle coast, west of the Lavaca, the arrival of new bands disrupted old subsistence arrangements. This led to increased conflict with Tejano rancheros over cattle stealing. At least one band, Prudencia's Cocos at the mouth of the Guadalupe, followed the model of their kin at the mouth of the Colorado.

For the Tonkawas, the location of Anglo-Texan settlement on the lower Brazos and lower Colorado had much different consequences. The Tonkawas, threatened by Comanche and Wichita expansion from the northwest and blocked from old trade ties to Louisiana by the immigrant American Indians, saw the Anglo-American settlers as potential military allies and trade partners. The more distant Tonkawas on the San Antonio and Guadalupe Rivers pursued a similar course of action toward the Mexican authorities and Tejano settlers. During the first years of Austin's colony, settler dependence on the Tonkawas for food and clothing helped bridge the chasm created by anti-Indian sentiment among the settlers. Austin and DeWitt, realizing the potential threat to their colonies from the Comanches and Wichitas, soon saw the Tonkawas as potentially valuable allies. Despite conflicts that arose between settlers and Tonkawas, Anglo-Texan and Tonkawa leaders resolved those conflicts.

The peace with the Tonkawas allowed them to introduce some of the Anglo-Texan settlers to the raiding and trading economy of the southern plains. In this economy participants supplemented hunting bison, cattle, deer, and other fur bearers and rounding up wild horses for trade with raiding for captives, horses, and pelts. As conflict between the Comanches and the Wichitas, on one side, and Anglo-Texans and Tejanos, on the other, increased, the raids took on a more political character. The Tonkawas served as guides and fighters in the raids against the Comanches and Wichitas; thus, they allied themselves with the settlers.

CHAPTER 3

❖ *The Political Economy of the*
❖ *Republic of Texas, 1836–45:*
❖ *Negotiation of Conquest*

The Karankawas' and the Tonkawas' negotiation of their survival with their Anglo-Texan conquerors during the Texas Revolution and the Republic of Texas took place in both an increasingly complicated political situation and in a rapidly changing economic environment. The period from 1836 to 1845 witnessed the transformation of Texas from a subdivision of a Mexican state to an independent republic to a state in the United States. An equally impressive economic transformation matched this political transformation. The political transformation took place through a revolt for local control and a decade of local rule, known to history as the Texas Revolution and the Republic of Texas.

INDIAN POLICY IN THE TEXAS REVOLUTION AND THE REPUBLIC OF TEXAS

Anglo-Texan settlers had attempted to wrest control of Texas from Mexico as early as 1827. This first attempt, the Fredonian Rebellion— led by empresario Haden Edwards of Nacogdoches, the tragic activist for American Indian rights John Dunn Hunter, and Western Cherokee leader Richard Fields—failed to gain support from other settlers from the United States. The revolt drew the active opposition of Austin, the Western Cherokee leader Duwali, and Mexican officials. The attempt to create an independent state for American Indians and Anglo-Americans ended with the exile of Edwards and the murders of Hunter and Fields. Other attempts at revolt, over tariff enforcement and disputes over land titles, developed on the upper coast, late in 1831, and culminated with the settler seizure of the Mexican fort at Velasco at the mouth of the Brazos in the summer of 1832. Yet, the crisis ended peacefully through negotiation. However, the revolt of 1835 and 1836 achieved widespread support in Texas. Coming after the suspension of Mexico's Federalist Constitution of 1824, in favor of a strong central government, the revolt in Texas that was widespread on the periphery of the Mexican state aimed to restore local control. As such, both Anglo-Texans and Tejanos supported the secessionist effort.[1]

The surprising and spectacular defeat of General Antonio López de Santa Anna's Mexican army by Sam Houston's Texan forces at San Jacinto on April 22, 1836, brought into being the Republic of Texas that had been declared on March 2 of that year. During the decade of Texas independence, the fledgling settler state faced numerous challenges to its existence. Foremost, Mexico refused to recognize the southern and western boundary of the new republic at the Rio Grande or even the legitimacy of the Texan state. In addition, the leadership of Texas had to deal with the American Indian inhabitants of their territory.

In East Texas, they faced the Texas Cherokees and other Indian refugees from the United States, as well as remnants of the Hasinais and the Bidais. In the west, the Comanches exercised complete control of the lands between the Rio Grande and the Arkansas River. The Wichita Confederacy, joined by the Keechis from East Texas, lived from the middle Brazos, near present-day Waco, northward to beyond the Red River. On the southwestern frontier of Texas, the Karankawas, Lipans, and Tonkawas survived along the fringe of Anglo-Texan settlement. The Karankawas occupied the outer coast between the Colorado and the Nueces Rivers. The Lipan hunting grounds extended from the Guadalupe River westward to beyond the Rio Grande. The western bands of the Tonkawas, who were encountered by Austin in 1821 and friendly with empresario Martín de León, lived on the lower San Antonio and lower Guadalupe Rivers. The eastern bands, who had developed close relationships with Austin's and DeWitt's colonies, lived on the headwaters of the Lavaca River and the middle Colorado River, above Columbus.

Official policy of the Republic of Texas alternated between Sam Houston's professed policy of accommodation toward Mexico and American Indians and Mirabeau B. Lamar's policy of overt hostility toward both.[2] The young republic, lacking the resources to exercise effective control over the vast territory it claimed, recognized the need to deal with its noncitizen, American Indian inhabitants. In order to do so, government officials had to ascertain two things: (1) How many Indians were in Texas? and (2) What was their orientation toward the settler state?

A report summarizing the status of American Indian groups in Texas was presented to President Houston by the Standing Committee on Indian Affairs of the Senate on October 12, 1837. It described the

Karankawas and the Tonkawas, along with the Lipans, as "part of the Mexican nation and no longer considered as a different people from that nation." Despite the implications of this report that the Karankawas and the Tonkawas were enemies of the Republic of Texas, Houston, as part of his policy of peace and trade with Indians, concluded a treaty with the western Tonkawas at San Antonio on November 22, 1837, and with the eastern Tonkawas at Houston the following April. Apparently, Houston failed to make a treaty with any of the Karankawa bands, though he did order the following gifts for each of the Karankawa chiefs on April 12, 1838: "one bolt of calico, some Vermilion, and sixteen pounds of Tobacco."[3]

Houston devoted his first term as president of the Republic of Texas, from October 22, 1836, to December 10, 1838, to maintaining peace with Mexico and the Indians of Texas. He attempted to achieve his goal of friendly relations with the Indians by guaranteeing them the same rights they had under Mexican rule, regulating trade and providing for the settlement of disputes between Anglo-Texans and Indians, and entertaining delegations from the Indian nations who came to Houston to trade or conduct official business.[4] Presbyterian minister W. Y. Allen recorded the following impressions of an "official visit" to the capital by a delegation of Tonkawas on the Fourth of July, 1838:

Wednesday, July 4th. Saw a delegation of Tonkawa Indians, about twenty-five. Many nearly naked. They stopped at the President's house, where they were received by the Secretaries of State and War. They were treated to whisky punch, noise, drinking, and fighting towards evening. And this the fourth of July . . . what will our government come to!

Thursday, July 5th. The Tonkawa Indians are, many of them, finely formed. Most of the men of the present delegation to Houston are almost entirely naked. All the costume of some of them is a long narrow strip of cloth passed between the legs, and held up before and behind by a string or a band around the lower part of the body. Some have an old blanket, some an old shirt, others a pair of leggings, mockasins, etc. Some of the women have a piece of leather or dressed buffalo skin fastened around the waist. Some an additional piece around the shoulders. Some of the younger females have tinkling ornaments fastened to the lower parts of their leather costumes. The men paint their faces hideously, wear their hair long, dressed with shining trinkets, some with long plaits of adscitious (sic) hair or cloth hanging down to the knees. Their language is a grunting jargon. They seem cheerful, sing considerably. Such singing as it is. They seem fond of whiskey, some of them are terribly drunk. They are a much better looking people than the Comanches. They are much demoralized by intercourse with the whites, learning their worst vices readily.[5]

Houston spent much of his second term, from December 12, 1841, to December 9, 1844, attempting to undo the consequences of President Lamar's aggressive policies toward Mexico and Native Americans during the intervening three years. Anson Jones, the last president of the Republic of Texas, continued Houston's policies during his brief term of office.

The inauguration of President Lamar in December of 1838 and local conditions in Texas, particularly along the southwestern border, made Houston's peace policy obsolete. However, the Lamar policy produced the most dramatic results. The ill-fated expedition to seize Santa Fe and the upper Rio Grande in 1841, the military alliance with the rebellious Mexican state of Yucatan, and the toleration, if not encouragement, of raiding into Mexico, culminated in Mexican retaliation in 1842. In March of that year, Mexican troops briefly captured Goliad and Victoria and looted San Antonio. In September, a better-equipped Mexican army led by General Adrian Woll reentered San Antonio and took much of the Anglo-Texan male population of that town captive. Eventually, Texan forces drove the Mexican army back beyond the Nueces.

These events forced the Houston administration to retaliate. A Texan army, commanded by General Alexander Somervell, left San Antonio on November 25, 1842, for Laredo. Upon reaching Laredo, Somervell had increasing problems maintaining military discipline over his army. A portion of the Texan force, after a night of intoxication on the "mescal, marihuana, and *aguardiente*," looted Laredo, a town claimed by the Republic of Texas. Eventually, dissension among the Texans over the goals of the expedition resulted in Somervell and 189 of his men returning to Texas in mid-December. The remainder, looking for more plunder and excitement, went on to Mier, where they were defeated and taken captive by the Mexican army.[6] Texan political control never reached beyond the Nueces during the republic, except at Kinney's settlement at Corpus Christi.

Lamar's Indian policies produced even more spectacular results. On December 21, 1838, in his first message to Congress, Lamar proposed that all Indians be removed from Texas. In January of 1839, he ordered an expedition of removal against the Cherokees in northeast Texas. The ostensible reason for such action lay in reports that the Cherokees intended to join Mexico in an attempt to retake Texas. However, Lamar and the Congress used the court decisions in the United States and Texas that declared that American Indians "are mere tenants at sufferance—that they cannot acquire rights in the soil" to legitimate their actions. This rumor of an alliance between the Cherokees and Mexico played upon the worst fears of Anglo-Texans.[7]

Although the prospect of alliance between American Indian nations and Mexico frightened many Anglo-Texans, others saw the prospect of an American Indian–Mexican alliance in a different light. In the aftermath of an alleged plot between Kickapoos and Tejanos to seize control of Nacogdoches in the summer of 1838, Isaac Watts Burton, a young lawyer from Nacogdoches, wrote to then Vice President Lamar: "The rebellion of Mexicans and their attempt to let loose the Indians on this frontier has created a great excitement among us—It is now over and we are daily catching the poor devils and I suppose we shall have a fine hanging frolick shortly."[8]

The expedition, led by Kelsey Douglas and Edward Burleson, defeated the Cherokees and burned their cabins and crops. Most of the Texas Cherokees crossed the Red River where they rejoined the Western Cherokees and met Eastern Cherokees forced from their homes in the southern Appalachians by Jackson's Indian Removal Act. Others went to Mexico or retreated to the west beyond the line of Anglo-Texan settlement. Burleson's men, including his Tonkawa allies, intercepted and murdered Cherokee leaders Egg and Duwali and their families on their way to Mexico.[9]

Flushed with success, the Douglas and Burleson expedition turned its attention to the other Indian people living in East Texas. By the end of July, 1839, only the Alabamas and the Coushattas, who came to Texas in the first decades of the nineteenth century, and the indigenous Bidais remained in eastern Texas.[10] The Anglo-Texans forced the Caddoans (including indigenous groups), Creeks, Choctaws, Delawares, Kickapoos, Seminoles, Shawnees, and other immigrant American Indian nations from the United States to retreat across the Red River into the United States or to move beyond the line of settlement in Texas or beyond the Nueces into effective Mexican territory.

The murder by Texas Rangers of much of the Peneteka Comanche leadership, known as the "Council House Fight," while in San Antonio under an agreement of truce in order to negotiate a hostage exchange precipitated the "Great Raid of 1840." The Comanches swept to the Texas coast and burned and sacked the port of Linnville. However, a hastily mobilized force of Anglo-Texan volunteers from the Colorado River settlements defeated the returning Comanches at the forks of Plum Creek, near present-day Lockhart, on August 12. As further retribution, an Anglo-Texan expedition led by John Moore followed the retreating Penatekas to the upper Colorado. At daybreak on October 24, Moore's men attacked a Comanche camp by surprise. In contrast to nine years earlier when Anglo-Texans refrained from killing women or children or burning the village in the raid against the Wichitas, Moore's forces killed more than 125 men, women, and children; burned and looted the village; stole more than 500 horses; and took 34 captives. In the wake of the events of 1840, the warfare between the Comanches and the Anglo-Texans continued with a renewed bitterness on both sides.[11]

One must also note that the actions and motives of the Anglo-Texan Rangers and settlers offended some of their contemporaries. German immigrant Gustav Dresel penned the following comments after observing a group of volunteers readying for an expedition to "chastise" the Indians in July of 1840: "It was a comical sight to observe these brave Texians appear on the drill ground. They were more like a gang of robbers about to undertake a raid than disciplined soldiers who risked time, money, and life to protect their fellow citizens from future invasions of the redskins."[12]

A visitor to the Republic of Texas, Francis C. Sheridan, left the following comments regarding the treatment of American Indians by Anglo-Texan settlers: "I cannot help thinking that the Indians have not received such fair play from the Texians, as the latter wish the world to suppose. . . . But the Texians appear to have long forgotten that they were human beings as well as themselves, and what is more human beings under the impression that they were wronged—and the bitterness of hatred borne towards the ignorant savages is best shown in the bloody revenges taken when opportunity occurs." Another visitor to Texas during the same period offered a similar observation on the plight of the Texas Indians: "The 'happy hunting grounds' indeed, can never be what they once were, to these poor people; yet peace and freedom from oppression, they have a right for."[13]

The aftermath of the revolt of 1836, the alleged Indian-Mexican conspiracies of 1838–39, and the invasions of 1842, saw a hardening of attitudes toward the Tejanos within Texas. Many Tejanos left Texas, and the Anglo-Texans gained almost total control of the state's politics and economy.[14] In addition, it became clear to Houston, and his successor Anson Jones, that only the United States could secure Texas' independence from Mexico, and they abandoned any pretense at restoring earlier American Indian rights and enforced a strict policy of separation.

By the Law of January 13, 1843, American Indians were to be removed beyond the line of settlement where they were to receive the full protection of the laws of the Republic of Texas. With the exception of the Alabamas and Coushattas, who received the lands their descendants now occupy by the Law of January 14, 1840, no American Indians were allowed within the line of settlement without permission from an Indian agent.[15] Likewise, whites, supposedly, could not pass beyond the line of settlement without the permission of the president. In addition, the law continued to emphasize the strict control of trade with Native Americans by establishing five government-licensed trading houses along the line of settlement and by banning unlicensed trade between settlers and Indians.

Houston, who was never adverse to making a profit from his friendship with Indians invested in Torrey's Trading House, the licensed firm for conducting the Indian trade in the Republic of Texas. For example, earlier, in 1830, he had bid on the contract to remove the Cherokees and the other American Indian peoples from the South. Apparently, President Jackson and Secretary of War John H. Eaton wanted to award the contract to Houston, in spite of the fact that he did not submit the lowest bid. The threat of political scandal prevented Houston from receiving the contract.[16]

Also, the law created a Bureau of Indian Affairs to supervise the Indians and continued the practice of periodic councils to settle disputes that arose between American Indian nations and between Indians and Anglo-Texans. Yet, the Republic of Texas, unwilling or unable to stop settler encroachment on Indian lands, recognized the ultimate futility of a line of separation. On September 29, 1843, the Republic of Texas concluded the Treaty of Bird's Fort with the Tonkawas and many other American Indian groups on the northwest Texas frontier. The treaty restated and expanded the provisions of the Law of January 13, 1843, to encourage the "civilization" of the Indians as part of the official policy of the Republic of Texas.[17] Apparently, Houston and Jones hoped that, by the time the line of settlement reached the farthest boundaries of Texas, the Indians would be able to live like Anglo-Texans among Anglo-Texans.

The contrast in the Indian policies of Lamar and Houston reflected the emergence of political and social differences among the Anglo-Texans along class and regional lines. Lamar and his policies had the strongest support in the frontier counties, where most of the Anglo-Texans were yeoman farmers and stock raisers, and among a clique of radical lawyers and land speculators. Houston's base of support lay in East Texas and the upper coastal plains among the planters and merchants.[18]

Also, Texas was not isolated from more global political trends. The American imperial agenda laid out in the Monroe Doctrine brought the United States into greater conflict with Mexico and the Great Powers of Europe, particularly the United Kingdom and Russia, both of which had claims or designs on western North America.[19] Through the period from 1836 to 1844, the intensifying debate over slavery tempered U.S. expansion. Eventually, the United States would make its push to the Pacific as its "natural" border.

A part of the ideology of westward expansion by the United States during the 1840s, which came to be termed "Manifest Destiny," was the notion that the Pacific Ocean was the "natural" western boundary of the United States. The "natural" southern and northern boundaries were less determined, but some argued for all of the western Hemisphere, or at least all of North America. For example, Sam Houston, in a speech to a Democratic Party gathering at Tammany Hall in New York during the Mexican War, remarked: "As surely as tomorrow's sun will rise and pursue its bright course along the firmament of heaven, so certain, it appears to my mind, must the Anglo-Saxon race pervade the whole southern extremity of the continent, and the people whom God has placed here in this land, spread, prevail, and pervade throughout the whole rich empire of this hemisphere."[20]

ECONOMIC GROWTH IN THE REPUBLIC OF TEXAS

Economic expansion continued despite the unsettled political conditions. Indian and Tejano removal freed new lands and created new opportunities for settlers from the United States and sources of revenue through land sales for the financially strapped republic. For example, within thirteen months of ordering the expedition to remove the Cherokees and other immigrant American Indian nations from Texas, President Lamar signed a bill into law authorizing the survey and sale of the lands granted to the Cherokees by Coahuila y Texas. The proceeds went to the republic.[21]

However, the center of growth continued on the lower Brazos and lower Colorado Rivers, where a plantation system rivaling other areas of the coastal South developed. By the end of the republic, Houston and Galveston had grown to be towns of considerable importance. In the remainder of Texas, settlement took place as yeoman stock farmers spread up the river valleys. By 1846, the line of settlement had reached west to Preston on the Red River north of present-day Pottsboro, Bird's Fort north of present-day Arlington, Bucksnort near the falls of the Brazos, Austin, New Braunfels, San Antonio, Castroville, and Corpus Christi.

Texas independence had set off a period of unparalleled land speculation that largely replaced the more orderly system of colonization during the period of Mexican rule. In the early 1840s, the republic briefly revived the practice of letting empresario contracts to encourage settlement. Peter's colony and Mercer's colony in North Texas, near Dallas, had settled more than 400 families from the Ohio Valley by 1845. Castro's colony resulted in the creation of the Alsatian settlement of Castroville in 1844. The large Fisher and Miller grant was sold to a German colonization group that founded New Braunfels in 1845 and brought more than 7,000 German emigrants to the Texas Hill Country by 1847. Besides the formal colonization policies of the 1840s, the republic and later the state allowed men to claim up to 320 acres of public land for fifty cents per acre.

Yet, land speculators operated with relative impunity, if not encouragement by the republic. An insightful comment on the nature of land speculation in the Republic of Texas comes from an anonymous visitor who traveled up the Colorado River to the site of the new capital in 1838: "Texas contains more *cities* than any other country in the world. Most of them scarcely contain a house—and many of them never will. But the proprietors give them high-sounding names, and the appellation of *city*, and talk of future greatness with as much earnestness as if they poesessed [*sic*] some of the importance which they imagined time would give them."[22]

While most Anglo-Texans raised little more than they consumed on their farms, the developing plantation economy produced 29,000 bales of cotton for export through the Gulf ports in the year ending October 31, 1845. The cotton was worth more than thirty times as much money as the republic's second-leading export, hides, through the same ports. This figure did not include cotton grown on smaller holdings in

East Texas, which was exported overland or down the Red River to the United States, or cotton smuggled out of Texas and into the United States. It would be the first year of statehood before the plantations on the upper coast, hampered by a chronic lack of capital, produced enough sugar for export. The prairies of the upper coast also saw the best-developed cattle-raising economy. Ranchers drove their cattle to New Orleans for sale, processing, and export to satisfy the growing world demand for hides, tallow, and beef.[23]

The expanding economy reflected the growing population. By the end of the republic there were possibly 120,000 Anglo-Texans, a four-fold increase over 1836, and they owned 40,000 African American slaves, an eight-fold increase over 1836.[24] Population figures for Tejanos and Indians are sketchier. Certainly, there were fewer Tejanos north of the Nueces River, and, except for the Alabama-Coushattas and a few highly acculturated Bidais, nearly all Indians had been forced beyond the Red River, the Nueces River, or the line of settlement.

RAIDING, TRADING, AND FRONTIER VIOLENCE

The southwestern border of Texas recovered slowly from the chaos and destruction wrought by the Texas Revolution, and it saw persistent violence as a way of life. Before turning to the struggle for survival by the western Tonkawas and the Karankawas in the chaos on the southwestern frontier and by the eastern Tonkawas on the Colorado River frontier, it is necessary to further explore the violence on the southwest frontier of Texas during the era of the republic.

Anglo-Texan frontiersmen easily adopted a pattern that had flourished on the northern frontier of New Spain for more than one hundred years. Raiding and illegal trading and their associated violence and excitement provided a powerful lure for the entrepreneurial Anglo-Texan who was trapped in the hard scrabble life of a frontier stock farmer. After the revolution, the violence became particularly acute on the southwestern frontier of Texas, where organized gangs of bandits, which used the hostilities between Mexico and Texas as an excuse for their actions, operated on both sides of the Nueces. Mexico's and Texas' lack of political control over the area between the Nueces and the Rio Grande further facilitated the violence. Although some of the bandit groups were ethnically based, such as the infamous "Cow-Boys" around Goliad and Victoria, others were not. For example, in the spring of 1849 one raiding party that had murdered Colonel Henry L. Kinney's driver outside of Corpus Christi was "about one hundred strong, and composed of mixed Indians, Mexicans, Negroes, *and whites.*"[25]

Anglo-Texans legitimated their participation in this wholesale live-stock theft on the grounds that the Mexican army had driven off large herds of cattle, horses, and mules from Texas ranches during the war. The persistent hostilities between the Republic of Texas and Mexico, the lack of effective law enforcement in the area, and an appeal to the Acts passed by the Consultation at San Felipe in 1835 and Section Eight of the General Provisions of the Constitution of 1836, which declared the property of all persons who failed to support the War of Independence in forfeiture, contributed to the general acceptance of the raiders' activities. The men engaged in "reclaiming" the "lost" cattle and horses called themselves "cowboys." Most of them saw themselves as within the law as long as they did not rob or murder Texas citizens. However, they frequently murdered Tejanos, Mexican traders, and American Indians. Prominent Victoria merchant John Linn said of the "Cow-Boys," after the particularly brutal murder of a party of Mexican traders outside of Victoria in 1842, that they should more properly be called "Men-Slayers."[26]

The cowboys continued their operations throughout the period of the republic. The merchants and speculators, whose interests lay in the development of trade with Mexico and population growth in Southwest Texas, soon persuaded Congress to outlaw the activities of the cowboys, their counterparts from Mexico, and Indians drawn to the raiding activities along the Nueces border. When the Third Congress met in January of 1839, it enacted a law that prohibited the driving off of livestock "which are not his or her legal property" from the largely depopulated counties west of the Guadalupe River, and a week later Congress made it a capital felony to "take, steal and carry away, any horse, mare, ass, mule, gelding, colt, foal, or filly, knowing the same not to be his own, or to aid in the theft or secretion of such property."[27]

Violence and dependence on raiding for economic gain also characterized the Colorado River portion of the southwestern frontier of Texas, which was a prime recruiting ground for raids against Mexico and American Indians. Near Bastrop, on his way to Austin in September of 1840, Secretary of the Treasury James Starr encountered a band of fifteen Texas "cowboys," who made their living off the people of Chihuahua by "murdering them, burning their houses, driving off the cattle, mules, and horses to this country in violation of a law of Congress and the Proclamation of the President inviting those Mexicans to trade on friendly terms with our people and offering them protection." The emboldened "cowboys" claimed that they owned "hundreds of cattle" and "boasted that no jury or court can be found to punish them." They even robbed their neighbors' melon patches with the expectation that the blame would fall on the Tonkawas.[28]

The Anglo-Texan men of the Colorado would also take the property of their fellow citizens, if the occasion presented itself. John Linn relayed the following account in the aftermath of the Battle of Plum Creek:

> Several hundred head of horses and mules were recaptured, as were also immense quantities of dry goods. "To the victors belong the spoils," and the "Colorado men" appropriated everything to themselves. [W. G.] Ewing recognized many of his goods in the captured property, but identification did him no good. Capt. J. O. Wheeler, though one hundred and fifty of the recaptured horses bore his brand, obtained with the greatest difficulty a horse to ride home.[29]

The raiding culture that developed beyond the Nueces and along the Colorado after the Texas Revolution seemed to be peculiar to certain conditions of incorporation through conquest. The cowboys developed in an area in which state control was absent or limited and contained a valuable and easily exploitable natural resource, but which was close enough to trade centers that the cowboys could sell their cattle, horses, and hides and have access to prey for their robberies. Economic distress and war on the Texas-Mexican frontier, runaway slaves, and disintegrating American Indian groups provided an ample source of recruits. In the 1850s, demobilized Texas Rangers were called the "curse of the frontier."[30]

The comparison to the buccaneers of the West Indies of the sixteenth century is compelling. Both groups operated in areas outside of formal state control. For both groups, the original economic base was in wild cattle, and they turned to robbery to supplement their incomes. Finally, buccaneers and cowboys both attracted men from a wide variety of ethnic backgrounds who found buccaneering and cowboying a refuge from downward mobility and shattered cultures. It is probably not accidental that, in the 1850s, antislavery advocate and Texas visitor Frederick Law Olmsted described the cowboys as "prairie pirates."[31]

The Karankawas and the Tonkawas negotiated their survival in the onslaught of the Anglo-Texan conquest in this complex local political scene, marked by rapid economic development and the full-flowering of the raiding culture on the margins of Texas.

KARANKAWA AND TONKAWA SURVIVAL IN THE REPUBLIC OF TEXAS

At the time of the Texas Revolution, Karankawa bands lived on the Texas coast from Matagorda Bay to Corpus Christi Bay. As discussed in the previous chapter, the Karankawas survived by pursuing traditional subsistence strategies, supplemented by work on the farms and ranches of the Anglo-Texan and Tejano settlers of the outer coastal plain. The western bands of the Tonkawas centered their activities on the lower San Antonio and lower Guadalupe Rivers. The western Tonkawas particularly favored Mission Valley, above Victoria, as a camping place.[32] The eastern bands of the Tonkawas camped about the headwaters of the Lavaca, east and north of Gonzales, and along the middle Colorado, above Columbus. The Tonkawas attempted to maintain their traditional hunting and raiding strategy, but the growing strength of the Comanches and the southward thrust of the Wichitas deprived them of horses and access to the buffalo range and trading posts. Therefore, the Tonkawas relied on a variety of subsistence strategies exploiting local resources and on trading the meat and hides of the game they killed to the settlers.

KARANKAWAS AND TONKAWAS IN THE TEXAS REVOLUTION

Much of the military action between the Texan separatists and the Mexican army during the Texas Revolution took place in or near the areas occupied by the Karankawas and the Tonkawas. For the Texans, it was of critical importance that they not be forced to fight American Indian nations and Mexico at the same time. Settlers planning for the war with Mexico saw guaranteeing Indian neutrality as a top priority. To achieve this end, Texan authorities went to both the Karankawas and the Tonkawas in the fall of 1835, and they asked them to remain out of the upcoming fight.[33]

For the most part, the Tonkawas stayed out of the hostilities, though evidence exists that some of the eastern Tonkawas fought alongside the Texans. Frank Collinson reported that he knew Tonkawa headman Campos at Fort Griffin in the 1870s and that Campos owned a "discharge" signed by Sam Houston soon after the Battle of San Jacinto. Campos's discharge thanked him and the other Tonkawas for their services in the Texas Revolution. Also the *Treaty between the Republic of Texas and the Tonkawa Indians*, signed at Houston with the eastern Tonkawas, referred to General Campos and Colonel Oquin [Ocquin].[34]

Along the southwestern border of Texas more dangerous conditions for bystanders prevailed. In the vicinity of Goliad, Refugio, and Victoria, the Tejano majority possessed divided loyalties between the secessionist or Federalist position and the Centralist position in the conflict. The western Tonkawas and the various Karankawa bands had, as a matter of survival, developed loyalties to individual settlers. These loyalties pulled each band to the position of its settler ally. The western Tonkawas, as the eastern Tonkawas had done with the Anglo-Texan empresarios Stephen F. Austin and Green DeWitt, cultivated the patronage of the empresario Martín de León. For example, de León had employed some Tonkawas to eliminate a Karankawa band from his ranch at Victoria in 1835 or 1836. Some of the surviving Karankawa bands had developed similar allegiances to Phillip Dimmitt, who lived at the mouth of the Lavaca River, and to Tejano rancheros, some of whom supported the Centralist position.[35]

The divided Tejano loyalties produced a bloody siege of neighbor-versus-neighbor violence around Goliad and Refugio in the winter of 1835–36. The Centralist rancheros and their Karankawa allies began guerrilla operations against Anglo-Texans, Federalist rancheros and their Karankawa allies. As a result, many Anglo-Texans and Federalist Tejanos saw all Karankawas as siding with the Mexican army and the Centralist Tejanos. The Mexican army considered the Karankawas traitors, supporting the secessionists, because of the loyalty of other Karankawa bands to Phillip Dimmitt, Texan commandant at Goliad during the late fall and winter of 1835–36. This division of loyalties among the Karankawas is the likely source of accounts of the Karankawas "switching sides" in the revolution. Seemingly, none of the Karankawas followed Phillip Dimmitt to the Alamo.[36] The western Tonkawas apparently avoided the predicament of the Karankawas. However, the results of the Texas Revolution would have more far-reaching impact than the actual fighting itself on both peoples.

WESTERN TONKAWAS IN THE REPUBLIC OF TEXAS

As noted earlier, the western Tonkawas had developed a close allegiance to the empresario Martín de León during the early 1830s. However in the anti-Mexican reaction after the Texas Revolution, de León lost most of his holdings and much of his influence around Victoria.[37] Without the protection of de León, the western Tonkawas became involved in the lucrative business of stealing cattle, horses, and other livestock that engaged the people of the southwestern border during the postwar years.

These activities attracted both the western Tonkawas and some Karankawas. The Tonkawas readily exploited the situation, because it meshed with their cultural orientation toward horses and raiding. The Karankawas, with their general lack of a horse tradition, found the transition to the raiding culture more difficult. It was not surprising to see a Tonkawa accused of murdering Jackson N. Parker, a "cowboy" collecting cattle for the Army of the Republic of Texas beyond the Guadalupe, in the summer of 1837. According to a contemporary newspaper account, Parker innocently chased some cattle into a mesquite thicket where he was killed by a Tonkawa, "who was so near him that the flash of the rifle burned his coat." A few months earlier, in November, 1836, some western Tonkawas, armed only with bows and arrows, had fought with the Texas military near San Antonio. They reportedly lost three men in the fight.[38]

During the late summer of 1838, some of the western Tonkawas accompanied a "ranging company" of volunteers from the lower Colorado and the lower Lavaca, led by Pinckney Caldwell, to the Nueces in search of a Mexican military force commanded by Manuel Savariego. After failing to locate Savariego, the Tonkawas and many of the Anglo-Texans went looking for horses to compensate them for their time. They found them in the ownership of a Mexican trader. On their way back to their homes, the Tonkawas drove their liberated horses through Goliad. Some of the residents of Goliad, led by Dr. Isaac Tower, a recent immigrant from New York and a member of Congress, followed the Tonkawas out of town a short distance. Claiming that the horses were stolen property, the men from Goliad took them from the Tonkawas at gunpoint and sold them to themselves at public auction at ridiculously low prices. By the next month, the citizens of Goliad, apparently jealous of the competition from the Tonkawas and spreading rumors of "depredations" on the upper Lavaca River, were said to be "in arms . . . and declaring it their intention to exterminate the Tonkawas," who were "living at this time at the mouth of the San Antonio and numbered about 200 warriors."[39]

Only a few weeks earlier, on June 12, 1838, the young Mary Maverick encountered some men from the western Tonkawas on the San Antonio River below San Antonio. She found them "loud and filthy." In addition, "They were in war paint, and well-armed, and displayed in triumph two scalps, one hand, and several pieces of putrid flesh from various parts of the human body. These were to be taken to the squaws to eat and dance around when these warriors rejoined the tribe." Their actions alarmed her. They admired her baby, "pretty and white," but she felt their real purpose was that "they, being cannibals, would like to eat my baby, and kill us all and carry off our horses." The Tonkawas rode along with Mrs. Maverick's party until after midnight without incident. Yet, Mrs. Maverick remembered the Tonkawas as "treacherous and cruel and noted thieves and murderers."[40]

There exists only an incomplete record of what happened on the lower San Antonio River in the fall of 1838, and there exists no further record of the western bands of the Tonkawas or the leaders Ouchcala and Gosata who signed the *Treaty between the Republic of Texas and the Tonkawa Indians* at the Post of Bexar in San Antonio a year earlier "in order to secure the blessings of peace." However, the western Tonkawas apparently were released at Victoria. Afterward, they "came across a company of Mexican soldiers, attacked them by surprise, captured all their horses, and a large quantity of provisions, and articles of merchandise. The Tonkawas appear to be elated with their success."[41]

Apparently the western Tonkawas had avoided total destruction at the hands of armed settlers through the intervention of Campos, who used the treaty and his "discharge" to turn back the Anglo-Texans bent on extermination. And, somewhat surprisingly, Pinckney Caldwell filed a suit against Samuel Williams, Dr. Tower, and others in the district court at Victoria for illegally taking the Tonkawas' horses.[42] Yet, despite support from some influential Anglo-Texans, at least some of the Tonkawas had been imprisoned at Victoria, and the western band of the Tonkawas was dispersed. After 1838, the story of the eastern Tonkawas and the story of the western Tonkawas merge. However, before going on to the account of the eastern Tonkawas during the Republic of Texas, we will turn to the Karankawas.

KARANKAWAS IN THE REPUBLIC OF TEXAS

The Karankawas, as pointed out earlier, were reluctant and ill equipped to join in the raiding and trading economy of the interior because of their orientation to the physical environment of the coastal marshes. The band around Matagorda Bay, as late as 1842, combined traditional subsistence activities with trading fish and game for food, blankets, whiskey, and other consumer goods. When the English naturalist William Bollaert observed them on the streets of Matagorda in the spring of that year, he noted:

> They do not like work; they fish and hunt enough to support them-selves and sell some. Now and then they bring in a panther's skin, or other peltries in exchange for blankets or whiskey. They now and then appropriate (steal is an ugly word). I saw some of them parading the town, walking almost naked, one after the other. They looked robust and in good health, but no smile or joy was seen in their looks. Texas . . . is fast becoming the grave of the tribes of Red Men.[43]

Overlooking Bollaert's fascination with the juxtaposition of physical vigor with inevitable extinction among the "primitive," we see the east-ernmost band(s) of the Karankawa maintaining an economic and cul-tural orientation that satisfied the demands of being Karankawa and coming to terms with the market economy and the European world. However, geographic location insulated the easternmost Karankawas to a considerable degree from the raiding and trading culture of frontier violence flowering on the middle Colorado River and along and west of the Guadalupe River.

For the Karankawas on the middle coast, the large herds of livestock along and beyond the Nueces provided a stronger lure. At least one or two bands of Karankawas, as well as an unknown number of individuals, abandoned the traditional Karankawa way of life along the coast for raiding in the interior. In March of 1842, some Karankawas joined the Lipans and Mescaleros in an attack on the retreating Mexican army of Ramón Valera below the Nueces. In December of that year, the Mier expedition encountered a band of forty Karankawas on the Rio Grande, a few miles below Guerrero. The Anglo-Texans disarmed the Karan-kawas and took twelve captives. They released the captives unharmed the next day. It was from this band that the Anglo-Texans acquired the Union Jack, which they carried into Mier, provoking a diplomatic inci-dent between Mexico and the United Kingdom. A "ranging company" led by Tejano ranchero Rafael Aldrete attacked another or this same band on the Nueces southwest of Refugio in 1844 or 1845.[44]

With entry into the raiding and trading culture of the interior likely to lead to the cultural, if not the physical, death of the Karankawas, most of the Karankawas of the middle coast attempted to follow the strategies that had prevailed during the Mexican period. However, this route became more difficult by the end of the republic. The Texas coast experienced rapid economic growth, particularly on the bayshore and the barrier islands that had heretofore been ignored by Anglo-Texans wanting to establish plantations and ranches. In 1838, the former empresario James Power located his ranch and trading house on Live Oak Point, and speculators laid out the town of Lamar across the channel connecting Copano and Aransas Bays. In the next five years, ranches proliferated, and speculators swarmed to the Texas coast. Anglo-Texans laid out towns, built ports, established trading houses, and planned roads, railroads, and navigation projects to take advantage of the expected boom coming with population growth in the interior and wresting the Mexican trade from Matamoros and Santa Fe.[45]

The text of the following clipping from the *Austin City Gazette* of October 30, 1839, inserted by Bollaert into his diary, furnishes a typical example of the preoccupation with the capture of the Mexican trade in the minds of the speculative interests in Texas:

> [The city of Austin] has many advantages of location not immediately discernible to the traveller who does not look beyond the spot itself for the mines of wealth destined to contribute their riches for the enlargement and decoration of our new Capital. It is located at the foot of a spur of the Cordilleras mountains, terminating in the valley of the Colorado. From this place the great road to Santa Fé will be laid out through a rich and well-watered country, abundant in game, and bees as numerous as the swarms of Hybla, and blessed with a climate to yield the Hesperian Fruit, which may be gathered here without the fear of the "sleepless dragon." Its proximity to the provinces of Mexico on the north and west borders of the Republic, with the aid of capital, which will soon find its way here, must attract all the valuable trade at present carried to St. Louis and Matamoros. Its distance from the largest trading towns on the Rio Grande does not exceed four or five hundred miles—one-third of the distance of the route at present travelled by the caravans from Missouri and Arkansas. We are barely permitted to glance at these advantages, satisfied that those interested in that valuable trade will soon turn their attention to this country.[46]

This orgy of progress left no room for the Karankawas. James Power and other merchants were calling for government protection from the Karankawas in the vicinity of Aransas Bay within a year of Power's location on Live Oak Point. Three years later, it was reported that a band of

Karankawas, numbering forty warriors, was robbing merchants around Lamar, supposedly at the instigation of Mexican authorities.[47]

With few exceptions, most of the Anglo-Texan developers on the Texas coast found the Karankawas an impediment to their dreams. Captain Thomas Bridges at Port Austin on Lavaca Bay at least tolerated the Karankawas in his settlement and, at times, hired them to do menial chores. Colonel Henry L. Kinney employed twenty-eight Karankawa men to help defend his trading house at Corpus Christi from an expected Mexican attack in March of 1842.[48] As the density of Anglo-Texan population increased on the outer coast and as the outer coast became more important as a center of ranching, trade, and transportation, it became difficult for the remaining Karankawas to sustain their traditional subsistence strategies. Chances for antagonistic encounters grew. Greater population movement through the coast, combined with a declining ability to sustain traditional nutrition, undoubtedly made the Karankawas more susceptible to disease.

The fortunes of the Karankawa bands became increasingly tied to the individual Anglo-Texan ranchers and promoters who claimed the hunting, fishing, and gathering territories of the Karankawas. In 1838, the *Houston Telegraph and Texas Register* relayed the following report from the new settlements adjacent to Aransas Bay:

> The Cronkawas have been encamped near Aransas during the summer, and have been exceedingly useful to the citizens of that place by furnishing a constant supply of fish, turtle, venison & c., for the inhabitants. The poor fellows appear humbled, and endeavor, by performing the most menial offices, to show their attachment to the whites.[49]

By the middle 1840s, desperate conditions prevailed for the Karankawas all along the coast. Phillip Power, who lived at Copano on Copano Bay, remembered that Indians "roamed the country either singly or in pairs begging food."[50] More dramatic is Mary Wightman Helms's recollection of the appearance of the remnants of a band of Karankawas in Matagorda, where she was visiting in 1843, after an absence of two years. This same band had sought shelter at her and her husband's plantation in the late 1820s and early 1830s, after the "Dressing Point" massacre:

> . . . they made their appearance in a most wretched, filthy condition, few in numbers, offering to trade fish for whisky. The young girl I had helped was dying. She formally gave away her only child to a white

woman and the whole tribe formed a procession to go and deliver the child before the mother's death.[51]

The *Houston Telegraph and Texas Register* gave the following account of the return of the Karankawas to Matagorda: "They professed much humility and are so anxious to obtain the protection of our citizens, that few are disposed to molest them. They have resumed their old occupations of hunting and fishing."[52]

James Power of Aransas apparently "adopted" two Karankawa children, Mary and Tom. They were still living at St. Mary's in Refugio County toward the end of the nineteenth century. However, Bollaert noted in 1842 that the young Indian boy of James Power resisted his new life.[53] It remains unclear how widespread or successful for the children the practice was of adopting Indian children.

The Karankawas not only suffered from disease, excessive use of alcohol, and loss of a finely tuned diet based on traditional subsistence patterns, but a renewal of settler violence exacerbated the physical and cultural collapse of the Karankawas in the mid-1840s. The best-documented event of settler violence from this period happened on the lower Guadalupe River between October, 1844, and January, 1845.

There are two versions of the story deriving from Anglo-Texan eye-witnesses to the events. Both accounts indicate that some Karankawas killed Captain John A. Kemper at his ranch on the lower Guadalupe in a dispute over some cattle, possibly because Kemper did not want Karankawas on his ranch, and they retaliated by killing his milk cow. Kemper's wife, mother-in-law, and children escaped unharmed. According to the Gus Black account, the Karankawas fled from the lower Guadalupe never to return in fear of the settlers' response, which was certain to be terrible.

However, Edwin Phelps stated that some men from Victoria joined the ranchers on the lower Guadalupe, including some that had been friendly to the Karankawas during Mexican rule, and attacked the camp of the Karankawas. The settlers drove the survivors out. Eventually they "cornered" them in a thicket, near where the town of Tivoli stands today. Only one Karankawa survived the second assault. He was a "veritable giant," and he fled into the bay. Phelps remembered: "this Indian stayed out in the brush along the bayshore for about a week, and then came into Refugio and surrendered. He then carried the mail between Refugio and some place, the name of which I do not remember, and died in Refugio."[54]

By the end of the republic, the western bands of the Tonkawas were no more and the Karankawas who survived gave the appearance of a people traumatized by the violence of conquest and its attendant evils of disease, starvation, and alcohol abuse. As Alice Bridges Oliver, who as a girl in Port Austin lived near the Karankawas, perceptively observed: "the spirit seemed to die within them and their degradation was complete."[55] Most of the survivors lost the option of being Karankawa. The loss of their coastal marsh homeland, which had provided the foundations for their economic and cultural well-being, and the relentless assaults of "civilization" virtually destroyed the Karankawas as a people.

EASTERN TONKAWAS IN THE REPUBLIC OF TEXAS

With the reins of political and economic control in Texas firmly in the hands of the Anglo-Texan settlers, the eastern Tonkawas, while not rewarded for their service in the Texas Revolution with land, were allowed to participate in the raiding activities of the settlers on the Colorado River frontier. The Anglo-Texan settlers on the Colorado were at the fore of the hostilities between the Anglo-Texans and their foes: Comanches, Wichitas, Mexicans, and Cherokees. The Tonkawas on the Colorado most certainly welcomed the opportunity to participate in the raids against their old enemies, the Comanches and the Wichitas, who had pushed them out of the richest buffalo hunting grounds and deprived them of the "vast droves of horses" that they had possessed thirty years earlier.

By 1838, the eastern Tonkawas, hereafter referred to as the Tonkawas, had located their main campsite on the east side of the Colorado River, below Alum Creek, on lands claimed by General Edward Burleson. The association between the Tonkawas, led by Placido and Campos, and General Burleson would sustain the Tonkawas through the turbulent years of the republic. In a pattern to be repeated, Placido and a small group of Tonkawa men accompanied the Burleson and Douglas expedition against the Texas Cherokees and other American Indian people in East Texas as scouts and fighters. For the next seven years, Placido and a hand-picked group of men were part of every major expedition led by Burleson against the Comanches and the Wichitas. They only rarely accompanied other Rangers after participating in John H. Moore's debacle on the San Saba in 1839. However, Houston considered Burleson's Tonkawa allies, as well as a similar cadre of Lipans, essential to his effort to turn back the Mexican invasion of 1842.[56]

Tonkawas, as well as Lipans, apparently chose certain Ranger leaders to follow on the basis of personal loyalty, in the same manner that they followed certain war chiefs among their own people. Intriguingly, the Rangers structured themselves around the same type of personal loyalty. The likely borrowing of leadership styles by the Texas Rangers from the Tonkawas, Lipans, and Comanches lies within the larger debate surrounding American Indian influence on Anglo-American institutions. Texas Ranger historian Walter Prescott Webb opened the door to such an investigation when he noted that Ranger organization was "something like a band of Comanche braves who followed their chief."[57] Yet, such an investigation has apparently not occurred.

Not only did the Tonkawa warrior corps serve as valuable scouts and able fighters for the Anglo-Texans, but they also served as shock troops in the war of terror between the Anglo-Texans and their American Indian enemies. Let me explain. The Anglo-Texan tactics against the Comanches and other American Indians would seem to terrorize the enemy. For example, one can examine Noah Smithwick's account of John H. Moore's raid on the Comanches on the San Saba River in 1839:

> When within a mile of the camp we dismounted and tied our horses. We then crept upon the sleeping Indians who were not dreaming of an attack. As soon as daylight gave us the exact situation of the camp we made a rush for it, pouring a volley right into the lodges. Taken completely by surprise the savages bounded from their lodges and scattered like partridges. Our men rushed in among the lodges. The women and children screaming, dogs barking, men yelling and shooting, in a moment transformed the peaceful scene on which the day had just dawned into a pandemonium.[58]

However, with their Tonkawa allies, the Anglo-Texans could employ a new element of terror—the threat of cannibalism.

The Tonkawas and their neighbors probably practiced some form of ritual cannibalism and torture of prisoners of war prior to the nineteenth century. During the nineteenth century, the indigenous people of the southern plains largely abandoned this practice with one notable exception—the Tonkawas. The Anglo-Texans had used the belief that the Karankawas were cannibals, despite little more evidence than that produced by the rumors of vicious cannibals passed around the hearths in the isolated cabins of the settlers, to justify their "wars of extermination" against them in the 1820s.[59] However, compelling evidence exists that Placido's Tonkawas practiced cannibalism in the war against the Comanches and the Wichitas.

Whether this was a continuation of an earlier Tonkawa cultural trait or a development arising from the demands of surviving the violence on the Texas, Comanchería, Mexico border remains unclear. First, scanty evidence of Tonkawa cannibalism prior to the 1830s exists. Second, some Anglo-Texan frontiersmen saw killing an Indian as no different from killing a wild animal and used their flesh for food with no less thought than they would eat a wild animal.[60] Finally, from existing accounts of Tonkawa cannibalism from this period, there is little doubt that it was associated with the scalp dance, tied to a warrior cult in which Tonkawas took on the characteristics of the wolf, and served both as a means for revenge and as a talisman for success in future battles.

Most nineteenth century observers of Tonkawa cannibalism recognized the ritual and symbolic aspects of the act.[61] Robert Hall saw the symbolic nature of Tonkawa cannibalism most clearly:

> They [the Tonkawas after Plum Creek] cut him [a dead Comanche warrior] into slices and broiled him on sticks. Curiously enough the eating of the flesh acted upon them as liquor does upon other men. After a few mouthfuls they began to act as if they were very drunk, and I don't think there was much pretense or sham about it. They danced, raved, howled and sang, and invited me to get up and eat a slice of Comanche. They said it would make me brave. I was very hungry, but not sufficiently so to become a cannibal. The Tonkaways were wild over the victory, and they did not cease their celebration until sunrise.[62]

Although Tonkawa cannibalism or tales of Tonkawa cannibalism may have frightened their enemies and enhanced their usefulness to their Anglo-Texan allies, the practice had a negative result for the Tonkawas. The Tonkawas became the mortal enemies of the Comanches and other American Indians of the southern plains. Many Indians on the southern plains in the nineteenth century saw Tonkawa cannibalism as depraved. A Choctaw named Puckshunnubbee wrote the following description of Tonkawa cannibalism in a letter to the Fort Smith *Herald* on January 24, 1851:

> The Tonkaways are cannibals eating the bodies of those whom they kill, and those of their own tribe who sicken and die. A short time ago, two or three weeks since, a young gentleman of my acquaintance

passed their camps on Red River, about sixty or seventy miles above Fort Washita, and they were eating one of their own people; and when they were asked about it, said that he was sick, and would have died, and that they had killed him to relieve him of his suffering, and themselves of hunger.[63]

Accusations of Tonkawa cannibalism led to and justified massacres of Tonkawas by other Indians, especially after 1859. Former Comanche captive Herman Lehmann gave a particularly vivid first-hand account of some Comanches murdering a group of Tonkawas in the 1870s accused of cannibalism.[64]

Also, Tonkawas apparently cultivated the role of outsiders among the American Indians of the southern plains. Perhaps taking on the role of "trickster," the Tonkawas frequently were accused of possessing and using negative magic by other Indians. Ranger Rip Ford recounted an incident in which the other Indians of the Brazos Reservation accused the Tonkawas of interfering with their rainmaking ceremonies: "The infernal Tonks, always bent on mischief, had stronger medicine than his [the rain king] and turned the cloud away. The Tonks were the black beasts of the agency and were made responsible for many such happenings."[65]

In addition Tonkawa cannibalism confirmed the moral superiority of the Anglo-Texans over the "savages," allies or enemies. The Anglo-Texans relished the stories of Tonkawa cannibalism with the same fervor that they did stories of Comanche and other Indian "atrocities." For example, in a supposedly eyewitness account of the aftermath of the Anglo-Texan and Comanche fight at Plum Creek that appeared in the pro-Lamar *Austin Texas Sentinel*, the reporter first regaled the reader with the lurid details of the deaths and injuries of the Anglo-Texan women captives at the hands of the Comanches. He concluded with this particularly ghoulish account of alleged Tonkawa cannibalism:

> Observing a crowd of Tonkawas, we rode out to see what it was that attracted them. They were gathered around the fallen chief, and hastily engaged in cutting off his hands and feet, and the choicest pieces of flesh from his body and with perfect indifference attaching it by string to their saddles, with the buffalo and venison they had prepared for the expedition. . . .
>
> The next morning we found the Tonkawas broiling and eating the fat yellow flesh of the Comanches, for their breakfast, reserving the feet, hands, and choice morsels as a treat for their squaws. We drew near

their campfire, and Placidore, the chief, holding up to us a nice piece of broiled Indian, cried out in broken Spanish, "*moucha wano—Comanche moucha wano*" which meant that the Comanche was very good.[66]

This delight in the savagery of the Indians took place in a discourse that also depicted them as objects of condescending pity. During the debate over Cherokee removal during January of 1840, the following observation appeared in the *Texas Sentinel:*

> But they only have to take a trip to the frontier, and see the Indian as he is, to strip him of his fancied nobility, and let him stand forth to the world, the *naked savage in his deformity.*
>
> An Indian has not one redeeming quality in his composition, the whole race are *thieves* and *murderers.*[67]

Only five months later, the *Telegraph and Texas Register* described the Indians of Texas as known for their "cowardice," as "objects of pity," and as "weak" and "imbecile."[68]

While Placido, Campos, and an elite warrior corps took part in the major events of the Anglo-Texan warfare with the Mexicans and Native Americans, most of the Tonkawas on the Colorado continued their struggle for survival. The Tonkawas labored seasonally on the farms in the rich bottom lands; traded game, hides, pecans, and crafts to the settlers; and hired out as guides for Anglo-Texans wishing to make the dangerous journey from Texas to Santa Fe.[69] When Bollaert visited Bastrop in August of 1843, he found:

> only one store for dry goods in the town, and this was full of Tonkaways bartering their buffalo robes, deerskins, moccasins, etc. for powder, cottonstuffs, beads, and such like finery for their squaws and an occasional bottle of whiskey from the tippling shop. This last is against *executive orders.*[70]

Relations between the Tonkawas and the Anglo-Texans around Bastrop were not always so idyllic. Disputes arose over matters as diverse as the ownership of horses and rights to the pecan crop. The Tonkawas, without citizenship rights in the new political and economic order, had no protection from the law and lived among Anglo-Texan settlers that saw "sporting" and "killing of Indians" as "synonymous terms."[71] As a result, in times of difficulty, they could only appeal to the intervention of friendly, powerful Anglo-Texans. However, such appeals did not always meet with success.

In 1842, the Tonkawa allies refused to accompany Burleson on an expedition after the murder of a Tonkawa man by an Anglo-Texan settler in an unfortunate, though all too common, incident based on mutual misunderstanding. The Tonkawa came to the settler's cabin to ask for a drink of water. The settler denied the request; the Tonkawa pointed an empty gun at the settler; the settler responded with a loaded gun and killed the Tonkawa. However, Burleson refused to intervene in the affair on behalf of the Tonkawas and threatened to evict the Tonkawas from the Colorado if they didn't provide him with scouts and fighters. With few alternatives, the Tonkawas ended the "strike" and provided Burleson with seven of their men for the raid.[72] This incident reveals the difference in the way Burleson and the Tonkawa warrior corps perceived their relationship. Burleson apparently saw the Tonkawas as something akin to mercenaries, employees who fought for him in return for food and shelter. The Tonkawas, however, perceived the relationship as one between allies with reciprocal rights and responsibilities.

Despite the economic and political ties between the Tonkawas and some of the Anglo-Texan settlers, anti-Indian feeling grew on the Colorado. Even as early as November of 1838, the settlers around Bastrop were calling for the removal of the Tonkawas and the Lipans from their vicinity, though "they are perceived as friendly." In May of 1843, the settlers around Bastrop accused the Tonkawas and the Lipans, who had camped near them, of stealing horses in the settlements for sale to white traders for resale on the Red River. Republic of Texas Indian Agent Ben Bryant resolved the dispute by attributing the story to an Anglo-Texan boy who had run away from home to live with the Indians. His conduct among the Lipans was "so bad" that Agent Bryant ordered them to return the Laughlin boy to his father in Austin. Apparently, the boy had spread the tale of Lipan and Tonkawa involvement in the horse theft ring in revenge for his betrayal by the Lipans.[73]

The question of Anglo-Americans abandoning their culture to live with Native Americans remains one of the most intriguing and poorly explored aspects of the long frontier experience in the United States. Apparently, an Anglo-Texan, David Warwick, earned the status of "war captain" among the Tonkawas in the mid-1840s.[74]

In the fall of 1843, the Tonkawas and the Lipans were camped together on Cedar Creek, outside of Bastrop. Some of them had "hired on" to the plantations in the Colorado bottom to pick cotton. Despite their military service and their willingness to "work," settlers were "worried" about their presence and requested their removal to the Little River.[75]

By the end of 1844, settler complaints about the Tonkawas and the Lipans forced the Jones administration to act upon the law separating Native Americans from the Anglo-Texans. On December 14, 1844, the agent for the Lipans and Tonkawas, Cambridge Green, reported to Superintendent of Indian Affairs Thomas G. Western:

> on the 27h of May, the Tonkawa in the vicinity of Gonzales—drinking liquor stealing cattle committing depredations which made it necessary that I should remain with them—I remained with them until the first of September. . . .
>
> as soon as I was able I returned to the Tonkawa camp on the Colorado—where I found the women picking out cotton and many of the men lying about Bastrop drunk—I Enquired of O'Quinn [Ocquin]— why they did not keep out of the settlements—He appeared—independent —saying a portion of their tribe was out west stealing Mexican horses—and that he felt assured that the people would sustain them—and that they were compelled to remain in the settlements to get subsistence—My indisposal required me to leave and so soon as I was able to ride again I came by Tonkawa Encamped on the head of Buckners Creek on the south for this place [Washington]. . . .
>
> The Inhabitants generally believe that the Lipan and Tonkawa commit depredations daily.[76]

In order to accomplish the removal of the Tonkawas from the settlements, Western appointed Robert S. Neighbors as agent to the Lipans and Tonkawas on February 12, 1845. Neighbors, a twenty-nine-year-old Virginian, had served in the Texas military from 1836 to 1842 and spent eighteen months imprisoned in Mexico after being captured by General Adrian Woll's army in San Antonio in 1842. He proved to be an effective agent and a valuable ally of Placido's Tonkawas.[77]

Superintendent Western ordered Neighbors to move the Tonkawas out of the settlements, preferably to the San Marcos River, near the San Antonio Road crossing, in order not to expose them to hostilities from the Comanches or the Wacos. Neighbors was to bring the Tonkawas to the next council to secure peace between the Tonkawas and the other Texas tribes. In addition, Western instructed Neighbors to have the

Tonkawas select a chief to be responsible to him and the government, to encourage the Tonkawas to continue their trade in hides and furs, but with the official trading house only, and to take up farming.

According to Superintendent Western's letter of instruction to Agent Neighbors on February 12, 1845, the Tonkawas were without a leader since "the death of their principal Chiefs." The letter gives no clue as to the cause of their loss. However, sixteen months earlier, the *Telegraph and Texas Register* reported: "A very fatal epidemic has prevailed among the Tonkawas during the last three months and the tribe heavily decimated." The disease was not smallpox. "Possibly it is the Grippe in an aggravated form."[78]

In order to accomplish Western's goals, Neighbors was to accompany the Tonkawas to the trading house on the Brazos, to repair their guns, and to provide them with gunpowder, hoes, and one hundred bushels of corn to sustain them. Most importantly, the Tonkawas were not to enter the settlements without a pass or seek war with the Wacos. Finally, Western warned Neighbors: "The white path [of peace] must not be Soiled with blood."[79]

As the spring and summer of 1845 passed, Neighbors tried to keep the Tonkawas out of the settlements and at peace with the Wacos, though the Wacos had murdered three Tonkawa men at the headwaters of Yegua Creek and a Tonkawa woman near New Braunfels and stolen most of the Tonkawas' horses. Earlier attempts to make peace between the Tonkawas and the Wacos failed as a result of Waco disgust over Tonkawa cannibalism. For example, in 1843, while visiting President Houston at Washington, the "Waco chief . . . requested the President to permit his warriors to attack the Tonkawas. He said they were cannibals, and he would never make peace with any 'Indians who eat Indians.'"[80]

However, the Tonkawas attended the council held at Tehuacana (Council) Springs during the full moon of September, 1845, with the Anadarkos, Caddos, Cherokees, Delawares, Ionis, Lipans, and Penateka Comanches. At the council, Campo (Campos), chief of the Tonkawas spoke:

> I have heard nothing today but what I am pleased with, for it is all good talk. It is not worth while for me to promise anything more than I have already promised, I have always been friendly with the whites, and have fought for them, and I shall continue to do so, and I want now to be friendly with all my Red Brothers, and walk with them the white path of peace. I want all our women and children to be no more

afraid in travelling about, either of their lives or property. All are welcome to come to my camp, and among my people, I will treat them well, and I want all to treat me and my people in the same way. If there are any of my Red Brothers here who have not made peace with my people I want them to do so now. If the young men of other tribes come among my people, I want them to dance with the young girls, and marry them, for I see no one here that I am not willing to meet as brothers. We are now here without horses, for the Waco came down and stole all we had, but we will soon have more, and then we intend travelling about and see our red brothers, and all live in peace. If the Great White Chief tells his people to make war with the Waco, I want them and all others who may make war against them, to try and get the horses which they stole from my people.[81]

In spite of the plea for the return of their horses, the Tonkawas received no assurances of their return. However, Mo-pe-chu-co-pe, a Penateka Comanche leader who attended the council, gave permission for the Lipans and the Tonkawas to relocate farther from the Anglo-Texan settlements on lands claimed by the Comanches. By the end of the year, the Tonkawas had moved westward to the Blanco River. In his last report to Superintendent Western, before the government of the Republic of Texas ended its existence through its union with the United States, an optimistic Neighbors found the Tonkawas in a "thriving and happy condition" and, having in a "great measure overcome their prejudice against planting corn . . . [and] anxious to be located on land that they can call their own and to be instructed in farming."[82] However, before Neighbors could complete his project of "civilizing" the Tonkawas, the acquisition of Texas by the United States would detonate events that would dramatically alter the processes of the Anglo-Texan conquest of the Karankawas and the Tonkawas.

Texas, during the decade of the republic, saw an intensification of the political and economic processes set in motion by the establishment of the Anglo-Texan colonies during the period of Mexican control. The Anglo-Texan leadership turned a local revolt, also supported by many Tejanos, against Centralist authority in Mexico into a revolution that secured Anglo-Texan domination. American Indians, as well as Tejanos, faced growing hostility from the Anglo-Texan majority during the decade of the republic. The official policies of the Houston and Jones administrations tended to ameliorate that hostility; those of the Lamar administration exacerbated it. For Indians, Houston advocated a version of the expansion-with-honor policy of the early years of the United States in hopes of reducing the violence between settlers and Indians along the frontier of settlement. By the end of the republic, Houston and his successor, Anson Jones, attempted to enforce strict geographic separation of Anglo-Texans and American Indians and control of trade between the two groups by bringing the Indian nations under greater administrative control. Lamar carried out a policy of Indian removal through forced expulsion from Texas or extermination. However, the official policies of the Republic of Texas sometimes meant little at a time when many of the people on the frontier—Anglo-Texan, American Indian, and Tejano—lived by raiding, and were under minimal state control.

Although Texas officials were aware of and exploited the more global political conditions of colonial expansion, which were manifested regionally by intrigue over the control of western North America, ties to the emerging global economy also proved to be important. The decade of the republic saw the growth of a slave-based plantation economy aimed at producing cotton for export to the United Kingdom and the United States in the fertile bottom lands of the lower Brazos and lower Colorado Rivers. Smaller scale cotton production spread almost to the limits of Anglo-Texan settlement. Commercial ranching developed on the prairies of the upper coast. The ranchers drove their cattle to New Orleans, where they could be slaughtered, processed, and shipped to meet the growing world demand for beef. A four-fold increase in the Anglo-Texan population and an eight-fold increase in the African American slave population accompanied the economic expansion.

For the Karankawas and the Tonkawas, both official policy of the Republic of Texas and the expansion of the global economy and its accompanying population growth had impacts, but it was in the raiding culture of the Texas frontier that they negotiated their survival during this phase of the Anglo-Texan conquest. For the Karankawas, the decade of the republic proved to be disastrous. After being caught up in the neighbor-versus-neighbor violence during the revolution, they faced a decade of Anglo-Texan economic development and population growth on the middle coast. By being outside of official treaty relations, the Karankawas became increasingly dependent on the goodwill of local ranchers, planters, merchants, and speculators. The Karankawas, tied by cultural and economic necessity to their coastal marshes, had few choices but to cope with the Anglo-Texans, though a few bands entered into the raiding economy of the interior of South Texas. Ultimately, the goodwill of Anglo-Texan settlers, always a scarce commodity, evaporated. Karankawa attempts at meshing with the new social order by doing ranch work and fishing and hunting for local markets failed in an onslaught of epidemics and massacres.

For the Tonkawas, the years of the republic proved difficult as well. Their cultural orientation toward horsemanship and raiding enticed them to enter the raiding culture. Despite treaty arrangements with the Republic of Texas, settlers, angry over their competition in the livestock stealing endemic west of the Guadalupe, broke up the western bands of the Tonkawas in 1838. The Tonkawas regrouped on the middle Colorado. By attaching themselves to a prominent local settler, Edward Burleson, and making their leading warriors available as guides and fighters in his campaigns against the Cherokees, Comanches, Wichitas, and Mexicans, they secured a tenuous acceptance by the Anglo-Texans of the middle Colorado. Despite their service to the Republic of Texas and their adaptation to the local economy as market hunters, farm laborers, guides, and suppliers of hides, horses, pecans, and crafts, Houston and Jones did not exempt the Tonkawas from their Indian policies. By the end of the republic, the Tonkawas were resettled outside the settlements and under the supervision of an agent. While their association with Burleson could not prevent epidemics, the Tonkawas did not suffer extreme settler violence, and they received some protection from their American Indian enemies. Finally, the Tonkawas, pressured by the needs of the state, became more of a tribe characterized by centralized authority in the hands of leaders associated with Burleson.

The Incorporation of Texas into the United States, 1846–59: Consolidation of Conquest

During the initial period of Texas statehood from 1846 to 1859, Anglo-Texans consolidated their conquest of both the Karankawas and the Tonkawas. During this period, Texas became a state in the United States through a complex series of actions that culminated in the Mexican War of 1846–48. It was the military defeat of Mexico by the United States that secured the incorporation of the Anglo-Texan colony into the United States. The political transformation ushered in sweeping cultural changes and explosive economic and population growth in Texas. Also during this period, Anglo-American and Anglo-Texan attitudes toward American Indians hardened, and these attitudes influenced public policy and private action toward Indians in Texas. Finally, the consolidation of the conquest of the Karankawas and the Tonkawas took place amid the more general violence associated with the establishment of American authority over the southern plains.

THE ENTRY OF TEXAS INTO THE UNITED STATES

After a complex series of political maneuvers during 1844 and 1845, the annexation of Texas became official on February 19, 1846, as President Anson Jones intoned these solemn words in front of the capitol in Austin: "The final act in this great drama is now performed: The Republic of Texas is no more."[1]

In 1844, the slavery question and Whig fears that the acquisition of Texas would lead to a war with Mexico torpedoed attempts to unite Texas with the United States. Many Northerners, and especially abolitionists, in the United States feared that the entrance of Texas, with its legalized slavery, into the union would strengthen the Southern and proslavery position. Despite the opposition engendered by the slavery question and more general Whig opposition to American expansion, John Tyler's secretary of state, John C. Calhoun, and Republic of Texas representatives James Pinckney Henderson and Isaac Van Zandt signed an initial agreement for the annexation of Texas to the United States on April 12, 1844. On June 8, 1844, the antislavery and anti-expansion sentiments prevailed in the U.S. Senate when it overwhelmingly rejected the agreement.

However, expansionist Democrat James K. Polk defeated Whig candidate Henry Clay in November of 1844 on a campaign platform of "Re-Annexation of Texas and Re-Occupation of Oregon," making it possible to forge a new agreement in 1845. On February 27, 1845, the U.S. Congress, in a joint resolution, approved the annexation of Texas. The joint resolution was signed by outgoing President John Tyler on March 1, and it was approved by the Congress of the Republic of Texas on July 4. On December 29, 1845, the U.S. Congress accepted a state constitution from Texas that provided for the continuation of legalized slavery in the new state. The Houston and Jones administrations skillfully played on American fears of British, French, and Russian colonial expansion in western North America to enhance the acceptability of the attainment of Texas in the U.S. Congress.[2]

However, "the final act" was followed by a bloody curtain call that cemented Texas' union with the United States. In both June and July of 1844, the Mexican foreign minister, José Bocanegra, warned the United States that Mexico would regard the annexation of Texas by the United States as a declaration of war. The annexation of a state that Mexico did not recognize as legitimate and one that claimed a large territory under Mexican administration hurled the United States into a confrontation with Mexico. On March 6, 1845, five days after lame-duck President Tyler signed the joint resolution and two days after President Polk's inauguration, the Mexican ambassador to the United States, Juan N. Almonte, broke off diplomatic relations with the United States. Unfortunately, the Polk administration's attempt to settle the controversy through diplomatic channels—a crude offer to buy not only Texas and the disputed lands between the Nueces and the Rio Grande, but also the lands between the Rio Grande and the Pacific—failed. Not only did this diplomatic maneuver fail, but it deeply offended the Mexican leadership. It made it virtually impossible for any Mexican official to negotiate with the United States over the Texas question. With vague promises of support from Great Britain and France, war fever consumed Mexico. In January of 1846, the new Centralist President, Mariano Paredes, vowed to defend the integrity of the national territory, including Texas and especially the disputed territory between the Nueces and the Rio Grande. By the end of March, 1846, all negotiations between the United States and Mexico had ended.[3]

In an attempt to strengthen its bargaining position, the Polk administration had sent a military force commanded by General Zachary Taylor to Corpus Christi, beyond the Nueces River in the disputed territory, in the late summer of 1845. Of course these actions further injured national pride in Mexico. Following the collapse of negotiations in the spring of 1846, Taylor's army marched southward to the mouth of the Rio Grande. There, they established military bases at Point Isabel and at Fort Brown, also in the disputed territory, across the Rio Grande from a Mexican army at Matamoros commanded by General Manuel Arista. The military action culminated in the defeat of Arista's forces north of the Rio Grande at Palo Alto on May 8, 1846, and at Resaca de la Palma on May 9. The U.S. Congress declared war on Mexico on May 11, 1846, and Polk signed the declaration on May 13. He cited American blood spilled on American soil.[4]

The U.S. forces dramatically seized the principal towns of Mexico and, with aid or lack of opposition by disgruntled local populations, occupied New Mexico and California. In the face of such an overwhelming military defeat, the Mexican government could do little but accept the terms offered by the United States. On February 2, 1848, the Treaty of Guadalupe Hidalgo officially ended the War of 1846–48. The military diplomacy of the United States rewarded it with title to all of Mexico north of the Rio Grande, the Gila River, and Baja California. In return, the United States paid Mexico fifteen million dollars and assumed all debts, totaling some three or four million dollars, owed to U.S. citizens by Mexico. In addition, the United States gave Mexican citizens in the conquered territories the right to become U.S. citizens and retain their property and pledged to protect the Mexican frontier from raids by "savage tribes" from within the United States.[5]

POPULATION AND ECONOMIC GROWTH IN TEXAS, 1846–59

With Texas secure from Mexican invasion and a part of the rapidly expanding economy of the United States, population growth and economic development accelerated. The discovery of gold in California in 1849 enhanced the political and economic importance of Texas as the eastern anchor of an all-weather land route to California. By 1850, the population of Texas had increased to more than 210,000, including more than 58,000 African American slaves. The frontier of Anglo-

Texan settlement extended from Corpus Christi to Castroville to Fredericksburg to Gatesville to Fort Worth to Gainesville. Additional Anglo-American settlements sprang up adjacent to the military posts on the Rio Grande.

The slave-based cotton economy in the river bottoms of the eastern half of Texas expanded and large-scale cattle ranching on the upper coast flourished. Yeoman farmers from the South and the Ohio River valley, aiming to raise corn, cattle, and a few bales of cotton, poured into the intervening uplands. At the same time, immigrants from central Europe competed with merchants from New Orleans and the Northeast in the growing trade centers of Galveston, Houston, Indianola, and San Antonio, and German settlers became the dominant element on the southwestern frontier around Castroville, Fredericksburg, and New Braunfels. Tejanos, despite persecution and subordination, continued to live southwest of the Colorado River.[6]

By 1860, the population of Texas increased to more than 600,000, including more than 180,000 African American slaves. The line of settlement had pushed west to Eagle Pass to Fort Clark to Fort Mason to Camp Colorado to Camp Cooper to the mouth of the Wichita River. At least a dozen towns in Texas contained more than 1,000 people, compared to only three or four in 1850. Economic growth matched population growth. By 1859, cotton production reached 431,000 bales, compared to only 58,000 bales ten years earlier. Commercial ranching spread from the upper coast to the prairies of the middle coast, beyond the Nueces, and west of the Post Oak Savannah as cattle drives to the Midwest and the mining camps of California and Colorado opened up new markets. Texas had more than 2,500,000 beef cattle and 750,000 sheep on its ranges in 1860.[7]

THE UNITED STATES AND AMERICAN INDIANS IN TEXAS

With the conquest of Texas, the American Indian people of Texas became the responsibility of the U.S. government. In Texas, federal Indian policy aimed to (1) prevent raids into Mexico as required by the Treaty of Guadalupe Hidalgo, (2) protect travelers and trade between Texas and California, and (3) secure the property of the settlers. To achieve these goals, the United States held a peace conference with the Indians of Texas. The conference culminated with the signing of a treaty on May 15, 1846, in which the American Indian nations and the United States agreed to the usual pledges of peace.

In addition, the United States established a chain of military posts on the border with Mexico: Fort Brown, Fort Ringgold, Fort McIntosh, Fort Duncan, and Fort Bliss. In addition, another line of forts bounded the frontier of settlement: Fort Inge, Fort Lincoln, Fort Martin Scott, Fort Croghan, Fort Gates, Fort Graham and Fort Worth. Fort Washita, across the Red River in Indian Territory, anchored this chain on the north. As the line of settlement pushed westward between 1851 and 1857, the U.S. Army abandoned many of these posts and established new ones. The military located other forts beyond the frontier of settlement to protect travelers and traders on the two main routes to California. On the southern route from San Antonio to El Paso, the United States constructed Fort Clark in 1852; Fort Hudson, Fort Lancaster, and Fort Davis in 1854; and Fort Stockton in 1859. On the northern route from Fort Smith, Arkansas, and North Texas to El Paso, the United States established Fort Belknap in 1851 and Fort Chadbourne in 1852.

By 1850, travel across the southern plains increased demand for meat and hides, and introduced bovine diseases had begun to impact the bison herds severely. The decline in the game coincided with an increased demand for Indian captives in New Mexico and for horses throughout the southern plains. These events led to an increase in raiding activities in Mexico, Texas, and the Southwest.[8] The Lipans and other Apaches, the Comanches and their allies, and the Wichitas were joined by newcomers from the East, most notably the Kickapoos and Cooacoochee's Seminoles. They raided from the Texas frontier westward into the border country of New Mexico, Arizona, Coahuila, Chihuahua, and Sonora. Outlaw gangs that had earlier been found largely between the Nueces and the Rio Grande spread westward. These gangs—made up of Anglos, Tejanos, Hispanos, Mexicans, runaway slaves, and refugees from the Indian Territory and the tribes shattered by Anglo-Texan conquest—further fueled the storm of violence raging along and beyond the frontier of settlement in Texas.

The push of settlement forced the Caddos, Hasinais (Anadarkos and Ionis), Keechis, Lipans, Penateka Comanches, Tonkawas, and Wichitas (including Wacos and Tawakonis) farther and farther west. For the agriculturists, it became more difficult to remain in one place long enough to raise a crop. For all, unfamiliar hunting territories, competition with outlaws, settlers, soldiers, and travelers for declining game, and exposure to violence and disease encouraged raiding and shattered traditional cultures. The entire area from well below the Rio Grande to the

Arkansas River, along and west of the line of settlement, became a haven for lawlessness centered around the stealing of captives and horses.

The creation of a coherent and workable Indian policy in Texas faced additional roadblocks. The state owned the public lands and saw the Indians as nuisances and as obstacles to the settlement of these lands. Thus, the United States could not guarantee title to American Indians for lands in Texas. Finally, the military tactics used to deal with the massive outlawry on the Texas frontier further contributed to the problem. The military responded to raids with punitive expeditions.

One hallmark of the military expeditions was a "no prisoner" policy in regard to the raiders. Major General Persifor F. Smith directed in general orders to his Texas officers in 1850: "All predatory Indians, no matter where discovered, will be pursued, attacked, and put to death. It is not advisable to take prisoners." A year later, the *Victoria Texian-Advocate* noted without comment that Indian prisoners were being shot by the U.S. military. Apparently the military failed to report accurately the deaths of women, children, and nonhostile American Indians. On other occasions, the deaths of noncombatant American Indians were described as a mistake, as in the following account of a fight near Fort Davis: Lieutenant Randall killed twelve Indians, including two forced "over a precipice sixty feet high," and captured a child, out of a total of fifteen. "The guide killed the chief and Lieutenant Randall scalped him. Eight horses were captured. About half the party were women, but dressed as men, and their sex was not known until after the killings."[9]

Because it was virtually impossible to know who committed the raids, the military sometimes attacked the first Indians found. The capricious branding of American Indians as "hostile" by the military had disastrous consequences for many Indian people in Texas. For example, the reputed Indian-hater General William S. Harney, who had been accused of atrocities in the Seminole War and the Mexican War, ordered Captain B. W. Armstrong to take a force of cavalry and march against the Lipans in December of 1852. The Lipans, who assumed that they were "at peace" with the United States, were unprepared for the brutal attack on their winter camp on the San Saba River. Attacking the Lipans while they slept, the soldiers fired indiscriminately into the lodges of the Lipans, burned the camp, and stole their horses. At least twenty-five people were murdered, and many other Lipans died from exposure and hunger that winter.[10]

In addition to the violence and the lack of an effective government policy to deal with it, the U.S. government and public abandoned any pretense of including American Indians in the social order of the United States. Indian-hating had triumphed by the 1850s. In fact, Indian-hating had become so well fixed in behavior and thought on the frontier of the United States that Herman Melville included an Indian-hater in the cast of social types in his novelistic exploration of American values, *The Confidence-Man*, published in 1857. The Indian-hater was a man who had lost family members to an Indian "raid." His grief turned to hate, and he held all Indians responsible for his loss. He then devoted his life to killing Indians wherever he found them, but his hatred and lust for revenge always proved to be insatiable.[11]

The last vestiges of the expansion–with–honor policy evaporated in the rush to conquer the continent. Both the American public and its political leadership had for the most part abandoned any belief in potential Indian equality. The belief that American Indians would be doomed because of their own inferiority and that their inevitable extinction would further world progress dominated private and public discourse about Indians in the United States.

This changing perspective concerning American Indians by Anglo-Americans who had previously had some sympathy for their plight became increasingly apparent in the 1840s and 1850s. For example, Sam Houston, in a speech supporting the Mexican War and the territorial ambitions associated with that effort, told a Democratic meeting in New York City: "Now the Mexicans are no better than Indians, and I see no reason why we should not go on in the same course now, and take their land."[12]

This shift in opinion was not confined to the United States. Instead, these ideas paralleled ideas current in England and Europe about "savagery and civilization" arising out of their ongoing conquests of Africa, Asia, Australia, and Oceania. A few years after Houston's speech, antislavery activist Frederick Law Olmsted, upon meeting Lipans and Tonkawas at Leona Springs, exhausted his own impressions of the Indians with "miserable squalor, foul obscenity, and disgusting brutishness."[13] Olmsted then quoted the first paragraph of an article written by Charles Dickens, nearly a year earlier, rebutting the idea of the noble savage:

> To come to the point at once, I beg to say that I have not the least belief in the Noble Savage. I consider him a prodigious nuisance and an enormous superstition. His calling rum and fire-water, and me a pale

face, wholly fail to reconcile me to him. I don't care what he calls me. I call him a savage, and I call a savage something highly desirable to be civilised off the face of the earth. I think a mere gent (which I take to be the lowest form of civilisation) better than a howling, whistling, clucking, stamping, tearing savage. It is all one to me, whether he sticks a fishbone through his visage, or bits of trees through the lobes of his ears, or birds' feathers in his head; whether he flattens his hair between two boards, or spreads his nose over the breadth of his face, or drags his lower lip down by great weights, or blackens his teeth or knocks them out, or paints one cheek red and the other blue, or tattoos himself, or oils himself, or rubs his body with fat, or crimps it with knives. Yielding to whichsoever of these cruel eccentricities, he is a savage—cruel, false, thievish, murderous; addicted more or less to grease and entrails, and beastly customs; a wild animal with the questionable gift of boasting, a conceited, tiresome, bloodthirsty, monotonous humbug.[14]

It was in these conditions and circumstances, the Anglo-Texans consolidated their conquest of the Karankawas and the Tonkawas.

THE DESTRUCTION OF THE KARANKAWAS

No Karankawas attended the peace council with representatives from the United States in 1846, and the Karankawas remained outside of the formal relationships with the United States. After the collapse of the early 1840s, most likely, only one or two functioning bands of Karankawas remained on the middle coast. Therefore, this division of the chapter focuses on the fate of those bands and their interaction with settlers and officials on the middle coast and the lower Rio Grande by continuing the development of the following three themes from the previous chapter: (1) destruction of Karankawa bands by armed settlers, (2) retreat to the Rio Grande, and (3) strategies for individual survival in cultural death.

The last record of the Karankawas on the middle Texas coast, in a scene that had become all too familiar to the Karankawas in their thirty-year encounter with Anglo-Texan settlers, dates from 1852. The increasing settlement of Refugio County and its development as a center of commercial ranching once again brought Karankawas into conflict with the settlers, who made them scapegoats for the cattle stealing endemic on the southwest frontier of Texas. After they discovered a Karankawa camp on the shore of Hynes Bay, William Kuykendall and his sons called together a posse to drive the Karankawas out of the county.

The posse of twenty-one men met at Fagan's ranch and elected John Hynes leader. These twenty-one men attacked the Karankawa camp by surprise. After stiff resistance to the unprovoked attack that resulted in the wounding of several of the settlers, the surviving Karankawas fled the area. The Hynes Bay massacre marked the end of the Karankawas as a social group on the middle Texas coast.[15]

If any Karankawa bands survived after 1852, they did so on the lower Rio Grande or lower coast. As described in the previous chapter, the Mier expedition encountered a Karankawa band on the Rio Grande between Guerrero and Mier in December of 1842; apparently, they had fled the middle coast after being accused of "depredations" at Live Oak Point. Earlier, Spanish officials reported that the Karankawas from Mission Refugio made yearly pilgrimages to the hills along the Rio Grande below Laredo to collect peyote.[16] Therefore, Karankawas knew the Rio Grande and had used it as a place of refuge.

At the time of the Mexican War, American and Texan soldiers believed that the only remaining Karankawas lived on Padre Island, off the lower coast. Although no eyewitness accounts placed the Karankawas on Padre Island, Karankawas, as noted earlier, had fled to the barrier islands of the upper coast in response to settler attacks in the late 1820s. Further lending plausibility to the reports of Karankawa survival on Padre Island, which was largely untouched by ranching or town-site speculation at this time, Karankawas from Mission Refugio had resorted to Padre Island as a place of refuge during the Spanish period.[17] However, they could not sustain themselves for long on the resources available on the barrier islands.

The evidence for brief Karankawa cultural survival outside of their homeland on the middle Texas coast remains circumstantial, but not unlikely, given their knowledge of the lower coast and the lower Rio Grande and their past responses to unbearable settler pressures. In fact, the Karankawa band massacred at Hynes Bay may have returned from exile on Padre Island or the lower Rio Grande, because the settlers felt that the retaliations in the aftermath of the Kemper incident of 1844–45, described in the previous chapter, had ridded the central coast of Karankawas.[18]

The most convincing evidence of Karankawa cultural survival after

1852 comes from the Rio Grande Delta. In May of 1852, Abbe Dome-nech, a French cleric in Brownsville, reported the following incident that had begun the previous fall:

> A band of Indians from the Mexican side committed shocking ravages all at once along the Texian banks of the Rio Grande, from Santa Rita to Galveston [in present-day southwestern Cameron County]. . . . As I was attending a sick person near Galveston, four Americans fell by the arrows of the Indians near the hut where I was.
>
> Outraged, forty Americans went to their camp, twenty-five miles upriver from Matamoros, but were beaten back by the Indians. The Americans complained to [Francisco] Avalos [the Mexican military commandant at Matamoros], who removed the Indians peacefully to Matamoros. . . .
>
> They were the mildest creatures in the world, at least in their new abode. They were of great stature and yellow copper-color. Each family was differently tattooed, and the men's entire dress was a towel. The women were better provided for. They sat the live long day fishing on the banks of the river; and at a certain motion of the water, they became aware of the presence of fish, invisible to civilized eyes. Off darted an arrow and in a moment there mounted to the surface a fish pierced right through. Avalos let them leave after a few months . . . and thenceforth no more was heard of them.[19]

The people described by Domenech fit to some degree other descriptions of the Karankawas. However, a number of indigenous groups in the Rio Grande Delta maintained their identity into the 1850s, and they possessed cultural traits, especially fishing with the bow and arrow, described by Domenech. British immigrant William Neale came to Matamoros to live in 1834, after visiting earlier, and spent the remainder of his life in the Rio Grande Delta. Neale remembered the following Native American groups in the region: Comanches, Lipans, Campaquas, Palomals, Zacatals, Ranchitos, Mesquitals, Arroyos, Las Tasas, and Carrizales. According to Neale, the first two groups, well-known raiders, infrequently visited the Delta. Of the indigenous people of the Delta, one can correlate the Campaquas with the Tampaquas, the Zacatals with the Zacatiles, and the Carrizales with the Carrizos.[20] The other groups likely represent place names of American Indian rancherías. Neale, a careful observer of and participant in life and events in the

Rio Grande Delta for more than sixty years, did not recall the existence of Karankawas in that area.

The question arises as to who Domenech observed at Matamoros during the winter of 1851-52. Existing evidence points to the Tampaquas, who lived near the settlement of Galveston and Lake Tampaquas (Campaquas), an oxbow of the Rio Grande immediately north of present-day Mercedes.[21]

The Tampaquas had several violent encounters with ranchers and travelers in the Rio Grande Delta during the 1850s. In the spring of 1852 forty men, both Mexicans and Indians, reportedly attacked seven Americans camped at Lake Campaquas, killing five of them. The attackers "cut off the right hands [of the victims] as trophies and took property belonging to Warren Adams."[22] Adams wrote a letter shedding further light on these events:

> [The Indians] belonging to the Carankaway and Campaquas tribes and being instructed by the authorities in Mexico to kill and plunder all American citizens near the frontier . . . acting under the instructions of the aforesaid authorities . . . mutilated the bodies of the murdered men, taking the right hand of each to testify that they were entitled to the reward of thirty or forty dollars offered by Mexico for each American they murder on this frontier.[23]

A few days later on May 17, 1852, two Americans were injured when the Indians fired on the steamer *Comanche* on the Rio Grande near Campaquas.[24]

These events occurred shortly after General Avalos released the Indians under his charge at Matamoros. Moreover, Adams's account associates the Karankawas with the Tampaquas. Whether or not the Karankawa-Tampaquas acted upon orders from Avalos remains unknown.

The Anglo-Texan settlers of the Rio Grande Delta continued to complain about the Tampaquas. On December 10, 1855, two Anglo-Texans, R. H. Hord and E. Basse, owners of Rancho Sal del Rey, near Lake Tampaquas, sent an appeal to Governor Elisha M. Pease demanding protection from the Indians of the Rio Grande Delta, particularly the "Tampaquash and Carcese," who "subsist chiefly by robbery and murder." Hord and Basse related how the Tampaquas and Carcese (Carrizos?) burned the ranch, murdered foreman Frank Frenzel, and drove off the livestock in the summer of 1853, with the ranch being under constant threat since that time.[25]

In 1873, the Mexican government sent a commission (Comisión Pesguisidora de la Frontera del Norte) to investigate the origins of the theft, robbery, and murder that had prevailed along the Rio Grande after the signing of the Treaty of Guadalupe Hidalgo in 1848. According to the *Reports* of that commission, the "Carancahuases, otherwise called Tampacuases," were at a place called "La Mesa" in 1852. General Avalos removed them from La Mesa to Burgos, in the center of Tamaulipas, because of their alleged involvement in theft, robbery, and violence along the border. However, they soon returned to La Mesa. On October 26, 1858, the Judge of Rosario, a settlement on the Mexican side of the Rio Grande about two miles east of present-day Nuevo Progresso, reported them to be at Uresteña, on the United States side of the Rio Grande. The *Reports* concluded: "The history of these Indians terminates with an attack made upon them in said year, 1858, by Juan Nepomuceno Cortina, then a citizen of Texas, along with other rancheros, when they were surprised at their hiding place in Texas, and were exterminated." Apparently Gatschet's widely cited conclusions concerning the fate of the Karankawas were based solely on findings of the *Reports* without considering the possibility that the Karankawas may not have been the Tampaquas.[26] In addition one must realize that the *Reports* explicitly sought to lay the blame, justly in many cases, for the violence and disorder along the Rio Grande on Texas and Texans and the failure by the United States to protect the border from raiders, of all ethnic groups, based in Texas. As a result, the *Reports* may be biased in favor of blaming the Karankawas, a people who lived in the United States, for the violence.

The question persists: Were the Tampaquas actually Karankawas? The ethnohistorical evidence strongly indicates that the Tampaquas were a people distinct from the Karankawas and residents of the Rio Grande Delta since at least the 1760s. The data from the 1850s suggest that the Tampaquas were resisting the destruction of their traditional homes by the development of commercial ranching in the Rio Grande Delta. However, the same data imply that at least a few of the Karankawas, dispossessed of their lands on the middle coast by settler violence, found refuge in the Rio Grande Delta with the Tampaquas. The Tampaquas shared similar cultural traits with the Karankawas and exploited a natural environment similar to that used by the Karankawas on the middle Texas coast. Even into the 1850s, a dense, verdant subtropical woodland covered the Rio Grande Delta. Resacas, or oxbow lakes, supported abundant fish, waterfowl, and alligators. Oyster reefs and extensive marshes occurred in the estuary of the Rio Grande.[27] Thus, the Tampaquas provided an ideal place of refuge for Karankawa survivors. Also, exploiting the political ambiguities of the border between Anglo-Texan and Mexican authority had been a Karankawa survival strategy since the 1820s. Yet in all likelihood, the history of the Karankawa as a people ended in the gunfire on Hynes Bay in 1852. Of course, individual Karankawas survived longer. Not only did they flee to the Tampaquas and possibly other American Indian groups, but also the mixed-ethnicity gangs of rootless people who stole livestock between the Nueces and the Rio Grande may have attracted others.

Those taken in as children by the settlers and raised as servants also lived beyond the destruction of their culture. For example, the young boy given up by the demoralized Karankawas to the people of Matagorda, as related in the previous chapter, grew up in the households of several Matagorda families. He became known as "Indian Tom" and apparently lost his life during the Civil War. According to stories told in the 1920s in Matagorda, the young man either died in the service of the Confederacy or was evacuated with his adoptive families by Union forces to a refugee camp in New Orleans. At the refugee camp he was supposedly murdered by a lieutenant in the U.S. Army for failing to respond to his orders to work. One of James Power's Karankawa children, Mary Amarso, married a settler, Charles Pathoff of St. Mary's, in Refugio County.[28] The fate of her brother, Tom Amarso, remains unknown. Finally, as the incident of the Karankawa man who dropped his weapons, surrendered to authorities, and later became a mail carrier in Refugio indicates, other Karankawas were sufficiently acculturated to enter into the Spanish-speaking, dark-skinned laboring class of the border country.

THE IMPOVERISHMENT AND
REMOVAL OF THE TONKAWAS

For the Tonkawas, the first year of statehood saw little change in their role in the political affairs of Texas. At least seventeen Tonkawa fighters accompanied their patron, Edward Burleson, as part of Governor James Pinckney Henderson's Texas Volunteers, to Matamoros to fight the Mexican army. Besides serving as scouts and fighters, the presence of the Tonkawas terrified the Mexican civilians. Apparently, the Tonkawas returned to Texas in November of 1846, with Burleson, Henderson, and the Texas Volunteers after the Battle of Monterrey.[29]

Prior to leaving for Mexico in the late spring of 1846, a delegation of fifteen Tonkawas, "chiefs, warriors, and women, armed with lances, bows, and quivers, red painted, flaps dragging the ground," arrived at the Council Springs to join representatives of the Anadarkos, Caddos, Ionis, Keechis, Lipans, Penateka Comanches, Tawakonis, Wacos, and Wichitas to conclude a treaty with the United States. The emissaries from the United States, Pierce M. Butler and M. G. Lewis, were accompanied by representatives from several of the American Indian nations in Indian Territory. For three months, the Council Springs became the site of a great fair. The Indians played games, celebrated, arranged marriages, and traded. By the date of the treaty signing on May 15, 1846, more than 3,000 Indians had received presents.[30] Never again would the Tonkawas and the other Indians of the southern plains gather as free people under such festive circumstances.

By the terms of the treaty, the Indians placed themselves under the protection of the United States and promised to trade only with traders licensed by the United States; to give up "all white persons and negroes [*sic*] who are now prisoners"; to give up any Indians guilty of murder or robbery of any citizen of the United States; to give up all horse thieves and stolen horses; to live in peace with the United States, its citizens, and other Indians who live at peace with the United States; and to turn over to the authorities of the United States anyone who "introduces ardent spirits or intoxicating liquors" among them. In return, the American Indian nations were to receive additional "presents in goods . . . to the amount of $10,000" and the "benefits" of blacksmiths, school teachers, and ministers who might be sent to them "at the discretion of the President of the United States."[31] The Indians of western Texas, including the Tonkawas, received no guarantee of title to their lands.

Within four years, the westward advance of the frontier of settlement and the increased amount of travel across the southern plains forever altered the lives of the Tonkawas and the other Indians of western Texas.[32] However, for the Tonkawas, the changing political order in Texas had almost as profound an impact as the loss of hunting grounds and the spread of disease associated with the westward movement of the settlers.

With the collapse of the Republic of Texas' policy of maintaining a line of demarcation between the settlers and the Indians, the Tonkawas retreated from the frontier of settlement. In February, 1848, Neighbors, who had acted as an unofficial Indian agent for Texas until his appointment as special agent for the Indians of Texas on March 20, 1847, found at least "fifty lodges of Tonkawas" in a Penateka Comanche camp on the upper Brazos, far to the northwest of the frontier of settlement. Apparently, many of the Tonkawas preferred to live with their old enemies, than to remain near the potential violence of the frontier. The newcomers who poured into Texas failed to appreciate the position the Tonkawas had held in the old order. For example, in the fall of 1846, a group of men from the United States on their way to fight in the Mexican War encountered a band of Tonkawas camped at Manchaca Springs, in southern Travis County, and falsely accused them of stealing their horses. The Tonkawas narrowly averted disaster by locating the horses.[33]

By 1849, the Tonkawas were asking the government for an annuity and horses to keep from starving. After his survey of conditions of the Texas Indians, Neighbors recommended that the U.S. government should take as much land from the Indians as the state needed for immediate use and set aside enough additional land for a reservation for the Texas Indians. In addition it should extend its intercourse laws to the Indians of Texas, establish an agency to serve the Indians; and establish military posts to assist the agents in carrying out all laws and treaties. Along with this program, Neighbors envisioned the government extending such services as vocational instruction, general education, and the supplying of livestock, seeds, and farm tools until the Indians could become self-sustaining.[34]

Neighbors arrived in Washington in August, 1849, to present his plan and learned that the change of administration following the election of Zachary Taylor had cost him his job. No longer special Indian agent for Texas, Neighbors returned to Texas and found a large body of Indians, including many Tonkawas, awaiting his arrival on the Clear Fork of the Brazos. They were supposedly eager to learn of their new relationship to the United States and were disappointed that Neighbors was no longer their official intermediary with the United States.[35]

For the next four years, U.S. Indian policy in Texas suffered from a lack of direction, inefficiency, and vacillation. The U.S. Army pursued its "no prisoner" policy toward American Indians suspected of raiding, and settlers bombarded the state government with complaints of "Indian depredations" and demands for action. The state government, both unwilling and lacking resources to act, largely refused to involve itself in Indian affairs. The settlers frequently implicated the Tonkawas in the raiding, disregarding their record of military service for the Anglo-Texans. For example, accusations that appeared in the press in the late summer of 1849 included such calls as "no other alternative remains but to wage war with all our might and carry it into the wigwams and villages of our barbarous foe."[36]

Public opinion about Indians, in general, continued to harden. The editor of the *Victoria Texian-Advocate* claimed that there were only two viable options for the U.S. government in dealing with the "Indian problem": (1) removal under government care until the Indians could be "civilized," or (2) extermination "by the revolver and the sword." The editor found removal to be the best option: "Aside from the inhumanity of the thing [extermination], this would cost the government infinitely more than it would to feed and civilize them." Earlier, David G. Burnet, who had lived with the Comanches as a young man, had written to Neighbors calling the U.S. government's removal of American Indians from Texas the "only practical substitute for the actual extermination of the Indians." The *Corpus Christi Star* exclaimed: "There is but one remedy for these things—war, an exterminating Indian war."[37]

Denied the stability of familiar hunting grounds and markets necessary to continue their hide trade, the Tonkawas starved.[38] With the death of their patron and ally in the state government, Edward Burleson, in 1851, the political and security position of the Tonkawas became as precarious as their deteriorating economic position.

For example, the Tonkawas and other American Indians received the following prices for their goods and services in the first years of statehood: bison hides–$3.00; deer hindquarters–2 for 25 cents; bear oil–$1.00/gallon; hunting–$1.00/day, plus the hides of the deer they killed. The main legal "Indian goods" they bought were woolen blankets, a coarse scarlet and blue wool cloth for breechclouts, printed calico for shirts, copper bracelets and anklets, knives, glass beads, powder, lead, and tobacco. Prices for many of the products the Indians sold had fallen in response to the worldwide decline in fur and hide prices in the 1840s and 1850s.[39] This decline in prices, along with the decline in game and increased competition for game further weakened their economic position.

Yet, at times, they earned food and money by aiding the growing number of travelers across western Texas. For example, several Tonkawas guided a party of gold seekers to the Sacramento Mountains of south-central New Mexico in the summer of 1853. In June, 1854, Tonkawas and Lipans helped Anglo-Texan drovers roundup strayed cattle being driven from San Antonio to California. However, fear of settler violence limited Tonkawa opportunities to benefit from the trade and travel across western Texas. Frequently, Tonkawas avoided contact with whites because of that well-grounded fear. One insightful observer of life on the southwestern frontier of Texas, noted: "Life sits lightly on a borderer. Neither his nor his friends' is spared any risk, and as for Indians, in his eyes they were only made to be killed."[40]

German scientist and political activist Julius Froebel's account illustrates the threat the Tonkawas felt from the settlers. In late January of 1854, Froebel, after joining some Anglo-Texan travelers, encountered an old Tonkawa man at Fort Inge. Froebel's companions accused the Tonkawa of being duplicitously hostile to them: "You talk now of friendship, but if one of us fell into your power you would cut his throat." The Anglo-Texans then "joked" that they would soon "visit the Tanko ladies." The old man, terrified that it was his throat to be cut, turned to Froebel, who was obviously not an Anglo-Texan "borderer." According to Froebel, "He stretched out his hand and embraced me, exclaiming repeatedly and in an expressive manner *Manito!*" The next day, when Froebel and his companions reached the Tonkawa camp on the Nueces, they found it abandoned following the old man's warning of their approach. Apparently American Indian fear of settler violence on the Anglo-American frontier of conquest was as strong as settler fear of "Indian attack."[41]

Because of their extreme impoverishment, the Tonkawas, at times, approached the military posts to beg for food. Apparently, the "charity" of the military overcame some of the fear engendered in the Indians by the "no prisoner" policy of the military. On his inspection of Texas military posts in 1853, Brevet Colonel W. G. Freeman encountered a band of Tonkawas at Fort Mason in August of that year:

Ft. Mason was the first post at which I met Indians. They were of the Tonkaway tribe some thirty in number, and had come to beg, and a more squalid, half-starved looking race I have never seen. It appears usual for the C.O.'s on such occasions to direct the issue to these poor creatures of small quantities of corn or damaged pork or bacon, though I believe there is no regulation authorizing such issue. Humanity, however requires them to be made, and the actual expense to the Government is really very trifling, as condemned provisions when sold by auction, conformably to the Subsistence Regulations, are invariably sacrificed—the sales seldom realizing much more than sufficient to cover the auctioneers fees.[42]

Apparently Colonel R. B. Marcy met the Tonkawas during this period. His widely quoted description of the Tonkawas offers further insight into their impoverishment:

> The Tonkawas . . . were generally regarded as renegades and aliens from all social intercourse with the other tribes . . . never attempting to cultivate the soil or build houses. They lived in temporary bark or brush tenements, affording but little protection from the weather, and derived a miserable, meagre subsistence from fish, small animals, reptiles, roots or anything else that afforded the least nutriment. They were the most ragged, filthy, and destitute Indians I have seen; and their ideas of comfort and their manner of living are but one grade above those of the brutes.[43]

Neighbors was reappointed special Indian agent for Texas following the federal authorization of a reservation system for Indians in the West in 1849 and the election of Franklin Pierce as president in 1852. This allowed Neighbors to pursue his agenda of establishing reservations for the Tonkawas and the other tribes on the Texas frontier.[44] A pragmatic concern over the persistent violence and a humanitarian concern over the welfare of the "remnant" tribes coalesced. In February of 1854, the legislature authorized the creation of Indian reservations from state-owned lands to be placed under federal control, under the stipulation that non-native Indians be removed from Texas and the reservation lands would revert to the state if or when the Indians no longer occupied them. The *Austin State Gazette* expressed the argument in favor of the reservations:

> The only means by which that ample and efficient protection to which they are certainly entitled, can be given to those of our citizens who reside upon the exposed frontier, is by making a reservation, having these Ishmaelites of the prairies collected within it, the non-intercourse laws of the United States extended over them, and all that horde of Savages that are hovering along the frontier who belong properly to the United States and Mexico, removed from our borders. Our own protection, and justice and humanity to the Indians equally demand it . . . [T]he title of the Indian will only be the right of occupancy, and when that is extinguished, land, jurisdiction and all will revert to Texas.[45]

However, it was to be more than a year before the Tonkawas could reach their reservation. The Tonkawas, along with the Lipans remaining in southwest Texas, were under the jurisdiction of Agent George Howard during 1854 and remained largely in the vicinity of Fort Inge. By that fall, Neighbors noted that the Tonkawas were ready to settle on the newly surveyed reservation and that they were "almost entirely destitute" and found "it difficult to subsist their women and children." By the following spring, Agent Howard had assembled 250 Tonkawas on the Nueces River and he was prepared to move them, with the help of seven wagons, to the Brazos Reservation at Fort Belknap by way of Bandera Pass, Fredericksburg, and Hamilton Valley. Throughout the year following the creation of the reservations, providing food and security for the Indian people to be settled on them had been a central concern of Neighbors.[46]

When Howard became ill, Neighbors went to the Nueces with the seven wagons to lead the Tonkawas to the Brazos Reservation. Upon his arrival on April 7, 1855, Neighbors realized one of his worst fears. The Tonkawas had disappeared. Three days before Neighbors reached the Nueces, a settler named Saunders, who lived near Fort Inge, along with eighteen other men, had gone to the Tonkawa camp with the intention of attacking them and stealing their horses. The Tonkawas had learned of the settlers' intentions and met them with a determined show of force. The settlers withdrew for reinforcements. The Tonkawa men joined the women and children who had earlier gone to the "mountains" for safety. The outraged Neighbors blamed both the military and Agent Howard for not protecting the massed Tonkawas, and he called for Agent Howard's dismissal.[47]

Many Tonkawas eventually made their way to the Brazos Reservation. The June 30, 1855, Census Roll showed 171 Tonkawas, 133 adults and 38 children, on the reservation.[48] On August 30, 1855, at the Brazos Agency, Tonkawa leaders Placidore (Placido?), Cha-pa-ton, Jimson, Simon, and White signed an amendment to the Treaty of May 15, 1846. The Tonkawas, along with representatives of the other tribes on the Brazos and Clear Fork Reservations, agreed to the following terms:

(1) to "abandon forever a roving and hunting life and . . . settle down permanently on the lands selected for us, as per act of the Legislature of the State of Texas approved February 6, 1854, and to devote all of our energies to the cultivation of the Soil and to raising stock as a means of subsistence for ourselves and families";   .

(2) "to establish laws and police regulations" in order to govern themselves;

(3) not to leave "the Reservation without the consent of the Indian Agent";

(4) to settle intertribal disputes in a council of "the U.S. Indian Agents and head Chiefs of said Tribes";

(5) not to allow other "Tribes or bands" to settle "on the Reservations" without the agreement of the agents and head chiefs and not to allow "absent members of the Tribes now settled" to visit or settle on the reservations, without permission of "the Agent under whose jurisdiction he resides" and "they agree to observe all the Articles of the Treaty and agreement . . . and acknowledge fully the authority of the Chief acknowledged by the Agents as the head of the Tribe";

(6) "to break off all intercourse with bands of Indians outside of the Reservations, . . . except . . . with the knowledge and consent of the Agents" and to report the arrival of all Indians to the agents and "assist the Agents in arresting all intruders or depredators"; and

(7) "to give assistance and protection to all farmers, laborers, and other employees of the Government on the reservations," and to protect all government property.

In return, the United States agreed:

> to protect and maintain all the members of the Tribes, parties to the agreement in the peaceable possession of the land embraced in the limits of said Reservations, and in their lives and property against injury and molestation from citizens of the United States while on said Reservation, and to afford such protection and aid in acclamation for injury from other Tribes of Indians [and] to furnish the said Tribes farmers to assist and instruct them . . . a Blacksmith and tools, . . . stock cattle and other domestic animals, . . . and to furnish them regularly with rations as may be deemed necessary to enable them to support their families, until they can subsist themselves by their own exertions; and the General Government is hereby pledged to pursue that course of policy with the settlers on these reservations, deemed best calculated to advance them as a self-sustaining people.[49]

At last, some Tonkawas, in the face of extermination by violence or starvation, relinquished their freedom and agreed to accept the "fruits of civilization" offered by the United States. Apparently, others preferred to remain with the Lipans and the other displaced Indian people along the middle Rio Grande. In the spring of 1854, Olmsted encountered some Tonkawas camped with the Lipans at Leona Springs, near

Fort Inge, and other Tonkawas at San Fernando, Coahuila, in the company of Comanches, Kickapoos, Lipans, Mescaleros, and Seminoles.[50] At the Lipan-Tonkawa camp, Olmsted found:

> nothing but the most miserable squalor, foul obscenity, disgusting brutishness . . . We spent an hour or two in the camp, visiting almost every hut. These were simply slight tents of poles and skins, of larger or smaller size. In each were a few rude utensils, scattered over a heap of skins and filthy blankets. The faces of both sexes were hideously streaked with paint, the features very coarse, nose large, and cheek bones particularly prominent . . . All [the children] were eager for a dime, and went through any amount of degrading nonsense to secure it. A few half starved Mexican horses were staked outside the camp.[51]

A few weeks later in San Fernando, Coahuila, a town apparently dependent on the Indian trade for its economic survival, Olmsted observed:

> The principal movement was given to the streets by the Indians, who were, in numbers, riding helter-skelter about, knocking down blackbirds with arrows, having trials of skill at cart-hubs, lying about in all postures of real or affected drunkenness, lounging in and out of every house, and carrying themselves with such an air as indicated they were masters of the town. . . . They entered every door, fell on every neck, patted the women on the cheek, helped themselves to whatever suited their fancy, and distributed their scowls or grunts of pleasure according to their sensations.[52]

Although the Tonkawas who chose to live off the reservation maintained their freedom, they faced numerous hazards beyond crushing poverty and the threat of starvation. With the creation of the reservation system, any Indian off the reservations without a pass became a "hostile," subject to the military's "no prisoner" policy and to settler violence.

On occasion, Anglo-Texan settlers shot Tonkawas on sight. At another time, some German Texan settlers in Fredericksburg lured a Tonkawa into a shed with offers of food and burned him to death. The murder of the Tonkawa at Fredericksburg produced a debate in the Austin newspapers. The young Edward Burleson defended the Tonkawa. The settlers at Fredericksburg countered that he was one of a party that "last year murdered an American and a German." Apparently, the murder intensified hostilities between Anglo-Texans and German Texans, for the

Austin State Gazette later reported that it was only a rumor that Burleson had gone to Fredericksburg and killed more than twenty German settlers in revenge.[53] It would take the divisions wrought by the Civil War before Anglo-Texans would openly murder their German-origin neighbors.

Interestingly, the Tonkawas did distinguish between Anglo-Texans and German Texans. For Tonkawas, Anglo-Texans were *pavotivos* or white men; German Texans were *moshotivos* or bearded men. For some years, they did not consider killing a *moshotivo* a crime. In fact, the Rangers on the Ford expedition asked Tonkawa scout O'Quinn [Ocquin], "You have eaten all sorts of people, what nationality do you think makes the best eating?" Ocquin replied, "a big fat Dutchman," who he and his men had killed on the Guadalupe River in 1849.[54]

In spite of the hazards, some Tonkawas remained in the border country. In the future, they would be joined by their kin disenchanted with reservation life and the protection offered by the U.S. government. Apparently, Tonkawas near Sabinas, Coahuila, some of whom had immigrated to Mexico after their second removal from Texas in 1883, maintained their ethnic identity as Tonkawas until at least the late 1920s.[55]

For the Tonkawas who chose to live on the reservation and be taught to farm and raise livestock, the next three years saw a cycle of crop failures due to drought and grasshoppers. The Brazos and Clear Fork Reservations lay immediately west of the 98th meridian. Beyond the 98th meridian the agricultural economy developed in the eastern United States during the nineteenth century became impracticable.[56]

However, the government rations and protection from settlers, outlaws, and Indians hostile to them gave the Tonkawas on the reservation security and the means for survival. Visitors to the Brazos Reservation came away enthusiastic about the "progress" being made by the reserve Indians: tending fields, gardens, and stock; building "American-style" houses; and attending church and school. Colonel Middleton T. Johnson reported to the *Dallas Herald:* "the feeding policy of Uncle Sam is succeeding admirably . . . The Indians in the reservations are becoming sleek and fat, and it is said that the wild Indians from the prairies can be distinguished from the domesticated Indians from his lank and lean appearance." Two months later, the *Dallas Herald* commented: "The domestication, civilizing, and evangelizing the wild Indians of Texas . . . will constitute a not unimportant evidence of progress and onward march of the age of humanity and religion." Yet, the Tonkawas resisted the demands of progress more than the other reserve Indians. They refused to farm or garden, attend church, send their children to school, or live in houses because "their religion forbade it."[57] However, Tonkawa leader Placido supposedly faithfully attended Methodist services while living on the Brazos Reservation and had earlier often attended camp meetings in the company of Edward Burleson.

However, the acculturation project at the Brazos and Clear Fork Reservations came to an early end in conflict with that other deeprooted attitude toward American Indians: Indian-hating. Throughout 1857 and 1858, horse stealing and murder plagued the northwest Texas frontier. The settlers, orchestrated by a recently dismissed Indian agent at the Clear Fork Reservation, John Baylor, blamed the Indian people on the reservations for the "depredations."

Apparently, John Robert Baylor, the nephew of Judge R. E. B. Baylor, for whom Baylor University is named, was an Indian-hater. He later commanded the Confederate forces that briefly occupied Arizona Territory. However, the Confederate government removed him from his command for instructing a subordinate to get rid of the "savage" Apaches by any method, poisoning if necessary. After Baylor was removed as agent at the Clear Fork Agency, he was accused of stealing horses from settlers and blaming it on his Comanche charges. He also led the white settlers in Weatherford, Texas, in their infamous "scalp dance" in the Parker County Courthouse, after a raid on a Comanche band in September, 1860.[58]

Strong evidence existed at the time that the thefts and murders were the work of the mixed-ethnicity gangs of outlaws that preyed on residents of the frontier. For example, the *Dallas Herald* reported that the gang that brutally murdered the Cameron and Ewing families in Jack County, enraging the settlers of the northwest Texas frontier against the Indians, was led by a man named Walker, "a red-headed Frenchman raised by the northern Indians." Earlier, the *Herald* had speculated that much of the theft, robbery, and violence on the northwest Texas frontier came at the hands of a gang of white horse thieves that operated from "the Agency into the Indian Nation, in Arkansas, and perhaps into Kansas Territory." Even the official Report of the Peace Commissioners to Governor Runnels in the spring of 1859 implicated white accomplices in the raids.[59]

However, in 1858, public opinion demanded that Governor Runnels call up a company of Rangers to defend the frontier settlements. The Ranger company, commanded by Captain John S. (Rip) Ford and accompanied by a number of men from the Brazos Reservation, including

Placido, Ocquin, and several other Tonkawas, traveled across the Red River and attacked a large Comanche camp. Ford said of his Tonkawa scouts: "These Indians were men of more than ordinary intellect who possessed minute information concerning the geography and topography of that country—all of Texas, most of Mexico, and all of Indian Territory and adjacent regions." Ford's memoir of the expedition against the Comanches furnishes a rich account of the interactions between the Tonkawas and Anglo-Texans on such expeditions. In addition, it clearly conveys the mutual respect engendered under these conditions. Despite the decisive victory of the Anglo-Texans, the raiding continued on the frontier.[60]

In the aftermath of the service rendered by the Indians from the Brazos Reservation, public opinion toward the reserve Indians softened. On May 26th, Governor Runnels stated that the "brave Indian allies . . . will be held in grateful remembrance by the people of Texas."[61] In addition, the *Austin State Gazette* urged the state to reward Placido with "a present of a small number of cows" for his invaluable service and his exemplary character:

> He is faithful and industrious. . . . He has done much by his example and by his conversation to encourage his countrymen to abandon their wild pursuits of the chase, and follow those of civilized life, and he has had, and continues to have much to contend against in the indolence and improvidence of the Indian character.[62]

Men from the Brazos Reservation, including Tonkawas, followed a young Sul Ross on a second expedition, commanded by Major Earl Van Dorn of the U.S. Army, against the Comanches in the fall of 1858, but the "grateful remembrance" did not long persist on the northwest Texas frontier.

On December 23, 1858, at least six white settlers—Peter Garland, Dr. McNeil (McNeal), Sam Stephens, William Motherell, Brown, and Hightower—attacked a hunting party of Indian men, women, and children, who were off the Brazos Reservation with the permission of the agent. They murdered seven people, including three women, in their sleep. In the ensuing fight, two more reserve Indians, a man and a woman, and Sam Stephens died. When the reservation farmer, J. J. Sturm, returned to the scene of the massacre with the survivors to reclaim the bodies, he found:

A more horrible sight I never expected to see. There on their beds lay the bodies of seven of the best and most inoffensive Indians on the reserves, their bodies pierced by buckshot and rifle balls, their eyes closed, and their bodies stretched at full length, their countenances indicating that they passed from calm sleep to sleep that knows no waking. One warrior lay outside the camp, he and his wife were both shot. After being shot he seized his gun and shot the murderer of his wife through the head. So murderer and murdered both fell together.[63]

After the murders on Keechi Creek, the anti-Indian sentiment on the northwestern frontier of Texas flared in anticipation of Indian reprisals. For example, in January of 1859, settler C. B. Underhill charged the agents and the "rascally reserve Indians" with plotting to kill a delegation of settlers sent to the reservation to resolve the dispute. In addition to the usual complaints of theft, harassment, and murder, Underhill accused "the red and white horse thieves" on the reservation of "debauchery, drunkenness, and abandoned conduct exhibited on the reserve, unfit to be put in print." Finally, playing on settler distrust of and dissatisfaction with the U.S. government, Underhill decried the government for supplying the Indians with arms, while neglecting frontier defense.[64]

Underhill's accusations may not have been totally unfounded. The teacher at the Brazos Agency, Zachariah Coombes, persistently complained in his diary of the moral climate on the reservation as interfering with the "civilizing" mission of the reservation system:

To civilize a savage requires a firm and decisive course ... [However] it seems to me that to eat, to sleep, to drink and be merry, also to race, gamble and cheat are the most striking and in fact are the examples which are daily and hourly set before them. And in addition to all this there are continually among the Indians a most degraded set of libertines who make it a boast that there is not nor has been any Indian female on this Reserve with whom they have not had or may not have illicet [sic] intercourse, precisely at their own will and pleasure.[65]

Of course, discussions of frontier Indian alcohol abuse, gambling, and sexual license must be framed in the context of similar behaviors among the Anglo-Americans. These behaviors appear to be little more than reflections of the observed white example.[66]

Despite open acknowledgment of their actions by the Keechi Creek murderers, Major Neighbors could not arrest them or indict them in this climate of hatred. The grand jury called to indict Peter Garland and his followers in the murders of Choctaw Tom and the other reserve Indians not only refused to indict the settlers for murder, but they indicted José Maria, chief of the Anadarkos, for horse theft.[67]

John R. Baylor once more came to the fore as the leader of the anti-Indian faction. On May 23, 1859, Baylor took 250 mounted settlers into the Brazos Reservation, with the purpose of breaking up the reservation and driving out its inmates. A detachment of the U.S. Army, commanded by Captain C. C. Gilbert, met Baylor's vigilantes. Baylor and his men backed down, but they did murder two elderly reserve Indians, including a woman tending her garden, during their foray.[68]

In the aftermath of Baylor's raid, the people on the reservation were in fear of their lives, and they were unable to hunt, roundup their stock, or farm. Neighbors despaired: "The reserves may be considered virtually broken up, all work is suspended. The Indians will not even cultivate their small gardens." With the Indians and whites on the reservation confined to close quarters in fear of attack, Neighbors found: "many sick, with three or four deaths per day, and the whole camp, both Indians and whites seriously threatened with an epidemic."[69]

The prospect of armed conflict between the U.S. Army and Anglo-Texan settlers over the safety of the Indians on the reservations forced Governor Hardin R. Runnels into action. On June 6, 1859, Runnels appointed a board of peace commissioners—George B. Erath, John Henry Brown, Richard Coke, J. M. Steiner, and J. M. Smith—to investigate the violence and restore the peace. In their report to the governor, the peace commissioners implicated white accomplices in the raiding, with only a few reserve Indians involved. Yet, they recommended removal: "We believe it impracticable, if not impossible, for tribes of American Indians, scarcely advanced one step in civilization, cooped up on a small reservation and surrounded by white settlers, to live in harmony for any length of time." Governor Runnels called up one hundred state troops to be commanded by John Henry Brown to separate the settlers from the American Indians on the reservations.[70]

The fear and hysteria continued. On May 5, 1859, E. J. Gurley, special counsel to prosecute the murderers of the reserve Indians, disclosed to Neighbors a settler plot to interfere with the removal of the reserve Indians: "They do not intend that they shall escape; but intend to kill them either at the reservation or before they get to the Red River."

Gurley also informed Neighbors that the settlers were planning to exploit the rifts between the Tonkawas and the other groups on the reservations and employ them in their plot for a promise of safety.[71] The incendiary anti-Indian rhetoric continued to appear in the press:

> We call upon you fellow citizens, in the name of all that is sacred, in behalf of suffering women and children, whose blood paints afresh, from the Red River to the Rio Grande, day by day, the scalping knife of the savage foe; in the name of mothers whose daughters have been violated by the "reserve Indians," and robbed of that virtue which God alone can give—come, come, fellow citizens; arouse, and take action before the deaths of tender infants, mothers, fathers, and aged grandsires is swollen to a more frightful extent by our sluggish action or supine indifference![72]

Yet, a debate emerged. George B. Erath and Middleton T. Johnson, respected figures on the Anglo-Texan frontier, traveled tirelessly and without regard to threats to their personal safety across northwest Texas to calm the fears of the settlers. On May 12, 1859, a large group of settlers gathered at the courthouse in Belknap to condemn the violence and urge restraint in the confrontation with the Indians on the reservations. The antiremoval argument centered on concerns that Indian removal would leave the frontier defenseless if U.S. troops stationed near the reservations left with their American Indian charges.[73]

In addition, the reservations and the troops furnished a substantial economic boon to the northwest Texas frontier. For example, in a single week, December 5 to December 13, 1857, the U.S. government bought 11,400 pounds of beef, 500 pounds of flour, and 105 pounds of salt at a cost of $570.91 for the use of 1,010 Indians at the Brazos Agency. The U.S. government expenditures at the Brazos and Clear Fork Agencies from 1855 through August, 1859, totaled more than $450,000. The fact that the two Indian reservations and associated military posts engendered local prosperity was not lost on the people of the area. The *Dallas Herald* noted that land in Belknap had "risen 150–200 per cent, and you can hear nothing now but contracts for building houses . . . *Vive la Belknap.*"[74] As late as February, 1859, the argument persisted that if the U.S. government removed the Indians at the Brazos and Clear Fork Agencies to Indian Territory and closed the associated military posts:

> We lose the large amount of public funds disbursed in maintaining those posts, the money disbursed by the Indian Agents in subsisting

the Reserve Indians—an amount in the aggregate that has been sufficient for several years past to furnish a market for surplus produce in the frontier counties that could not have been found elsewhere, and that has put dollars into every man's pocket, who has a bushel of corn, or a bale of oats, a rack of hay or a beef to sell.[75]

The pro-Indian argument continued to be advanced along humanitarian lines as well, as in this newspaper account of a meeting with Placido:

> Placido, the old chief asks, 'Where am I to take my little band! No friends, no money, no home, no hunting grounds: he says his only friends are Texians and that he does not wish to leave the country.' It is painful to hear him talk, he manifests so much feeling, and rarely speaks of the matter without shedding tears. He says that it makes him sorry to hear that the Texans are anxious to murder his little tribe, after they fought so hard for their country.[76]

On June 11, Neighbors received orders from Washington to move the Indian people on the Texas reservations across the Red River to Indian Territory. Indian-hating had triumphed over security, economic, and nascent humanitarian concerns. Despite the feuding between Neighbors and Brown, the state militia maintained order.[77] On August 1, 1859, the Tonkawas, along with the other Indians on the Brazos and Clear Fork Reservations, loaded much of their portable personal property onto ox-drawn wagons for the trek north, out of Texas. They were escorted by the agency personnel and U.S. Army troops commanded by Major George Thomas. On August 8, 1859, they safely crossed the Red River into Indian Territory.

Major Neighbors, obsessed and exhausted with his mission to civilize and protect his Indian charges, described the departure of the Tonkawas and the other reserve Indians across the Red River to his wife in the following Biblical terms:

> I have this day [August 8, 1859] crossed all the Indians out of the heathen land of "Texas" and am now "out of the land of the Philistines."
>
> If you want to hear a full description of our Exodus out of Texas read the Bible where the children of Israel crossed the Red Sea. We have had about the same show, only our enemies did not follow us to R[ed] River. If they had—the Indians would have in all probability sent them back without the interposition of Divine Providence.[78]

Reportedly, Placido "cried like a child" when Neighbors left and placed the Tonkawas under the care of Agent Samuel Blain at the Washita Agency.[79] The Anglo-Texans had completed their conquest of the Tonkawas.

EPILOGUE TO THE REMOVAL

The Tonkawas who chose reservation life remained at the Washita Agency for three years. With the outbreak of the Civil War, the agency and nearby Fort Cobb fell to Confederate administration. The Confederate government appointed John Leeper, who had been in charge of the Clear Fork Agency in Texas, as Indian agent for the Washita Agency. In late October of 1862, some Indians from the Kansas Agency—Delawares, Osages, and Shawnees who were loyal to the Union—joined with other Indians from the Fort Cobb Agency who were angered over rumors that some Tonkawas murdered and ate a Caddo boy. They attacked the Washita Agency. More than half the Tonkawas died, including Placido.[80]

The survivors returned to Texas. Some went to the ranch of Shapley S. Ross, former Indian agent for the Brazos Agency; others returned to "Tonk Valley," the Anglo-Texan settlement that had grown up at the site of the old Tonkawa village on the Brazos Reservation. Those who survived the massacre and the difficult war years through the charity of a few Anglo-Texan friends congregated at Fort Griffin after the Civil War. The Tonkawas at Fort Griffin received military rations, and the men worked for the U.S. Army as scouts in the campaigns against the Comanches and other American Indians on the southern Great Plains. When Fort Griffin closed in 1881, the Tonkawas lived on a nearby ranch for two years. However their destitution and complaints by settlers eventually compelled the U.S. government to remove the Tonkawas once more to Indian Territory, though some individuals joined their kin in Coahuila.[81]

The United States first settled the Tonkawas on the Iowa Agency, but the Iowas refused to accept the Tonkawas. The government then removed them to the Oakland Agency, near the present-day town of Tonkawa, Oklahoma. Ten years later, following the Dawes Act, the Tonkawas had their lands allotted. Each family received 160 acres; the balance was opened to Anglo-American settlement. Through the remainder of the nineteenth century and the first half of the twentieth century, the Tonkawas declined in numbers and lost their language and much of their traditional culture. However, like many other American Indian tribes, the last half of the twentieth century has seen growth in numbers, a resurgence in interest in their traditional culture, involvement in pan-Indian cultural and political activities, and attempts to secure legal redress for earlier wrongs.[82]

The military annexation of Texas by the United States enhanced some patterns and trends that had emerged during the previous twenty-five years; at the same time, it smashed or altered others. The security provided by the conquest of Mexico promoted even more rapid population growth. Texas became a magnet not only for Anglo-American immigrants from the southern United States with their African American slaves, but for immigrants from all of the western United States and from central Europe. Population growth both fueled and reflected economic expansion, as Texas cotton, sugar, and beef began to assume growing importance in the world-economy.

The demographic, economic, and political transformation of Texas altered life for Texas' Indians. First, population growth pushed American Indian people out of their traditional homes. Second, population growth and more intensive economic development led to a reduced demand for Indian labor and devalued American Indian economic contributions based on hunting and gathering activities. Third, the larger and more distant United States became responsible for regulating affairs between the settlers and the Indians. Finally, the demographic, economic, and political changes took place in a period of Western imperial expansion marked by a growing disdain for non-Western peoples. In the United States and Texas, the attitudes toward American Indians coalesced around two, not always mutually exclusive, avenues of action: cultural destruction through civilization and physical destruction by extermination.

For the Karankawas, population growth and economic development on the middle Texas coast left no room for their subsistence activities. Anglo-Texans who had tolerated Karankawas in their midst in the 1830s and early 1840s now ridded their ranches of them with the same vigor they applied to killing predatory animals. In a world that had no use for "savages," no voice was raised to stop the destruction of the Karankawas. By the end of the period, Karankawas no longer existed in interaction with one another as an ethnic community; only a few dispersed individuals survived.

For the Tonkawas, population growth, economic development, and settler intolerance pushed them westward beyond the line of settlement. There, they suffered from disease, starvation, and violence. The transfer of responsibility for the Tonkawas to the United States offered some hope for the Tonkawas, who had lost what little political influence they had with the death of Edward Burleson and the passing of a generation of Texans that remembered their service to the Anglo-Texans in earlier years. The Tonkawas' entrance into treaty relations with the United States and close ties with Special Indian Agent for Texas Major Robert Neighbors enabled them to survive as an ethnic community. Their survival came at the price of relinquishing their independence, accepting confinement to a reservation to be "civilized," and their eventual removal from Texas at the insistence of hostile Anglo-Texan settlers.

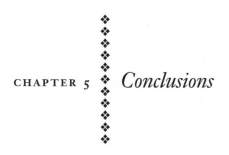

CHAPTER 5 ❖ *Conclusions*

The purpose of this case study of the Anglo-Texan conquest of the Tonkawas and the Karankawas between 1821 and 1859 has been to better understand the processes of conquest. It attempted to answer four broad questions relating to the processes of conquest that emerged from a theoretical orientation that combined global and local perspectives concerning social change. These four questions bear repeating:

(1) How does geopolitical location, especially the degree of state control, alter the processes and outcomes of conquest?

(2) How does the degree of incorporation into world-economic relations influence conquest?

(3) What are the cultural orientations of the conquered and conquering groups toward the other and toward the form of social violence known as conquest? How do they change during the processes of conquest?

(4) Can individual or collective human actors make a difference, and what limits or encourages the opportunity to make a difference?

GEOPOLITICAL LOCATION

In comparing the experience of the Karankawas and the Tonkawas in Spanish Texas, geopolitical location effectively shaped the processes and outcomes of conquest. During the Spanish period, the Karankawas along the coast served as a useful barrier against French, English, and Anglo-American intrusion into Spanish Texas. Probably not accidentally, the period of greatest Spanish hostility toward the Karankawas coincided with the time of greatest Spanish security in Texas from other European powers, immediately after the French cession of Louisiana to Spain and before U.S. expansion to the Mississippi. For the Tonkawas, cooperation with the Spanish peaked at the height of the Lipan threat to the Spanish. When the Spanish became allied with the Lipans, as a result of mutual concern over the Comanche invasion from the north-west, the Spanish-Tonkawa alliance turned to warfare. However, the strategic position of the Tonkawas along the Camino Real between San Antonio and Louisiana meant that the Spanish had to deal effectively with the Tonkawas. Unable to conquer them militarily, the Spanish adopted a policy of supporting Tonkawa leaders friendly to them and eliminating hostile leaders, as in the case of El Mocho. For both Karankawas and Tonkawas, the encounter with Spanish authority enhanced political centralization, though the details remain poorly known.

After 1821, the Anglo-Texans quickly removed the Karankawas from the upper coast, the area of their greatest economic interest. Karankawa subsistence activities could not mesh with Anglo-Texan plans for plantations and ports. The almost absolute powers granted to Austin as an empresario enhanced the ability of the Anglo-Texans to complete their project. However, Karankawa ties with the missions, intervention by Mexican authorities, and the unofficial border between Anglo-American Texas and Mexican Texas that lay across the lands occupied by the Karankawas resulted in the survival of some Karankawa bands, especially outside of Austin's colony. Undoubtedly, without this intervention, the history of the Karankawas as a people would have ended much sooner. For the much different encounter between the Anglo-Texans and the Tonkawas in Mexican Texas two geopolitical factors stand forth: (1) The Tonkawas occupied lands in the interior that were of marginal utility to the Anglo-Texans; and (2) The Tonkawas served as useful barriers between the Anglo-Texans and the Comanches and Wichitas of the interior.

The comparison between the Karankawas and the Tonkawas again proves revealing during the period of the Republic of Texas. The Karankawas, now restricted to the middle coast, saw intensive economic development spread to their diminished homeland. This focus of growth left the Karankawas with few alternatives. They could abandon the middle coast, but they would no longer be Karankawas without their coastal marshes around which they oriented both their spiritual life and economic life. The nearest other suitable environment for Karankawa survival was far to the south at the mouth of the Rio Grande, occupied by Mexican rancheros and indigenous American Indian groups. With Anglo-Texan economic and political domination, the Karankawas had to accommodate themselves to the new order or abandon the middle coast. The Tonkawas found themselves similarly squeezed. Anglo-Texan settlement reached the western edge of the Post Oak Savannah by the first years of the republic. To the west lay terrain that was less amenable to Tonkawa subsistence activities and, more critically, occupied by their enemies, the Penateka Comanches. However, the Tonkawas insured their survival by allying themselves with powerful Anglo-Texans in their campaigns against Indians and Mexicans.

During the period from 1846 to 1859, geopolitical location continued to affect the ability of the Karankawas and the Tonkawas to survive during the consolidation of the conquest. The Karankawas on the middle coast could not retreat in the advance of Anglo-Texan settlement, although evidence points to the possibility that some Karankawas joined culturally similar American Indian groups in the Rio Grande Delta. The Tonkawas on the western frontier could physically remove themselves to the west, but only at great cost. For the Karankawas, the lack of political ties to the state continued to plague their chances for survival during the period of U.S. administration. Without treaty relations with the United States, the Karankawas depended almost entirely on the precarious goodwill of the Anglo-Texan settlers who lived among them. The Karankawa-Tampaquas band on the lower Rio Grande attempted to exploit the political ambiguities of the border for their survival, but they too eventually fell victims to settler violence. The Tonkawas lost much of their political advantage with the passing of the Republic of Texas. The state no longer needed their services. However, the Tonkawas entered into treaty relations with the United States that would eventually secure their survival, at the cost of their freedom.

From the above analysis, it is indisputable that the geopolitical location of the American Indian peoples played a critical role in the processes of the Anglo-Texan conquest. While this analysis pays considerable attention to the location of American Indian groups in relation to capitalist development, it suggests other factors of geopolitical location at work.[1] First, borders played a central role. Karankawas exploited the unofficial border between Anglo-American Texas and Mexican Texas during the period of Mexican rule, and the Karankawa-Tampaquas exploited the official border between the United States and Mexico during U.S. rule. In both instances, they appealed to Mexican authorities to extricate them from difficulties with Anglo-Texan settlers and authorities. The Tonkawas used their position as borderers between Anglo-Texans and Comanches in a somewhat different manner. By allying themselves with the Anglo-Texans in their wars with the Comanches and Wichitas, the Tonkawas gained both a degree of insulation from Comanche aggression and a privileged position among American Indian peoples in Anglo-Texas during the period of Mexican rule and the republic.

In addition, this analysis centers around the type of state and degree of state control over settlers and American Indians.[2] The weak state control over Anglo-Texans in Mexican Texas and the weak settler-controlled state apparatus present during the republic allowed for more extreme processes. Karankawas could be harried to the edge of extermination without state intervention. At the same time, social space existed that allowed the Tonkawas to flourish. By the time the United States established more effective political control over Texas, the Karankawas had been reduced to remnants that could neither be readily protected by the United States nor seek protection from the United States as a people. Ironically, increased state control after the Mexican War led to diminished prospects for the Tonkawas. They lost their role as allies of the Anglo-Texan settlers when responsibility for the frontier wars shifted to the U.S. Army. Ultimately, they were given a choice of being forced to be hunted as outlaws or accept U.S. authority and confinement to a reservation. However, in the disturbances at the Brazos and Clear Fork Agencies in 1858 and 1859, the U.S. government prevented the potential destruction of the Tonkawas, and the other reserve Indians, at the hands of armed settlers. Yet, they were forced to accept removal to Indian Territory.

WORLD-ECONOMIC TIES

Incorporation into the trade relations of the developing world-system played a greater role in the historical development of the Tonkawas than it did for the Karankawas. The lack of trade opportunities with the Spanish in San Antonio encouraged the Tonkawas to disassociate themselves from the Spanish and turn toward the French, and later the English and the Anglo-Americans, as trading partners, especially after 1782 when Anglo-American traders along the Mississippi supplemented the well-developed entrepôts in Louisiana. The decline in hostilities among American Indian groups in Texas, east of Comanchería, during the last two decades of the eighteenth and first two decades of the nineteenth century may be partially attributable to the denser web of trade networks at this time. Such a turn contradicts many analyses of the role of European traders in Native America as agents of violence and social disorganization.[3] The Tonkawas, at the time of El Mocho, attempted to use their pivotal position in the exchange of firearms from the Mississippi Valley for horses from western Texas to take a leadership role in the proposed pan-Indian alliance.

Despite the more deleterious aspects of the North American fur trade for American Indian peoples, gifts and goods cemented alliances between American Indian nations that could lead not only to greater prosperity and cooperation, but also to new ethnic group formation. In Texas, this process never reached full development. Despite the efforts of leaders such as El Mocho, American Indian ethnic distinctions remained sharp through the Spanish period. Finally, were Juan Rodriquez, El Mocho, and José María widely accepted as leaders among their people arising out of the demands of conquest or incorporation into the world economy or does their importance represent a fiction arising from the Spanish need to deal with powerful leaders?[4] The experience with Yaculchen suggests that the latter case was true at times.

The Karankawas, isolated on the middle coast, probably had fewer trade opportunities than before the Spanish arrived in Texas and disrupted indigenous trade links with the people of the Rio Grande Plains. The Cocos on the upper coast were better positioned to participate in the new Texas trade networks.

In Mexican Texas, incorporation into trade relations of the expanding world-economy also played an important role in shaping the conquest. For Anglo-Texans, it furnished the economic rationale for transplanting the plantation economy of the Old Southwest to Texas. The only way Karankawas could find a place in the new economic organization on the upper coast was to abandon Karankawa ethnic identity and become slaves. Since the plantation organization was poorly developed in Mexican Texas, some Karankawa bands maintained their identity by attaching themselves to a plantation in return for security. The maintenance of the band organization prevented them from being amalgamated into the African American slave community. However, the center of Karankawa survival lay west of Austin's colony in an area in which their subsistence strategies could better mesh with Tejano cattle raising. Tonkawas, in Mexican Texas and on the frontier of Anglo-Texan settlement, were incorporated into a raiding and trading economy that developed in conjunction with the larger fur trade between North America and Europe.[5] This economy had appeal to elements of the Anglo-Texan community who did not have the resources or the interests to compete in the plantation economy. Thus, participation in the raiding and trading economy by Tonkawas and by some Anglo-Texans cemented relations between the two groups.

Both Karankawas and Tonkawas altered their economic activities to meet the new demands of the economic boom associated with the independence of Texas. However, the Karankawas' ability to provide menial chores on cattle ranches and fish and game to settlers proved to be marginal to the settlers, especially as population growth and integration into regional and world transportation systems increased the labor supply and the availability of food. For the Tonkawas, the persistent isolation of the settlements on the middle Colorado throughout the period made their economic role as laborers and suppliers of commodities more valuable. However, the strength of the Tonkawas in the processes of negotiating the conquest lay in their willingness to help the Anglo-Texan state in the struggles with its enemies that threatened its survival and blocked its expansion into western North America.

During the period of U.S. administration, ties to the world-economy by the Karankawas and the Tonkawas impacted the processes of conquest in a much different manner than in the past. As Texas became more deeply incorporated into the world-economy, the role of Karankawas and Tonkawas as day laborers and providers of fish, game, and hides became less consequential. By the end of the period, Anglo-Texan and Western commitment to progress and belief in the irrelevance of "savages" to the attainment of progress led to widespread public demand and acceptance of removal or extermination as the solution for dealing with Indians in Texas. In the case of the Tonkawas, removal triumphed even in the face of compelling economic advantage to maintaining the reservations in northwest Texas.

Integration of the Karankawas and the Tonkawas into the world-economy seemed to be less critical in shaping the processes of the Anglo-Texan conquest than did their geopolitical location. However, I must offer two caveats. First, politics and economy are excruciatingly intertwined in the modern world-system, even on and beyond the periphery. For example, in the eighteenth century the Tonkawa leader El Mocho used the advantages of his trade ties with the West to plan a pan-Indian political movement that would have expelled the Spanish from Texas. In Mexican Texas, Tonkawa access to the raiding and trading economy of the southern plains may have been a greater factor in their acceptance by Anglo-Texan settlers than their barrier position between the settlers and the Comanches. Second, as Anglo-Texas became more integrated into the world-economy, the economic and political position of Karankawas and Tonkawas become more marginal as economic niches that they could fill while maintaining their ethnic identity disappeared. This happened first on the lower Brazos and Colorado in the 1820s. It spread to the middle coast by the 1840s and to the frontier after statehood, though government expenditures for frontier wars and reservations provided a powerful economic incentive for tolerating American Indians in the 1850s. Yet, Indian-hating among Anglo-Texans overcame the pecuniary benefits associated with keeping the Tonkawas and other reserve Indians in Texas.

CULTURAL CONSTRUCTIONS

In analyzing the role of cultural constructions in the Anglo-Texan conquest of the Karankawas and Tonkawas, we must first accept the fact that we only have a record of Anglo-Texan constructions of Karankawas and Tonkawas. In addition, these constructions took place in the wider context of Anglo-American experience with Indians and of Westerners with non-Western people. Also, as others have noted, these constructions took place within a specific political and economic environment and were used by the dominant group to defend their actions. In addition, these constructions had roots in myth and emotion that may have had little to do with political and economic motivation.[6] For example, for the Anglo-Americans encountering the Karankawas and the Tonkawas, the degree of incorporation into European-oriented trade relations became important for another reason: the cultural construction of the other. Because neither Karankawas nor Tonkawas farmed, the other economic activity in which they engaged that transcended the Western category of savagery was trade.

For the Spanish, the cultural construction of the Karankawas and the Tonkawas as savages took another turn. The leading exponents of Karankawa and Tonkawa savagery were the clerics. For them, the constructions of savagery provided the rationales for new mission efforts in a time of diminished financial support for missions and their military protection. Thus, cultural constructions cannot be divorced from their political and economic contexts.

The use of cannibalism as a cultural construction by Anglo-Texans in Mexican Texas most clearly illustrates the use of cultural constructions in shaping conquest. Despite the fact that there is much stronger evidence of cannibalism as a normative practice among Tonkawas than among Karankawas, Anglo-Texans used alleged Karankawa cannibalism to legitimate their destruction of the Karankawas. Anglo-Texans in Mexican Texas paternalistically portrayed Tonkawas as harmless beggars and petty thieves. They largely ignored evidence of cannibalism among their Tonkawa allies. Both constructions overlaid deeply rooted Anglo-Texan beliefs about the savagery of Indians, who had to be exterminated or civilized. The construction of Karankawas as cannibals allowed Anglo-Texans to exterminate them. The construction of Tonkawas as beggars and petty thieves allowed Anglo-Texans to tolerate them as long as they were useful, with some hope that they might become "civilized."

By the time of the republic, Anglo-Texans tended to see both groups as "savages" who were dirty, treacherous, and lacked full mental capabilities. Those more distant from the two groups, in line with contemporary thinking about Indians, regarded them as "poor fellows," who were doomed to extinction by civilization and progress. Most of those nearer them, saw them as nuisances to be removed from their midst. For the Karankawas, removal took the form of massacres by settlers. For Tonkawas, although disputes at times ended in murder, settlers complained to the government. More intriguing are the later Anglo-Texan constructions of Indian cannibalism. After the Texas Revolution, accusations of Karankawa cannibalism almost disappeared. During the same period, Anglo-Texan association with their Tonkawa allies in battle forced them to confront Tonkawa cannibalism. However, the utility of Tonkawa cannibalism as an element of terror against the Comanches and the fear that reports of Karankawa or Tonkawa cannibalism would discourage settlement and investment led to little public discussion of the subject, except for an occasional point in arguing for the universal savagery of Indians. Individual Anglo-Texans came to view Tonkawa cannibalism as a normal part of the brutal wars they fought with their enemies.

Probably the central factor in the processes of the Anglo-Texan conquest of the Karankawas and the Tonkawas during the period of U.S. administration was the acceptance, among all strata of Anglo-Texans and Anglo-Americans, of two alternatives in dealing with American Indians: civilization or extermination. The growing economic and political powerlessness of Karankawas and Tonkawas in Texas tended to substantiate the Anglo-Texan ideology concerning the fate of "savages." As increased incorporation into the political and economic dimensions of the modern world-system limited political choices for Karankawas and Tonkawas and made their labor less valuable, increased cultural connections to the West limited the range of Anglo-Texan attitudes and beliefs about American Indians. By the 1850s, the Western discourse of savagery and civilization channeled almost all interaction between settlers and Native Americans.

HUMAN ACTORS

Finally, did any actors make a difference? In Mexican Texas, Karankawa band leaders, such as Prudencia, who held their bands together and attached them to prominent settlers, prolonged the survival of their bands. Antoñito used his ties with Mexican officials and clerics to arrange a peace that offered hope for Karankawa survival. Tonkawa leaders, such as Caritas and Joyoso, saw that the main hope for Tonkawa survival in the face of Comanche, Wichita, and immigrant American Indian expansion lay in alliances with Mexican officials, including Anglo-Texan and Tejano empresarios, and Anglo-Texan and Tejano settlers.

However, the most interesting example of social actors altering conquest comes from Stephen F. Austin's judgments about Karankawas and Tonkawas upon his first meeting with them. These judgments dominated Anglo-Texan discourse concerning both groups. It was his pronouncement that Karankawas were the "universal enemies of man," that "they killed of all nations that came into their power, and frequently feast on the bodies of their victims," and that "there will be no way of subduing them but extermination" which set the agenda for the Anglo-Texan conquest of the Karankawas. At the same time, Austin's dismissal of the Tonkawas after his first meeting with them as harmless "beggars" persisted as a common theme in relations between Anglo-Texans and Tonkawas throughout the period.[7] Yet, the interrelationship between personal influence, cultural construction, and the demands of the political economy remain intriguingly intertwined in the Anglo-Texan encounter with the Karankawas and Tonkawas in Mexican Texas.

Austin's and the Anglo-Texans' divergent cultural constructions of the Karankawas and Tonkawas are of unusual theoretical interest. First, how did Austin's constructions achieve such dominance? Second, where did Austin's constructions come from? Did he know that Karankawas occupied valuable lands and Tonkawas would be useful friends? Were the judgments the product of some mixture of his experience, personality, and culture that happened to mesh with economic and political needs of his colony? Undoubtedly, Austin wielded more influence and authority than any Anglo-Texan of his time, though the evidence suggests that there were Anglo-Texans who did not share his perceptions of Karankawas and Tonkawas. For example, the Wightmans sheltered Karankawas at their plantation, and Gabriel Snyder and his neighbors embarked on their own campaign of extermination against a nearby Tonkawa camp. Thus, the complex interrelationships between personal influence, cultural constructions, and the demands of the political economy impacted the Anglo-Texan conquest of the Karankawas and Tonkawas in Mexican Texas. However, the end of Mexican Texas and the creation of the Republic of Texas altered the political and economic landscape and brought in new cultural constructions and new social actors that structured the Karankawas' and Tonkawas' negotiation of conquest with the Anglo-Texans.

During the period of the republic, the Karankawas' lack of leadership able to deal with the republic, after the Texas Revolution cut old ties to Mexico, and their inability to forge alliances with powerful local Anglo-Texans weakened their ability to negotiate their survival. For the Tonkawas, adept leaders such as Campos, Ocquin, and Placido used ties developed to Houston in the Texas Revolution to establish treaty relations with the republic and to extricate their kin from serious confrontations with settlers. The alliance with political leader and Ranger Captain Edward Burleson further strengthened the Tonkawas' negotiation for survival during the decade of the republic. Under U.S. authority, the personal efforts of Tonkawa leaders, such as Placido, and one Anglo-Texan, Robert Neighbors, prevented the physical destruction of the Tonkawas in the 1850s and allowed the Tonkawas to survive as an ethnic community.

Once more, I must return to the theme of social space in discussing the role of human agency. As Texas became more entwined in the political, economic, and ideological dimensions of the modern world-system, it became more difficult for human actors to find the space they needed to effect social change.

The period of U.S. administration in Texas provides an example of the intertwined nature of political, economic, and cultural domination in the consolidation of conquest. After Anglo-Texans achieved more secure political control of Texas at the end of the 1840s, integration into the world-economy deepened and eliminated economic spaces that Karankawas and Tonkawas could exploit. At the same time, Anglo-Texans attempted to destroy all traces of the conquered peoples on the basis of an ideology that constructed those conquered peoples as savages. Anglo-

Texan domination left no room for counter ideologies. Only two avenues for Karankawa and Tonkawa survival remained: (1) They could physically escape into regions where Anglo-Texan dominance was contested, which the Karankawas did in the Rio Grande Delta and Tonkawas did in the borderlands of Coahuila and Texas; or (2) They could attempt to renegotiate their survival with the state. Placido's Tonkawas were able to choose the second option, and their success, such as it was, came from personal efforts by Tonkawas and their few Anglo-Texan allies at finding spaces in the hegemonic system for ethnic survival.

It is appropriate that the one person who deserves the most credit for saving the Tonkawas from destruction during the events of 1858 and 1859, Robert Neighbors, was not a war chief or a Ranger captain or an empresario. Robert Neighbors was the superintendent of Indian Affairs for the Texas Agency of the Bureau of Indian Affairs. He accomplished his goals through effective campaigns of letter writing and personal influence in the newspapers and in the bureaucracy of the United States and the state of Texas.

In summary, the case study not only illuminated the variability and uncertainty of the processes of conquest, but the manner in which those processes changed when they were part of the larger transformation from beyond the periphery of the modern world-system to the core. Rather than being unidimensional, the Anglo-Texan conquest of the Karankawas and Tonkawas illustrates the twists and turns taken by individual and collective social actors faced with massive social change: the conquest of western North America by the United States; incorporation into an industrializing, capitalist world-economy; immersion in the developing mass culture of the modern world-system; and the bureaucratization associated with the development of the modern state, economy, and media.

During the formative years of sociological thinking, European sociologist Ludwig Gumplowicz presented a powerful argument for the centrality of conquest—social violence over access to resources resulting in arrangements of domination and subordination—in the ordering of human affairs. Gumplowicz based his conquest hypothesis on the assumptions that groups of people would inevitably be in conflict with one another, that these groups centered themselves around cultural relationships as well as material relationships, and that intergroup conflict leading to conquest was a primary shaping force of human social arrangements.[1]

In the United States, as well as in Europe, Gumplowicz's conquest hypothesis became enormously influential in the social sciences at the turn of the century. It provided the foundations of sociology's focus on the outcomes of intergroup conflict. Sarah Simons borrowed directly from Gumplowicz in formulating the concept of social assimilation, and that concept came to define the assimilation model of ethnic relations that continues to dominate the sociology of racial and ethnic relations in the United States.[2] Also at the turn of the century, the historian Frederick Jackson Turner, in a parallel development, emphasized the importance of conquest in creating and revitalizing the society and culture of the United States:

> This nation is formed under pioneer ideals . . . The first ideal of the pioneer was that of conquest. It was his task to fight with nature for the chance to exist . . . Facing each generation of pioneers was the unmastered continent. Vast forests . . . mountainous ramparts . . . desolate, grass-clad prairies . . . arid deserts, and a fierce race of savages all had to be met and defeated.[3]

However, the nineteenth century colonial expansion and accompanying conquest of non-Western people provided the empirical basis for the development of a related analytical concept that was to have a much greater impact than Gumplowicz's conquest hypothesis. English social philosopher John A. Hobson coined the term "imperialism" to describe the Western conquest of the non-Western world for economic gain. Hobson, at the turn of the century, argued that worldwide economic exploitation by the West arose inevitably out of nineteenth-century technological advances in the West and the demands of capitalist expansion in the West. Despite its inevitability, imperialism, with its "mission of civilization," was ultimately destructive, according to Hobson. In the conquered lands, the imperial project either destroyed indigenous people or transformed them into a servile class, depending upon their utility for the colonial power. Hobson also viewed imperialism as destructive to the West. Imperialism encouraged, even demanded, an extreme nationalism in which militarism and the concentration of political and economic power would lead to disaster for the West. Hobson's analysis of imperialism failed to persist in mainstream sociology, even though it powerfully influenced a whole generation of European Marxists: Bakunin, Hilferding, Kautsky, Lenin, and Luxembourg.[4] The reintroduction of imperialism as an analytical concept into mainstream sociology came with the development of world-system theory in the 1970s. However, world-system theory largely stripped the concept of imperialism from its cultural components and reformulated it as a strictly political and economic process.

At the end of World War I, Joseph Schumpeter provided an elaboration on imperialism and conquest as social processes. Schumpeter, echoing Gumplowicz, argued that imperialism and conquest were as ancient as human political arrangements. Unlike Gumplowicz's interpretation, Schumpeter separated conquest from ethnicity, and, unlike Hobson's interpretation, Schumpeter divorced imperialism from economic calculation, though ethnic nationalism and economic gain could be motivations for conquest and imperialism. In his final analysis, Schumpeter saw conquest and imperialism—"the object disposition on the part of a state to unlimited forcible expansion"—as social atavisms resulting from the interests of a warrior class.[5] These interests could at times dominate the values of a state leading to conquest for the sake of conquest, as Schumpeter argued was the case in ancient Assyria. Nevertheless, at other times, the nationalistic, the religious, or the economic interests of other classes could fuel the imperial drive. Unlike the pessimistic conclusions of Gumplowicz and Hobson, Schumpeter's conception of conquest and imperialism as vestigial forms of human social action led him to believe that conquest and imperialism would wither under fully developed modern capitalism.

At mid-century, with imperialism flourishing in the presence of capitalist world domination, another sociologist attempted to elucidate the sociological dimensions of conquest and imperialism. W. E. B. DuBois proposed that the central organizing feature of the world since the end of the Napoleonic Wars, but with roots extending back to the first voyages of European exploration at the end of the fifteenth century, was white conquest of nonwhite people for material gain. Although DuBois agreed with Hobson that world peace and imperialism were mutually incompatible, DuBois differed from Hobson by focusing on the deleterious effects of Western conquest on non-Western people.[6] Yet, as happened to the insights of Gumplowicz, Hobson, and Schumpeter into the centrality of conquest in organizing human social relations, those of DuBois remained marginal to sociology.

By the 1970s, sociology experienced a renewed flurry of interest in the development of conquest as an analytical concept. The emergence of conflict theory challenged the prevailing notion of stability as central to social organization. Other than new editions of works by Gumplowicz and Hobson, little interest surfaced in the idea of conquest from conflict theorists. Some possible reasons for this lack include the following: (1) its ahistorical interest in abstract social systems inherited from its origins in structural functionalism, as developed by Ralf Dahrendorf, Randall Collins, and Johnathan Turner, or (2) its preoccupation with small-scale social interactions, as also pursued by Randall Collins from an ethnomethodological, phenomenological, and rational choice orientation.[7]

The revitalization of neo-Marxian social theory, especially the elaboration of world-system theory, during this period furnished another opportunity for bringing conquest into sociological theory. World-system theory allowed for process and history in the understanding of social change and stimulated interest in the processes and outcomes associated with the encounter between the modern world-system, centered in northwestern Europe, and the rich mosaic of cultural, economic, and political entities that lay outside of northwestern Europe. Yet, the world-system model attracted intense criticism. The most widely voiced of these critiques included the limited and passive role relegated to precapitalist and non-Western social entities, the subordination of cultural explanations to economic and political explanations, and explicitly leaving out the role of human agency in moving social change.[8] Most scholars

working in the world-system or political economy framework continued to collapse the complex, multilayered processes of conquest into
Western-centered economic and political relationships.

Another promising theoretical vehicle for the reintroduction of
conquest into contemporary sociological theory came with Michael
Hechter's internal colonialism model. As in the related world-system
model, economic and political relationships tended to overshadow cultural explanations and human agency in understanding the processes of
conquest that led to ethnic subordination within nation states. However,
a small group of scholars in the United States used the internal colonialism model as a point of departure in formulating their argument for
the primacy of the conquest experience in understanding the past and
present of African Americans, Mexican Americans, and American Indians in the United States.[9]

Despite the limited interest in the idea of conquest in contemporary
sociology, conquest commands center stage in the theoretical and analytical presentations of anthropology and history. The scope of the
research oriented around conquest varies from Stanley Diamond's interpretation of state conquest of nonstate peoples as a defining charac-
teristic of human experience to the more local problems of how conquest has shaped the contemporary American West, the American
character on the frontier, and contemporary political processes in the
United States. However, today we see sociologists and anthropologists
making the parallel argument in favor of placing the history of racial and
ethnic groups and the complex processes of ethnic group creation,
change, and death in a broader sociological context.[10]

Methodological Issues ❖ APPENDIX 2

This book addresses three contemporary methodological debates within historical sociology: (1) the tension between historical particularity and sociological generalization, (2) the related debate over the use of primary sources versus summarizing secondary sources, and (3) the ability to overcome the biases inherent in using data that are the products of the dominant group. First, sociological generalization demands a different unit of analysis than historical particularity. Sociologists are interested in studying processes.[1] Thus, this book has the conquest of Karankawas and the Tonkawas as its unit of analysis, and, as such, the book has different interests than if it used historical categories such as Indian history or Texas history or Western history, though it shares some commonalities with works that do have those units of analysis.

In addition, John H. Goldthorpe proposed that, although there is a tendency to particularize in history and generalize in sociology, history should set the limit to sociological generalization. As a result, the availability and applicability of historical data limit the development of sociological theory through the use of historical cases. To avoid this problem historical sociologists frequently base their findings on a summary of historical interpretations. Although historical sociologists treat historical interpretations, secondary sources, as historical facts, secondary sources remain interpretations of historical data. Immediately two questions arise: How can the historical sociologist know how much support exists for the historical interpretation in question? and How does one gauge accuracy in historical interpretations, conflicting or not? The only answers for those who choose to do historical sociology are to ask questions that can be illuminated by the available primary sources and to rework and familiarize themselves with the primary sources on which significant historical interpretations are derived.[2] In Chapter 1 and in the opening discussions of the political and economic contexts of conquest in Chapters 2 through 4, I rely heavily on secondary sources for these macrosociological analyses and discussions. Thus, my choice of secondary sources strongly influences my understanding of the formation of the Karankawas and the Tonkawas and the political economy of nineteenth-century Texas. In all cases, the secondary sources employed can lead the interested reader to a greater understanding of issues only briefly touched upon in the book.

However, the details of the Anglo-Texan conquest that make up the bulk of Chapters 2 through 4 were largely gleaned from a rich variety of primary sources. The more detailed analyses and discussions of the Anglo-Texan conquest of the Karankawas and the Tonkawas overwhelmingly rely on primary sources: (1) diaries, memoirs, and reminiscences of Anglo-Texan settlers; (2) travelers' accounts from the period; (3) newspaper accounts; and (4) official correspondence. The first two sources have much in common. First, they are unique productions of the authors that are not subject to review or standardization. As such, they reflect the eccentricities, idiosyncrasies, and whims of the remarkably varied people who produced them. Some of the characters encountered in this exploration of the diaries, memoirs, and travelers' accounts from nineteenth-century Texas include the stuffy, the flamboyant, the brutish, the sensitive, the scholarly, the barely literate, the snobbish, and the plain. One of the more fascinating and revealing accounts is Mary Wightman Helms's *Scraps of Early Texas History*. However, she hid her story of her relations with the Karankawas at Matagorda in an unusual religious tract that criticized the "excesses" of nineteenth-century evangelical Protestantism, especially those of the Campbellites, and explicated her own religious philosophy. She based her beliefs upon the religious works "divinely revealed" to her in the Gulf surf during her lonely years at her and her husband's Matagorda County plantation.

Thus, one can question the validity of such documents. In order to confirm validity, I always attempted to find additional accounts of any incidents that strained credulity, and the book offers conflicting interpretations and reports when such occurrences surface. The diaries and travelers' accounts are particularly useful in that they are more immediate than memoirs and reminiscences, and, of course, travelers can offer insights that persons more familiar with the scene take for granted. I must note that without Marilyn Sibley's *Travelers in Texas, 1761–1860* locating these accounts would have been a much more arduous task than it was.

Memoirs and reminiscences have the drawback of being written years after the fact. Thus, they can be and usually are influenced by a sense of historical inevitability, other accounts, and editing, by oneself or others, of events that might seem unsavory or embarrassing at the time of writing. During the period from 1870 to 1910, when most of the memoirs I used were written, no apparent shame or embarrassment accrued to recounting the violence between Anglo-Texans and American Indians in the nineteenth century. Noah Smithwick's widely used *The Evolution of a State*, first published in 1900, had the advantage of being written by an author who left Texas at the onset of the Civil War. Therefore, his absence insulated him from the outpouring of Texas settler reminiscences and memoirs after 1870. John Holland Jenkins's remarkably candid *Recollections of Early Texas*, written in the 1870s and 1880s, also possesses great value in understanding the Anglo-Texan–American Indian violence. Although containing factual errors, J. W. Wilbarger's *Indian Depredations in Texas*, which has served as a mythic recounting of the six decades of Anglo-Texan conquest of the Indian nations of Texas for Anglo-Texan readers since its original publication in 1889, captures the essence of Indian-hating by Anglo-Texans on the Texas frontier.

Newspaper accounts from the period again offer the advantage of immediacy. In addition, the act of reading newspapers from the period immerses the researcher in the life of the period—political debates and economic activities—in a way that reading even the best-written diaries, journals, memoirs, or secondary works cannot accomplish. Of course, one must interpret newspaper articles in light of the political agenda and the economic interests of the newspapers' owners and editors.

Official documents also have the advantage of immediacy and give structure, meaning, and insight into official actions. Yet, they must also be interpreted in light of the political and economic agendas of the authors. Chapter 2 could not have been written without *The Austin Papers*, edited by Eugene Barker; Chapter 3, without *The Indian Affairs Papers of Texas and the Southwest, Volumes I and II*, edited by Dorman Winfrey and others; and Chapter 4, without *The Indian Affairs Papers of Texas and the Southwest, Volume III*, edited by Dorman Winfrey and James Day, and the Letters Received by the Office of Indian Affairs, Texas Agency. In addition to the ethnohistories of the Karankawas and the Tonkawas (Preface, Endnote 2), the most helpful secondary sources in understanding and leading me to the details of the Anglo-Texan conquest of the Karankawas and the Tonkawas are John Milton Nance's impeccably researched *After San Jacinto* and *Attack and Counterattack*, Kenneth F.

Neighbours's *Indian Exodus*, and Hobart Huson's *Refugio: A Comprehensive History from Aboriginal Times to 1953.*

An even thornier problem, incorporating the perspective of the powerless, looms when using historical evidence. The premier historical evidence is the written account. Yet surviving written accounts almost always represent the point-of-view of the powerful. Attempting to reconstruct the perspective of the powerless, in contrast to accepting that of the powerful, becomes even more problematic when the case involves the conquest of a nonliterate people by a literate population. The researcher works only with the conquerors' point-of-view. In such an instance, the researcher must utilize to the fullest the human ability to take on the role of the other in order to interpret the documentary evidence critically.[3]

The ability of the researcher to take on the role of the other becomes even more laden with difficulty when the researcher approaches the powerless from personal, group, and institutional locations of relative power. Norma Williams and Andrée Sjoberg advanced the following methodological considerations when confronted with this problem: First, we must ask "questions as 'How are the data collected?' and 'How are they constructed?'" and Second, the research project should not advance the researcher's goals by portraying the other as exotic or devaluing the other. Instead, the project should ask questions and produce results that can further the cause of the other or cause the powerful in society to question or reexamine their own legitimacy.[4]

In this analysis of the Anglo-Texan conquest of the Karankawas and the Tonkawas, I have attempted to employ as many techniques as possible to broaden the range of perspectives. These vary from using as wide a variety of data as possible, in order to provide a richer context surrounding the social processes under examination and reveal rifts within the dominant group, to taking new multiple perspectives and viewpoints in relation to the research problem.

Probably the greatest challenge to taking new perspectives faced in the book lies in extricating the narrative from the settler discourse of Indian "depredations" and settler "chastisement" and the counter-discourse of European American brutality and American Indian innocence. As James Axtell noted, the language we use in presenting accounts of social conflict inevitably reveals moral judgments by the writer. Rather than recoil from making moral judgments, this book is written within a sociological tradition that sees sociology as a moral science as well as a social science. In addition, it lies in agreement with Axtell that any moral judgment should place greater responsibility on the actions of European Americans for four reasons: (1) They took American Indian lands; (2) They obliterated American Indian cultures; (3) They benefited from American Indian losses; and (4) They set themselves a higher moral standard in what they perceived as the contest between "civilization" and "savagery."[5]

Notes

Preface

1. Terence K. Hopkins and Immanuel Wallerstein, "Structural Transformation in the World Economy," *World-System Analysis: Theory and Methodology*, pp. 121–43.

2. For the Karankawas, see Albert S. Gatschet, *The Karankawa Indians. The Coast People of Texas*; Ed Kilman, *Cannibal Coast*; Mildred P. Mayhall, *The Indians of Texas: The Atákapa, the Karankawa, and the Tonkawa*; William W. Newcomb, *The Indians of Texas: From Prehistoric to Modern Times*; Robert Arthur Ricklis, *The Karankawa Indians of Texas: An Ecological Study of Cultural Tradition and Change*; Richard P. Schaedel, "The Karankawas of the Texas Gulf Coast," *Southwestern Journal Of Anthropology* 5 (1949): 117–37; Thomas Wolff, "The Karankawa Indians: Their Conflict with the White Man in Texas," *Ethnohistory* 16 (1969): 1–32. For the Tonkawas, see Robert Haskaarl, "The Culture and History of the Tonkawa Indians," *Plains Anthropologist* 7 (1962): 217–31; William K. Jones, *Notes on the History and Material Culture of the Tonkawa Indians*; Mayhall, *The Indians of Texas*; Debra Lamont Newlin, *The Tonkawa People from the Earliest Times to 1893*; Thomas F. Schilz, *People of the Cross Timbers: A History of the Tonkawa Indians*; and Andrée F. Sjoberg, "The Culture of the Tonkawa, A Texas Indian Tribe," *Texas Journal of Science* 5 (1953): 280–304.

3. See Ludwig Gumplowicz, *The Outlines of Sociology*; John Hobson, *Imperialism, a Study*; Immanuel Wallerstein, *The Modern World-System: Capitalist Agriculture and the Origins of the European World-Economy in the Sixteenth Century*; Michael Hechter, *Internal Colonialism: The Celtic Fringe in British National Development*.

4. Compare to Wilma Dunaway, "Incorporation as an Interactive Process: Cherokee Resistance to Expansion of the Capitalist World-System," *Sociological Inquiry* 66 (1996): 455–70.

5. Compare to Thomas D. Hall, "Historical Sociology and Native Americans," *American Indian Quarterly* 13 (1989): 223–38. Compare to Charles Tilly, *Big Structures, Large Processes, and Huge Comparisons*, pp. 1–59. Compare to Duane Champagne, *American Indian Societies: Strategies of Political and Cultural Survival*, p. 1; John Swanton, "Remarks," *Proceedings of the International Congress*

of Americanists 20 (1922): 53–59; Sjoberg, "The Culture of the Tonkawas"; William W. Newcomb, Jr., "A Reappraisal of the 'Cultural Sink' of Texas," *Southwestern Journal of Anthropology* 12 (1956): 145–53.

6. Champagne, *American Indian Societies*, pp. 2–4; Darcy Ribeiro, *The Americas and Civilization*.

7. Thomas D. Hall, "Incorporation into the World-System: Toward a Critique," *American Sociological Review* 51 (1986): 390–402; Christopher Chase-Dunn and Thomas D. Hall, *Rise and Demise: Comparing World-Systems*, pp. 59–77; Champagne, *American Indian Societies*, pp. 5–7; See Walter Prescott Webb, *The Great Plains: A Study in Institutions and Environment;* T. R. Fehrenbach, *Lone Star: A History of Texas and Texans;* Andreas Reichstein, *The Rise of the Lone Star.*

8. See Talal Asad, "Conscripts of Western Civilization," *Civilization in Crisis: Anthropological Perspectives, Volume 1 of Dialectical Anthropology: Essays in Honor of Stanley Diamond*, pp. 332–52; Champagne, *American Indian Societies*, pp. 5–7; Hall, "Incorporation into the World-System"; Chase-Dunn and Hall, *Rise and Demise*, pp. 59–77; Richard White, *"It's Your Misfortune and None of My Own": A History of The American West*, pp. 328–53.

9. See Eric Wolf, *Europe and the People without History*. Of course, incorporation of non-state peoples into state dominated political and economic relations predates the origins of the modern world-system, see Christopher Chase-Dunn and Thomas D. Hall, *Core/Periphery Relations in Pre-Capitalist Worlds;* Christopher Chase-Dunn and Thomas D. Hall, "Comparing World-Systems: Concepts and Working Hypotheses," *Social Forces* 71 (1993): 851–56; Chase-Dunn and Hall, *Rise and Demise*, pp. 59–77.

10. See Henry F. Dobyns, *Their Number Became Thinned: Native American Population Dynamics in Eastern North America;* John C. Ewers, "The Influence of Epidemics on the Indian Population and Cultures of Texas," *Plains Anthropologist* 18 (1973): 104–15; Russell Thornton, *American Indian Holocaust and Survival: A Population History since 1492.*

11. For example, see Thomas D. Hall, *Social Change in the Southwest: 1350–1880;* Sandra D. Faiman-Silva, *Choctaws at the Crossroads: The Political Economy of Class and Culture in the Oklahoma Timber Region*, Chase-Dunn and Hall, *Rise and Demise*, pp. 59–77.

12. For example, see Elizabeth A. John, *Storms Brewed in Other Men's Worlds: The Confrontation of Indians, Spanish and French in the Southwest, 1540–1795.*

13. See Richard Drinnan, *Facing West: The Metaphysics of Indian-Hating and Empire-Building;* Francis Jennings, *The Invasion of America: Indians, Colonialism, and the Cant of Conquest;* James J. Rawls, *The Indians of California: The Changing Image;* David Svaldi, *Sand Creek and the Rhetoric of Extermination: A Case Study in Indian-White Relations.*

14. Dunaway, "Incorporation as an Interactive Process," Chase-Dunn and Hall, *Rise and Demise*, pp. 59–77; Thomas D. Hall, "The World-System Perspective: A Small Sample from a Large Universe," *Sociological Inquiry* 66 (1996): 440–54; David Montejano, *Anglos and Mexicans in the Making of Texas, 1836–1986*, p. 318.

15. For example, see Randall Collins, "On the Micro-Foundations of Macro-Sociology," *American Journal of Sociology* 86 (1981): 984–1014; See George H. Mead, *Mind, Self and Society;* Gideon Sjoberg and Ted R. Vaughan, "The Bureaucratization of Sociology: Its Impact on Theory and Research," *A Critique of Contemporary American Sociology*, pp. 54–113; R. Brian Ferguson and Neil L. Whitehead, "The Violent Edge of Empire," *War in the Tribal Zone: Expanding States and Indigenous Warfare*, p. 17.

16. The Indian point-of-view that emerges so clearly in recent works on large, well-studied groups such as the Cheyenne, Sioux, Choctaw, Pawnee, and Navajo depends on the availability of diverse range of historical documents, a rich ethnographic literature, and a vibrant oral tradition. For example, see John H. Moore, *The Cheyenne Nation: A Social and Demographic History;* Gary Clayton Anderson, *Kinsmen of Another Kind: Dakota-White Relations in the Upper Mississippi, 1650–1862;* Richard White, *Roots of Dependency: Subsistence, Environment, and Social Change among the Choctaws, Pawnees, and Navajos.* For the problems faced by researchers dealing with groups who were destroyed or virtually destroyed by Western conquest, see Phillip P. Boucher, *Cannibal Encounters: Europeans and Island Caribs, 1492–1763.*

17. Compare to William Roseberry, "Political Economy," *Annual Review of Anthropology* 39 (1988): 161–15; William Roseberry, "La Falta de Brazos: Land and Labor in the Coffee Economies of Nineteenth Century Latin America," *Theory and Society* 20 (1991): 351–82; Hall, "World-System Perspective."

18. See John H. Peterson, Jr., "The Indian in the Old South," *Red, White, and Black: Symposium on the Indians in the Old South*, pp. 116–33.

19. In particular, Spanish personal names follow the spellings in Adan Benavides, *The Bexar Archives, 1717–1836: A Name Guide.*

Chapter 1. Texas in 1821: Prelude to Conquest

1. Juan Antonio Padilla, "Texas in 1820," *Southwestern Historical Quarterly* 23 (1919): 47–68, 61.

2. For example, see Zebulon M. Pike, *An Account of Expeditions to the Sources of the Mississippi, and through the Western Parts of Louisiana, . . . and a Tour through the Interior Parts of New Spain*, p. 272.

3. Odie Faulk, *The Last Years of Spanish Texas, 1778–1821*, p. 101; Donald Chipman, *Spanish Texas, 1519–1821*, pp. 207–27; Padilla, "Texas in 1820," p. 64; Pike, *An Account of Expeditions*, p. 272.

4. Eugene C. Barker, *The Life of Stephen F. Austin: Founder of Texas 1793–1836: A Chapter of the Westward Movement of the American People*, pp. 37–38.

5. See Carlos E. Castañeda, *Transition Period: The Fight for Freedom, 1810–1836. Vol. VI, Our Catholic Heritage in Texas, 1519–1836*, pp. 1–174; Chipman, *Spanish Texas*, pp. 216–41; Faulk, *Last Years*, 132–40; Julia Kathryn Garrett, *Green Flag over Texas: The Last Years of Spain in Texas.* Compare to Juan Gómez-Quiñones, *Roots of Chicano Politics, 1600–1940*, pp. 65–85.

6. Castañeda, *Transition Period*, pp. 173–74.

7. Odie Faulk, "The Comanche Invasion of Texas, 1743–1836," *Great Plains Journal* 9 (1969): 10–50; See Thomas W. Kavanagh, *Comanche Political History: An Ethnohistorical Perspective, 1706–1875*.

8. Dan Flores, *Journal of an Indian Trader: Anthony Glass and the Texas Trading Frontier, 1790–1810*, p. 92.

9. See Padilla, "Texas in 1820."

10. Mattie Austin Hatcher, *The Opening of Texas to Foreign Settlement, 1801–1821*, pp. 73–76; Padilla, "Texas in 1820."

11. Roy H. Pearce, *Savagism and Civilization: A Study of the Indian and the American Mind*, pp. 3–4.

12. Bernard W. Sheehan, *Seeds of Extinction: Jeffersonian Philanthropy and the American Indian*, pp. 68, 174.

13. Robert F. Berkhofer, *The White Man's Indian: Images of the American Indian from Columbus to the Present*, p. 152.

14. Thomas Jefferson, *The Complete Jefferson*, p. 459.

15. Ibid., pp. 497–98.

16. Quoted in Ronald Takaki, *Iron Cages: Race and Culture in Nineteenth-Century America*, p. 62.

17. Reginald Horsman, *Race and Manifest Destiny: The Origins of American Racial Anglo-Saxonism*, p. 114.

18. Takaki, *Iron Cages*, pp. 56, 69–79.

19. Reginald Horsman, *The Frontier in the Formative Years, 1783–1815*, pp. 50–83.

20. Takaki, *Iron Cages*, pp. 94–96; Sam Houston, *The Autobiography of Sam Houston*, pp. 9–14.

21. Quoted in Takaki, *Iron Cages*, p. 103.

22. See Wolf, *Europe and the People without History*, pp. 267–85. See Douglass Cecil North, *The Economic Growth of the United States, 1790–1860*, pp. 122–34, 182–88; Horsman, *The Frontier in the Formative Years*, pp. 166–88.

23. Berkhofer, *The White Man's Indian*, p. 75; Pearce, *Savagism and Civilization*, pp. 58–59.

24. See Oren R. Lyons, "The American Indian in the Past." *Exiled in the land of the Free: Democracy, Indian Nations, and the United States*, pp. 13–42.

25. See William W. Newcomb, Jr., "The Karankawa," *Handbook of North American Indians, Volume 10, Southwest*, pp. 359–67; Ricklis, *The Karankawa Indians*, pp. 99–124; Ricklis, *The Karankawa Indians*, pp. 1–110, Lawrence E. Aten, *Indians of the Upper Texas Coast*; Herman Smith, "Origins and Spatial/Temporal Distribution of the Rockport Archeological Complex, Central and Lower Texas Coast," *Midcontinental Journal of Archeology* 9 (1984): 27–42.

26. See Kathleen Gilmore, *The Keeran Site: The Probable Site of La Salle's Ft. St. Louis in Texas*; Robert S. Weddle, *Wilderness Manhunt: The Spanish Search for La Salle*.

27. The Aranamas remained associated with the mission Espíritu Santo de Zúñiga at La Bahía until its secularization in 1830. By 1830, the Aranamas lived

by farming and stock raising and had adopted the dress and many of the customs of their Tejano neighbors. They considered themselves superior to their "savage" Lipan, Karankawa, and Tonkawa neighbors. The Aranamas apparently accompanied the Tejano residents of Goliad to the Rio Grande when they abandoned the town in the aftermath of the Texas Revolution. See Jean Louis Berlandier, *The Indians of Texas in 1830*, p. 165; James Linn, *Reminiscences of Fifty Years in Texas*, p. 336. Compare to Beth White, *Goliad Remembered, 1836–1940*, pp. 2–3; Kathleen Gilmore, "The Indians of Mission Rosario: From the Books and from the Ground," *Columbian Consequences, Volume 1*, p. 224. See William H. Oberste, *History of Refugio Mission*.

28. Herbert E. Bolton, *Athanase de Mézières and the Louisiana-Texas Frontier*, pp. 298–302.

29. Ibid., pp. 104, 111, 298–302.

30. See Ricklis, *Karankawa Indians*, pp. 159–66. Compare to Faulk, "Comanche Invasion"; Oberste, *History of Refugio Mission*, p. 342.

31. Aten, *Indians of the Upper Texas Coast*, pp. 84–85.

32. Ricklis, *Karankawa Indians*, p. 156; Robert Arthur Ricklis, *Aboriginal Life and Culture on the Upper Texas Coast: Archaeology at the Mitchell Ridge Site, 41GV66, Galveston Island*.

33. Jose Antonio Pichardo, *Pichardo's Treatises on the Limits of Louisiana and Texas, Volume I*, pp. 393–96; Bolton, *Athanase de Mézières*, pp. 18–19, 165; John Sibley, "Historical Sketches of Several Indian Tribes in Louisiana South of the Arkansas River and River Grand," *Travels in the Interior Parts of America Communicating Discoveries Made in Exploring the Missouri River, Red River, and Washita . . .*, pp. 40–53; Padilla, "Texas in 1820."

34. See David B. Gracey, II, "Jean Lafitte and the Karankawa Indians," *East Texas Historical Journal* 2 (1964): 40–44; Aten, *Indians of the Upper Texas Coast*, p. 58; J. O. Dyer, *The Lake Charles Atakapas (Cannibals), 1817–1920*.

35. Gatschet, *Karankawa Indians*, p. 18; Annie P. Harris, "Memoirs of Mrs. Annie P. Harris," *Southwestern Historical Quarterly* 40 (1937): 231–46.

36. See Aten, *Indians of the Upper Texas Coast*, pp. 75–76, 89–96; Fray Gaspar José de Solís, "Diary of a Visit of Inspection of the Texas Missions Made by Fray Gaspar José de Solís in the Year 1767–1768, *Southwestern Historical Quarterly* 35 (1931): 28–76.

37. Compare to Ewers, "Influence of Epidemics"; Harris, "Memoirs," p. 242.

38. See Gatschet, *Karankawa Indians*, p. 63; Gilmore, "The Indians of Mission Rosario."

39. Walter L. Williams, *The Spirit and the Flesh: Sexual Diversity in American Indian Culture*, p. 2; Kathy Weston, "Lesbian/Gay Studies in the House of Anthropology," *Annual Review of Anthropology* 23 (1993): 339–67.

40. Alvar Nuñez Cabeza de Vaca, *The Journey of Alvar Nuñez Cabeza de Vaca and His Companions from Florida to the Pacific, 1528–1536*, p. 127. See de Solís, "Diary of a Visit"; Gatschet, *Karankawa Indians*, p. 131. Compare to Williams, *Spirit and the Flesh*, pp. 108, 181–92.

41. Berlandier, *Indians of Texas*, p. 149, Plates 15 and 16.

42. See Gilmore, "Indians of the Mission Rosario"; Berlandier, *Indians of Texas*, p. 149; Mary S. Helms, *Scraps of Early Texas History*, p. 43.

43. Henri Folmer, "De Bellisle on the Texas Coast," *Southwestern Historical Quarterly* 44 (1940): 204–31; Berlandier, *Indians of Texas*, pp. 57, 148.

44. Berlandier, *Indians of Texas*, pp. 148, 175, Figure 28. See Gilmore, "Indians of the Mission Rosario"; Sibley, "Historical Sketches," p. 45.

45. For example, see Stephen F. Austin, "Journal of Stephen F. Austin on His First Trip to Texas, 1821," *Quarterly of the Texas State Historical Association* 7 (1904): 287–307.

46. For example, see Newcomb, "Karankawa"; Cabeza de Vaca, *Journey*, pp. 54–98; Folmer, "De Bellisle," p. 219.

47. See Berkhofer, *White Man's Indian*, pp. 1–31; Boucher, *Cannibal Encounters*, pp. 6–7.

48. de Solís, "Diary of a Visit," pp. 42–43.

49. Johnathan Goldberg, *Sodometries: Renaissance Texts, Modern Sexualities*, pp. 179–222.

50. Sibley, "Historical Sketches," p. 45; John Sibley, *A Report from Natchitoches in 1807*, p. 95.

51. T. N. Campbell and T. J. Campbell, *Indian Groups Associated with the Spanish Missions of the San Antonio National Historical Park*; William W. Newcomb, Jr., "Historic Indians of Central Texas," *Bulletin of the Texas Archeological Society* 64 (1993): 1–63.

52. See LeRoy Johnson, "The Reconstructed Crow Terminology of the Titskanwatits, or Tonkawas, with Inferred Social Correlates," *Plains Anthropologist* 39 (1994): 377–414; Herbert E. Bolton, "Tonkawa," *Handbook of American Indians North of Mexico, Part 2*, pp. 778–83; Sjoberg, "Culture of the Tonkawa"; See William W. Newcomb, Jr., and T. N. Campbell, "Southern Plains Ethnohistory: A Re-Examination of the Escanajaques, Ahijados, and Cuitoas," *Pathways to Plains Prehistory: Anthropological Perspectives on Plains Natives*, pp. 29–43.

53. See Campbell and Campbell, *Indian Groups*; LeRoy Johnson and T. N. Campbell, "Sanan: Traces of a Previously Unknown Language in Colonial Coahuila and Texas," *Plains Anthropologist* 37 (1992): 185–212; Newcomb and Campbell, "Southern Plains Ethnohistory"; Newcomb, "Historic Indians of Central Texas."

54. See Alex D. Krieger, *Culture Complexes and Chronology in Northern Texas with Extension of Puebloan Datings to the Mississippi Valley*, pp. 165–68; Karl H. Schlesier, "Commentary: A History of Ethnic Groups in the Great Plains, AD 150–1500," *Plains Indians, AD 500–1500: The Archeological Past of Historical Groups*, pp. 308–51, 355; Newcomb, "Historic Indians of Central Texas"; Jones, *Notes on the History*.

55. For insight into the events that led to the Spanish occupation of Texas and the southern plains and their impacts on Native Texas, see Chipman, *Spanish Texas*, pp. 43–126; Nancy Parrott Hickerson, *The Jumanos: Hunters and*

Traders of the South Plains; John, *Storms Brewed*; David J. Weber, *The Spanish Frontier in North America*.

56. See Herbert E. Bolton, "The Founding of the Missions on the San Gabriel River," *Southwestern Historical Quarterly* 17 (1914): 323–78.

57. See Hickerson, *Jumanos*, pp. 205–207; Newcomb, "Historic Indians of Central Texas"; Herbert Eugene Bolton, "Ranchería Grande," *Handbook of American Indians North of Mexico, Part 2*, p. 354; Herbert Eugene Bolton, "San Xavier de Náxera," *Handbook of American Indians North of Mexico, Part 2*, p. 438.

58. Compare to Bolton, "Ranchería Grande." See Herbert Eugene Bolton, "San Xavier de Horcasitas," *Handbook of American Indians North of Mexico, Part 2*, pp. 437–38; Newcomb, "Historic Indians of Central Texas." Compare to F. Todd Smith, *The Caddo Indians: Tribes at the Convergence of Empires*, p. 57.

59. See Bolton, "Founding of the Missions"; Herbert E. Bolton, *Texas in the Middle Eighteenth Century*.

60. Compare to N. M. Miller Surrey, *The Commerce of Louisiana during the French Regime, 1699–1763*, pp. 98, 226–30.

61. See Henry Easton Allen, "The Parilla Expedition to the Red River," *Southwestern Historical Quarterly* 43 (1939): 53–71; John, *Storms Brewed*, pp. 698–700.

62. In addition to Allen, "The Parilla Expedition," other complete treatments of the destruction of the Spanish mission to the Lipans on the San Saba River and the subsequent Ortiz expedition, can be found in Bolton, *Texas in the Middle Eighteenth Century*; William Edward Dunn, "The Apache Mission on the San Sabá River: Its Founding and its Failure," *Southwestern Historical Quarterly* 17 (1914): 379–414; Robert S. Weddle, *The San Sabá Mission, A Spanish Pivot in Texas*. For an English translation of the documents relating to the San Sabá mission, see Paul D. Nathan (translator) and Leslie Byrd Simpson (editor), *The San Sabá Papers: A Documentary Account of the Founding and Destruction of the San Sabá Mission*.

63. William W. Newcomb, Jr., "The Ethnohistorical Investigation," *A Lipan Apache Mission: San Lorenzo de Santa Cruz, 1762–1771*, pp. 141–80; de Solís, "Diary of a Visit."

64. John, *Storms Brewed*, p. 426; Schilz, *People of the Cross Timbers*, pp. 99–126.

65. Alice C. Fletcher and Herbert E. Bolton, "Mayeye," *Handbook of American Indians North of Mexico, Part 1*, pp. 824–25; Sibley, "Historical Sketches."

66. Bolton, "Tonkawa," pp. 781, 782; John, *Storms Brewed*, pp. 635–36, 644, 652–53; Smith, *Caddo Indians*, pp. 80–81, 158.

67. John, *Storms Brewed*, pp. 698–99.

68. See Faulk, "Comanche Invasion"; Kavanagh, *Comanche Political History*.

69. Andrée F. Sjoberg, "Lipan Apache Culture in the Historical Perspective," *Southwestern Journal of Anthropology* 9 (1953): 76–98. See and compare to William B. Glover, "A History of the Caddo Indians," *Louisiana Historical Quarterly* 18 (1935): 872–946; Sibley, "Historical Sketches"; Smith, *Caddo Indians*.

70. See Faulk, "Comanche Invasion"; Joaquin Arredondo, "Joaquin

Arredondo's Report on the Battle of the Medina, Aug. 18, 1813," *Quarterly of the Texas State Historical Association* 11 (1908): 220–32; Chipman, *Spanish Texas*, p. 235; Schilz, *People of the Cross Timbers*, pp. 132–38.

71. Grant Foreman, *Indians and Pioneers: The Story of the American Southwest before 1830*, pp. 50–53.

72. Sibley, "Historical Sketches," p. 46.

73. Bolton, *Athanase de Mézières*, pp. 278–79. See Johnson, "Reconstructed Crow Terminology"; Sjoberg, "Culture of the Tonkawa."

74. Pike referred to the river we know today as the Colorado River as "Red river," a literal translation of the Spanish name. Pike called the river we know as the Red River, "the Red River of Natchitoches."

75. Pike, *Account of Expeditions*, p. 272 and Appendix III, p. 33.

76. See Sjoberg, "Culture of the Tonkawa."

77. Ibid.

78. Ibid., pp. 296–97.

79. Ibid.

80. Flores, *Journal of an Indian Trader*, p. 112.

81. For example, see John Salmon (Rip) Ford, *Rip Ford's Texas*, p. 229; Sjoberg, "Culture of the Tonkawa."

82. See Jones, *Notes on the History*; Berlandier, *Indians of Texas in 1830*, p. 51, Plate 5; Ferdinand Roemer, *Texas*, pp. 99–263.

83. Berlandier, *Indians of Texas in 1830*, p. 43.

84. See Roemer, *Texas*, p. 201.

85. For another anthropological perspective toward Western reports of cannibalism by non-Western people that suggests that there is no convincing evidence of cannibalism as a normative practice, see W. Arens, *The Man-eating Myth: Anthropology and Anthropophagy*. Arens argues that the belief in cannibalism existing among some "other" approaches a cultural universal. Thus social science insistence on the widespread presence of cannibalism among the people of the non-Western world represents a piece of ethnocentric folk wisdom embedded in social science. For a review of anthropological perspectives on cannibalism, see Peggy Reeves Sanday, *Divine Hunger: Cannibalism as a Cultural System*, pp. 3–26.

86. See Sjoberg, "Culture of the Tonkawa."

87. Compare to David J. Wishart, *An Unspeakable Sadness: The Dispossession of the Nebraska Indians*, pp. 92–99.

88. See Chase-Dunn and Hall, *Rise and Demise*, pp. 59–77; Ferguson and Whitehead, "Violent Edge of Empire"; Hall, "World-System Perspective."

89. See Dunaway, "Incorporation as an Interactive Process."

Chapter 2. The Political Economy of Mexican Texas, 1821–35: Initiation of Conquest

1. See Hatcher, *The Opening of Texas*; Weber, *Spanish Frontier*, p. 281–82.

2. It is of note that Stephen F. Austin's father, Moses, who inaugurated the Texas project, had earlier developed a lead mine in Spanish Upper Louisiana, now Missouri. The elder Austin's actions positioned the family for greater prosperity when Upper Louisiana became an American territory after the Louisiana Purchase. For the details surrounding the development of Austin's Colony, see Barker, *Life of Stephen F. Austin*, pp. 3–118.

3. David J. Weber, *The Mexican Frontier, 1821–1846: The American Southwest under Mexico*, pp. 161–62.

4. The Spanish land measurements standardized by the Texas Legislature in 1919 and commonly applied to Mexican Texas are as follows: One *labor* equals 177 acres or 1,000,000 square *varas;* one *sitio* equals 25,000,000 square *varas,* 4,428 acres or one square league. A *vara* equals 33.33 inches; a league equals 5,000 *varas,* 13,857.5 feet, or 2.63 miles. However, the Coahuila y Texas Colonization law specified the *vara* at three feet or 36 inches. Thus, *labors* and *sitios* may have been substantially larger in Mexican Texas. See Weber, *Mexican Frontier,* p. 340.

5. Weber, *Mexican Frontier,* p. 163.

6. Ibid., p. 170.

7. Ibid., pp. 176–77, 213.

8. See William H. Oberste, *Texas Irish Empresarios and Their Colonies: Power and Hewetson, McMullen and McGloin, Refugio and San Patricio.*

9. Weber, *Mexican Frontier,* p. 166.

10. See Joseph Carl McElhannon, "Imperial Mexico and Texas," *Southwestern Historical Quarterly* 53 (1949): 117–50.

11. Faulk, *Last Years,* pp. 97–98.

12. Chipman, *Spanish Texas,* p. 204; J. Villasana Haggard, "The House of Barr and Davenport," *Southwestern Historical Quarterly* 49 (1945): 66–77.

13. Eugene C. Barker, "A Glimpse of Texas Fur Trade in 1832," *Southwestern Historical Quarterly* 19 (1916): 279–82; Flores, *Journal of an Indian Trader,* pp. 3–50.

14. See Kavanagh, *Comanche Political History,* pp. 278–84. Compare to Grant Foreman, "Early Trails through Oklahoma," *Chronicles of Oklahoma* 3 (1925): 99–119; Frank McNitt, *The Indian Traders,* pp. 25–43.

15. Compare to Alan M. Klein, "Political Economy of the Buffalo Hide Trade: Race and Class on the Central Plains," *The Political Economy of North American Indians,* pp. 133–60.

16. For example, see North, *Economy of the United States,* pp. 122–34; Wolf, *Europe and the People without History,* pp. 268–85; Weber, *Mexican Frontier,* p. 141; Terence Jordan, *North American Cattle Ranching Frontiers: Origins, Diffusion, and Differentiation,* pp. 151–56.

17. Weber, *Mexican Frontier,* p. 227.

18. See Richard W. Slatta, *Comparing Cowboys and Frontiers,* pp. 45–48. See and compare to Hall, *Social Change in the Southwest,* pp. 157–63; Kavanagh, *Comanche Political History;* Charles L. Kenner, *A History of New Mexico-Plains Indian Relations,* pp. 53–97.

19. Austin to Bustamante, May 10, 1822, in Eugene C. Barker, *The Austin Papers, Volume I*, p. 508.

20. Anonymous, *A Visit to Texas*, p. 251. Compare to Howard R. Lamar, *The Trader on the American Frontier: Myth's Victim*, pp. 52–53; William B. DeWees, *Letters from an Early Settler of Texas*, p. 125.

21. DeWees, *Letters*, pp. 125–27.

22. See and compare to Lamar, *The Trader on the American Frontier*, pp. 16–29.

23. See Mary Austin Holley, *Texas*, pp. 161–73; Noah Smithwick, *The Evolution of a State or Recollections of Old Texas Days*, p. 43.

24. See and compare to Lamar, *The Trader on the American Frontier*, p. 52. For example, see Wilma Dunaway, *The First American Frontier: Transition to Capitalism in Southern Appalachia, 1700–1860*; Klein, "Political Economy"; Wolf, *Europe and the People without History*, pp. 158–94; Patricia C. Albers, "Symbiosis, Merger, and War: Contrasting Forms of Intertribal Relationship among Plains Indians," *The Political Economy of North American Indians*, pp. 94–132.

25. Anonymous, *Visit to Texas*, p. 240.

26. The brackets are the editor's; apparently, the parentheses and the ellipses are Austin's. Austin, "Journal," pp. 304–305.

27. Smithwick, *The Evolution of a State*, p. 13.

28. Ibid., pp. 13–17.

29. Charles Adam Gulick and Katherine Elliot, *The Papers of Mirabeau Buonaparte Lamar, Volume IV*, pp. 245–46.

30. DeWees, *Letters*, pp. 37–40.

31. Ibid., p. 40.

32. Ibid.

33. See James Axtell and William Sturtevant, "The Unkindest Cut of All, or Who Invented Scalping," *William and Mary Quarterly*, 3d series, 37 (1980): 451–72.

34. Jesse Burnam, "Reminiscences of Capt. Jesse Burnam," *Quarterly of the Texas State Historical Association* 5 (1901): 12–18.

35. Compare to Michael Taussig, "Culture of Terror—Space of Death, Roger Casement's Putumayo Report and Explanation of Torture," *Comparative Studies in Society and History* 26 (1984): 467–97.

36. Andrew Jackson Sowell, *A History of Ft. Bend County*, p. 56; DeWees, *Letters*, p. 44.

37. Barker, *Life of Stephen F. Austin*, p. 117.

38. Horatio Chriesman, "Recollections of Capt. Horatio Chriesman," *Quarterly of the Texas State Historical Association* 6 (1903): 236–41.

39. See the following documents from Barker, *Austin Papers, Volume I*, pp. 759–895: Proclamation, Mar. 31, 1824; Austin to Military Commandant, Apr. 20, 1824; Rawls to Austin, June 13, 1824; Austin to Rawls, June 14, 1824; Cummings to Austin, Aug. 25, 1824; and Coles to Dimmitt, Sept. 14, 1824.

40. Barker, *Austin Papers, Volume I*, p. 1198.

41. John C. Marr, *History of Matagorda County*, pp. 34–36; J. W. Wilbarger, *Indian Depredations in Texas*, p. 210.

42. Kilman, *Cannibal Coast*, p. 224; J. H. Kuykendall, "Reminiscences of Early Texans," *Quarterly of the Texas State Historical Association* 6 (1903): 236–53; John Holland Jenkins, *Recollections of Early Texas: The Memoirs of John Holland Jenkins*, p. 188. The quotation marks in the text are Jenkins's. Also, see and compare to Drinnan, *Facing West*, pp. xvii–xix.

43. Barker, *Austin Papers, Volume I*, pp. 1639–41.

44. Sowell, *History of Ft. Bend County*, p. 91.

45. Ibid.

46. Barker, *Austin Papers, Volume I*, p. 1220; Annie Fagan Teal, "Reminiscences of Mrs. Annie Fagan Teal," *Southwestern Historical Quarterly* 34 (1930): 317–28.

47. During the early 1830s, several observers commented on epidemics among the Karankawas who survived Austin's war. For example, in the Bexar Archives, see Aldrete to de la Garza, July 24, 1833, and de la Garza to Alcalde at Goliad, July 25, 1833. Also, see Elizabeth McAnulty Owens, *Elizabeth McAnulty Owens: The Story of Her Life*, pp. 3–4.

48. Mayhall, *Indians of Texas*, pp. 302–12, furnishes a guide to the communication in the Bexar Archives between the Tejano rancheros and the Mexican authorities in Goliad and San Antonio regarding problems between the rancheros and the Karankawas. For example, see Elozúa to Cosío, July 15, 1831, Bexar Archives; Placido Benavides to the Political Chief at Bexar, June 12, 1834, Bexar Archives.

49. See Teal, "Reminiscences."

50. Helms, *Scraps of Early Texas History*, pp. 41–42.

51. Ibid.

52. Holley, *Texas*, p. 160.

53. Wilbarger, *Indian Depredations*, p. 214.

54. Austin, "Journal," p. 297; DeWees, *Letters*, pp. 44–45: Gibson Kuykendall, "Recollections of Capt. Gibson Kuykendall," *Quarterly of the Texas State Historical Association* 7 (1903): 29–40.

55. Austin to Luciano Garcia, Oct. 20, 1823, in Barker, *Austin Papers, Volume I*, pp. 701–702: Gibson Kuykendall, "Recollections."

56. Compare to Richard White, *The Middle Ground: Indians, Empires, and Republics in the Great Lakes Region, 1650–1815*.

57. Austin to Saucedo, May 19, 1826, in Barker, *Austin Papers, Volume I*, pp. 1341–44.

58. Ibid., p. 1342.

59. William Rabb to Austin, Nov. 12, 1828, in Barker, *Austin Papers, Volume II*, pp. 144–45.

60. Austin to Ahumada, Apr. 26, 1826 in Barker, *Austin Papers, Volume I*, pp. 1304–1305. Also, see John Henry Brown, *Indian Wars and Pioneers of Texas*, p. 526.

61. Gulick and Elliot, *Lamar Papers, Volume IV*, pp. 248–49.

62. See the following documents in the Bexar Archives relating to the Tonkawas retreat to the San Antonio River in 1820 and 1821: Ramírez to Martínez, July 1, 1820; Salinas to Martínez, Mar. 30, 1821; García to Martínez, June 19, 1821. See the following documents in the Bexar Archives for the events surrounding Joyoso's journey to Mexico: López to Martínez, Apr. 15, 1822; Carrasco to Iturbide, May 25, 1822; and "Passport issued to Salvador Carrasco to conduct home Cabra, alias el Hoyoso, Chief of the Tonkawas," Aug. 1, 1822.

63. José María Sánchez, "A Trip to Texas in 1828," *Southwestern Historical Quarterly* 29 (1926): 249–88.

64. DeWitt to Musquiz, Apr. 23, 1829, Bexar Archives.

Chapter 3. The Political Economy of the Republic of Texas, 1836–45: Negotiation of Conquest

1. For a sympathetic analysis of this unique and ultimately quixotic attempt to create an independent state for European Americans and Native Americans beyond the borders of the United States, see Richard Drinnan, *White Savage: The Case of John Dunn Hunter*, pp. 155–229. One can locate the Declaration of Independence of the Fredonian Republic, which guaranteed freedom and equality between "Red" and "White" in Hans P. M. N. Gammel, *The Laws of Texas, 1822–1904, Volume I*, pp. 109–10. See Eugene C. Barker, *Mexico and Texas, 1821–1835*, pp. 101–14; Reichstein, *The Rise of the Lone Star*, p. 196; Weber, *Mexican Frontier*, pp. 30–37.

2. See Anna Muckleroy, "The Indian Policy of the Republic of Texas," *Southwestern Historical Quarterly* 25 (1922): 229–60; 26 (1922): 1–29, 128–48, 184–206.

3. Dorman H. Winfrey, et al., *The Indian Papers of Texas and the Southwest, 1825–1916: Volume 1, 1825–1843*, pp. 24, 28–29, 48–49.

4. See Gustav Dresel, *Gustav Dresel's Houston Journal: Adventures in North America and Texas, 1837–1841*, pp. 33–35.

5. W. Y. Allen, "Extracts from a Diary of W. Y. Allen, 1838–1839," *Southwestern Historical Quarterly* 17 (1913): 43–60.

6. John Milton Nance, *Attack and Counterattack: The Texas-Mexican Frontier, 1842*, pp. 427–524; Sam W. Haynes, *Soldiers of Misfortune: The Somervell and Mier Expeditions.*

7. Gulick and Elliot, *Lamar Papers, Volume II*, pp. 352–54; *Austin Texas Sentinel*, Jan. 18, 1840; John Milton Nance, *After San Jacinto: The Texas-Mexican Frontier, 1836–1841*, pp. 113–41.

8. Gulick and Elliot, *Lamar Papers, Volume II*, pp. 208–209.

9. See Dianna Everett, *The Texas Cherokees: A People Between Two Fires*; Walter Prescott Webb, *The Texas Rangers: A Century of Frontier Defense*, pp. 54–55.

10. The Alabama-Coushattas have remained in East Texas to this day. The

last attempt at removal in the late 1850s was thwarted by the violence at the Brazos Agency discussed in Chapter 4. Also see Dorman H. Winfrey and James M. Day, *The Indian Papers of Texas and The Southwest 1825–1916: Volume III, 1846–1859*, pp. 287–89, 292–94, 315–16. The Bidais suffered numerous epidemics after Anglo-Texan settlement began in their traditional homelands in the upper San Jacinto and lower Navasota River basins. The survivors became increasingly acculturated to the Anglo-Texan world in the 1830s and 1840s. Apparently in the 1850s, some of the remnants of the Bidais went to the Brazos Reservation with their neighbors: the Anadarkos, Caddos, Ionis, and Keechis. The reservation experience completed the destruction of Bidai ethnic identity. See Andrée F. Sjoberg, *The Bidai Indians of Southeastern Texas*, pp. 40–46.

11. Wilbarger, *Indian Depredations*, pp. 183–85. For example, see Rupert N. Richardson, *The Comanche Barrier to South Plains Settlement: A Century and A Half of Savage Resistance to the Advancing White Frontier*. As a corrective, see Kavanagh, *Comanche Political History*.

12. Dresel, *Gustave Dresel's Houston Journal*, p. 103. The purposeful destruction of Native American people by Anglo-Texan settlers recounted in this book should not obscure the fact that they had shared beliefs with Europeans who remained at home or who conquered other indigenous people elsewhere on the globe. Therefore, this tale of ferocious violence toward a dark-skinned other by European-origin people provides a common thread in the history of Europe and European expansion. For example, see Donald Kenrick and Gratton Puxon, *The Destiny of Europe's Gypsies* and Tzvetan Todorov, *The Conquest of America: The Question of the Other*. However, the method and intensity of the violence has varied by time and geographic area. As a result, the problem demands more comparative studies.

13. Francis C. Sheridan, *Galveston Island or, A Few Months Off the Coast of Texas*, pp. 107–108; Matilda Houstoun, *Texas and the Gulf of Mexico, Yachting in the New World*, pp. 227–28.

14. See Montejano, *Anglos and Mexicans*, pp. 26–30.

15. Gammel, *The Laws of Texas, Volume II*, pp. 842–45, 371–72.

16. See Roger Conger, "Torrey's Trading House," *Handbook of Texas, Volume II*, pp. 790–91; Michael Paul Rogin, *Fathers and Children: Andrew Jackson and the Subjugation of American Indians*, p. 302.

17. Winfrey, et al., *The Indian Papers, Volume I*, pp. 241–46.

18. Fehrenbach, *Lone Star*, p. 254–65.

19. Compare to Richard Rollin Stenberg, *American Imperialism in the Southwest, 1800–1837*, pp. 142–69.

20. Sam Houston, *The Writings of Sam Houston, Volume V*, p. 35.

21. Gammel, *Laws of Texas, Volume II*, pp. 358–63.

22. Fehrenbach, *Lone Star*, pp. 282–95; Anonymous, "A Visit Up the Colorado River: Extracts from an Anonymous Diary, 17–25 July 1838," p. 4.

23. William R. Hogan, *The Texas Republic: A Social and Economic History*, pp. 18–21.

24. Ibid., pp. 21–22, 291.

25. *Corpus Christi Star*, May 5, 1849.

26. Gammel, *Laws of Texas, Volume I*, pp. 542, 1079; Nance, *After San Jacinto*, p. 48; Linn, *Reminiscences*, p. 323.

27. Gammel, *Laws of Texas, Volume II*, pp. 53, 166–67.

28. Johnathan Nathan Cravens, *James Harper Starr: Financier of the Republic of Texas*, pp. 48–49.

29. Linn, *Reminiscences*, p. 343.

30. See *Corpus Christi Star*, May 12 and May 26, 1849; *Victoria Texian-Advocate*, Apr. 20, 1856.

31. See and compare to Immanuel Wallerstein, *The Modern World-System, II: Mercantilism and the Consolidation of the European World-Economy, 1600–1750*, pp. 157–61; Frederick Law Olmsted, *A Journey through Texas, or a Saddle-Trip on the Southwestern Frontier*, pp. 443–44.

32. Linn, *Reminiscences*, p. 333–35; Owens, *Elizabeth McAnulty Owens*, p. 5.

33. Dimmitt to Austin, Oct. 27, 1835, in Barker, *Austin Papers, Volume III*, pp. 213–14; Hobart Huson, *Phillip Dimmitt's Commandancy of Goliad: An Episode of the Mexican Federalist War in Texas Usually Referred To as The Texian Revolution*, pp. 82–85.

34. See Frank Collinson, "The Tonkawas," *Ranch Romances*, July 8, 1938, pp. 128–30; Winfrey, et al., *The Indian Papers, Volume I*, pp. 46–48.

35. Huson, *Captain Phillip Dimmitt*, pp. 42, 82–85, 234, 293–94; See Owens, *Elizabeth McAnulty Owens*, p. 6–7; Teal, "Reminiscences."

36. Huson, *Captain Phillip Dimmitt*, pp. 70, 234–35.

37. Linn, *Reminiscences*, p. 260.

38. *Houston Telegraph and Texas Register*, Aug. 22, 1837; Gulick and Elliot, *Lamar Papers, Volume IV*, p. 229.

39. *Houston Telegraph and Texas Register*, Sept. 29, 1838; also, see Nance, *After San Jacinto*, pp. 54–59.

40. Mary A. Maverick, *Memoirs of Mary A. Maverick*, pp. 18–20.

41. Winfrey, et al., *The Indian Papers, Volume I*, pp. 28–29; *Houston Telegraph and Texas Register*, Nov. 3, 1858.

42. See George W. Bonnell, "Report of G. W. Bonnell, Commissioner of Indian Affairs, Third Congress of the Republic of Texas, First Session, November 3, 1838," *Communication from the Commissioner of Indian Affairs, and Other Documents in Relation to the Indians of Texas*, pp. 38–50; Gulick and Elliot, *Lamar Papers, Volume V*, p. 225.

43. William Bollaert, *William Bollaert's Texas*, p. 73.

44. Nance, *Attack and Counterattack*, p. 44; George B. Erath, "The Memoirs of George Bernard Erath, III," *Southwestern Historical Quarterly* 27 (1923): 27–51; Thomas J. Green, *Journal of the Texian Expedition Against Mier*, p. 73; William Preston Stapp, *The Prisoner of Perote*, p. 31; John Milton Nance, "Was There a Mier Expedition Flag?" *Southwestern Historical Quarterly* 95 (1989): 543–57; Hobart Huson, *Refugio: A Comprehensive History from Aboriginal Times to 1953, Volume 1*, p. 488.

45. See and compare to Montejano, *Anglos and Mexicans*, pp. 15–21.

46. Bollaert, *William Bollaert's Texas*, pp. 193–94.

47. Nance, *After San Jacinto*, p. 67; *Houston Telegraph and Texas Register*, Sept. 21, 1842.

48. See Gatschet, *Karankawa Indians*, pp. 65–68; Nance, *Attack and Counterattack*, p. 43.

49. *Houston Telegraph and Texas Register*, Nov. 3, 1838.

50. Huson, *Refugio, Volume I*, p. 554.

51. Helms, *Scraps of Early Texas History*, p. 43.

52. *Houston Telegraph and Texas Register*, June 7, 1843.

53. Huson, *Refugio, Volume I*, p. 554; Bollaert, *William Bollaert's Texas*, p. 41.

54. Huson, *Refugio, Volume I*, pp. 488–90.

55. Gatschet, *Karankawa Indians*, p. 16.

56. Kenneth Kesselus, *History of Bastrop County, before Statehood*, p. 203. Compare to Webb, *Texas Rangers*, pp. 44–62; Nance, *Attack and Counterattack*, pp. 223–24.

57. Compare to Lyons, "American Indian in the Past"; Webb, *Texas Rangers*, p. 79.

58. Smithwick, *Evolution of a State*, pp. 217–18.

59. According to Ewers, "Influence of Epidemics," the abandonment of cannibalism by other peoples of the southern plains may have been the result of increased value placed on captives to replenish populations decimated by disease. Compare to Taussig, "Culture of Terror," p. 494.

60. For example, Jenkins, *Recollections of Early Texas*, pp. 193–94, relates the following incident from the early days of the Republic, as told by a participant, Rufus Perry. A ranging company, commanded by W. W. Hill, attacked an Indian camp in what is now Burleson County and killed three people:

> We were somewhat surprised and puzzled just after the fight to see a member of our company, an old backwoods man named David Lawrence, step up and cut off the thigh of one of the slain Indians. I asked him what he intended to do with it. "Why," he answered, "I am going to take it along to eat. If you don't get some game before noon tomorrow we'll need it."

See Taussig, "Culture of Terror," pp. 495–96, for the provocative idea that colonial pressure may stimulate, if not create, cannibalism among colonized people.

61. For example, see George Bird Grinnell, *The Cheyenne Indians: Their History and Way of Life, Volume I*, p. 200; Jenkins, *Recollections of Early Texas*, pp. 77–78; Robert L. Miller, *The Life of Robert Hall: Indian Fighter and Veteran of Three Great Wars*, pp. 52–53; Smithwick, *Evolution of A State*, pp. 245–46. However, a few attributed Tonkawa cannibalism more to depravity and the need for food. For example, see Rudolph L. Biesele, "Early Times in New Braunfels and Comal County," *Southwestern Historical Quarterly* 50 (1946): 75–92; George W. Bonnell, *Topographical Description of Texas to Which Is Added an Account of the*

Indian Tribes, p. 38; Collinson, "The Tonkawas"; Grant Foreman, *Advancing the Frontier, 1830–1860*, p. 255; James Mooney, "Our Last Cannibal Tribe," *Harper's Monthly Magazine* 103 (1901): 550–55; Edwin Waller, "Reminiscences of Judge Edwin Waller," *Quarterly of the Texas State Historical Association* 4 (1900): 33–53. Bonnell, Collinson, and Waller were first-hand observers. However, Waller's editor misattributed Waller's account of Tonkawa cannibalism to the Karankawas. Biesele, Foreman, and Mooney wrote secondary accounts of Tonkawa cannibalism.

62. Miller, *Life of Robert Hall*, pp. 52–53.
63. Foreman, *Advancing the Frontier*, p. 254.
64. See Herman Lehmann, *The Last Captive*, pp. 107–109.
65. Ford, *Rip Ford's Texas*, p. 238.
66. *Austin Texas Sentinel*, Mar. 11, 1841.
67. Ibid., Jan. 25, 1840.
68. *Houston Telegraph and Texas Register*, June 10, 1840.
69. Brown, *Indian Wars*, p. 497; Col. Wilson T. Davidson, "A Comanche Prisoner in 1841," *Southwestern Historical Quarterly* 45 (1942): 335–42; Kesselus, *History of Bastrop County*, p. 203; Smithwick, *Evolution of a State*, p. 247.
70. Bollaert, *William Bollaert's Texas*, p. 190.
71. Smithwick, *Evolution of a State*, p. 247; Anonymous, *Texas in 1840, or The Emigrants Guide to the New Republic*, p. 47.
72. *Houston Telegraph and Texas Register*, Sept. 7, 1842.
73. Gulick and Elliot, *Lamar Papers, Volume II*, pp. 303–307; *Houston Telegraph and Texas Register*, May 17, 1843.
74. Compare to Lyons, "American Indian in the Past"; Statement of Luis Sanchez as Taken by Walter Winn, May, 1844, in Dorman H. Winfrey and James M. Day, *The Indian Papers of Texas and The Southwest 1825–1916: Volume II, 1844–1845*, pp. 64–66.
75. *Houston Telegraph and Texas Register*, Oct. 4, 1843.
76. Winfrey and Day, *Indian Papers, Volume II*, pp. 150–51.
77. Kenneth F. Neighbours, *Indian Exodus: Texas Indian Affairs, 1835–1859*, p. 42.
78. Winfrey and Day, *Indian Papers, Volume II*, p. 198; *Houston Telegraph and Texas Register*, Oct. 18, 1843.
79. Western to Neighbors, Feb. 12 and Mar. 2, 1845, in Winfrey and Day, *Indian Papers, Volume II*, pp. 197–98, 205–206; Neighbours, *Indian Exodus*, p. 206.
80. *Houston Telegraph and Texas Register*, May 17, 1843.
81. Winfrey and Day, *Indian Papers, Volume II*, p. 341.
82. J. C. Neill, Thomas I. Smith, and E. Morehouse to Anson Jones, Sept. 27, 1845, in Winfrey and Day, *Indian Papers, Volume II*, pp. 369–70; William G. Cooke to Anson Jones, Dec. 12, 1845, Winfrey and Day, *Indian Papers, Volume II*, pp. 422–23; Neighbors to Western, Feb. 4, 1846, in Winfrey and Day, *Indian Papers, Volume III*, p. 13.

Chapter 4. The Incorporation of Texas into the
United States, 1846–59: Consolidation of Conquest

1. Ernest Wallace and David Vigness, *Documents of Texas History*, p. 160.

2. The term "re-annexation" was used to support the position that Texas had been a part of the Louisiana Purchase that had been frivolously given away in the negotiations of the Adams-Onís Treaty with Spain. See Reichstein, *Rise of the Lone Star*, pp. 171–80.

3. See Sanford H. Montaigne, *Blood over Texas*, pp. 101–36; See Richard Griswold del Castillo, *The Treaty of Guadalupe Hidalgo*, pp. 1–29; Reichstein, *Rise of the Lone Star*, pp. 178–80.

4. See Griswold del Castillo, *Treaty of Guadalupe Hidalgo*, for causes of the war, Polk's military diplomacy, and consequences of the Treaty of Guadalupe Hidalgo.

5. See Hall, *Social Change in the Southwest*, pp. 189–95; Griswold del Castillo, *Treaty of Guadalupe Hidalgo*, pp. 183–99.

6. See D.W. Meinig, *Imperial Texas: An Interpretive Essay in Cultural Geography*, pp. 28–65.

7. *Texas Almanac and State Industrial Guide, 1966–1967*, p. 390.

8. See Dan Flores, "Bison Ecology and Bison Diplomacy," *Journal of American History* 78 (1991): 465–85; Hall, *Social Change in the Southwest*, p. 217.

9. Thomas T. Smith, "Fort Inge and Texas Frontier Military Operations," *Southwestern Historical Quarterly* 96 (1992): 1–25; *Victoria Texian-Advocate*, May 12, 1851; *Austin State Gazette*, Aug. 25, 1855.

10. For General Harney's reputation as an Indian-hater, see Samuel E. Chamberlain, *My Confession: Recollections of a Rogue*, pp. 226–27; and compare to John K. McMahon, *History of the Second Seminole War, 1835–1842*, pp. 282–84; Thomas F. Schilz, *The Lipan Indians in Texas*, pp. 54–55.

11. Herman Melville, *The Confidence Man: His Masquerade*, pp. 168–90. For a description of an Anglo-Texas Indian-hater, by noted Indian and Mexican killer and tall-tale teller Big Foot Wallace, see Wilbarger, *Indian Depredations in Texas*, pp. 129–38.

12. Houston, *Writings, Volume 5*, p. 36.

13. Olmsted, *Journey through Texas*, p. 289.

14. Charles Dickens, "The Noble Savage," *Household Words* 7 (1853): 337–39.

15. Huson, *Refugio, Volume II*, p. 353.

16. See George R. Morgan and Omer C. Stewart, "The Peyote Trade in South Texas," *Southwestern Historical Quarterly* 87 (1984): 269–96.

17. William Seaton Henry, *Campaign Sketches of the War with Mexico*, p. 14; Samuel Chester Reid, *The Scouting Expeditions of McCulloch's Texas Rangers*, p. 46; Oberste, *History of Mission Refugio*.

18. Huson, *Refugio, Volume I*, pp. 552–53.

19. Emmanuel Domenech, *Missionary Adventures in Texas and Mexico. A Personal Narrative of Six Years' Sojourn in Those Regions*, pp. 347–49.

20. Martin Salinas, *Indians of the Rio Grande Delta: Their Role in the History of Southern Texas and Northeastern Mexico*, pp. 62–113, 116–24; William Neale and William A. Neale, *Century of Conflict, 1821–1913*, pp. 11–19.

21. See the following maps: "Brownsville and Matamoros Area, 1872" in Neale and Neale, *Century of Conflict*, p. 80; USGS Texas (1:20,000), Mercedes and Santa Maria Sheets, 1956.

22. *Brownsville American Flag*, May 15, 1852.

23. Ibid.

24. *Victoria Texian-Advocate*, June 12, 1852.

25. Winfrey and Day, *Indian Papers, Volume III*, pp. 260–62.

26. La Mesa and Uresteña were apparently located along the Rio Grande immediately east or downriver from present-day Reynosa. See the following maps: "Porciones Maps" in Rio Grande Valley Historical Center at the University of Texas–Pan American; and USGS Texas (1:20,000), Progresso Sheet, 1956. Comisíon Pesquisidora de la Frontera, *Reports of the Committee of Investigation Sent in 1873 by the Mexican Government to the Frontier of Texas*, pp. 406–407; Gatschet, *Karankawa Indians*, pp. 50–51.

27. T. N. Campbell, "Pakawa Indians," *Handbook of Texas, Volume III*, pp. 690–91; T.N. Campbell, "Tampaqua Indians," *Handbook of Texas, Volume III*, p. 950; Salinas, *Indians of the Rio Grande Delta*, pp. 12–13, 62–63; Del Weniger, *The Explorer's Texas: The Lands and Waters*, pp. 158–70.

28. Marr, *History of Matagorda County*, pp. 46–47; Huson, *Refugio, Volume I*, p. 554.

29. *Niles National Register* 70 (June 27, 1846): 259; Charles Spurlin, "Mobilization of the Texas Militia for the Mexican War," *Military History of Texas and the Southwest* 15:3 (n.d.): 21–44; John Holmes Jenkins and Kenneth Kesselus, *Edward Burleson: Texas Frontier Leader*, pp. 359–63.

30. Elijah Hicks, "Journal of Elijah Hicks," *Chronicles of Oklahoma* 13 (1935): 68–99; Neighbours, *Indian Exodus*, p. 51.

31. Winfrey and Day, *Indian Papers, Volume III*, pp. 43–52.

32. Compare to Ewers, "Influence of Epidemics"; Flores, "Bison Ecology and Bison Diplomacy"; Richardson, *Comanche Barrier*, pp. 164–77.

33. Neighbours, *Indian Exodus*, pp. 58–60; Neighbors to Medill, Feb. 16, 1848, Letters Received by the Office of Indian Affairs, Texas Agency; See William A. Matlock, "Journal of a Trip through Texas and Northern Mexico in 1846 and 1847," *Southwestern Historical Quarterly* 34 (1930): 20–37.

34. *Houston Telegraph and Texas Register*, Apr. 12, 1849; Neighbours, *Indian Exodus*, p. 64.

35. Ibid., p. 65.

36. See Lena Clara Koch, "The Federal Indian Policy in Texas, 1845–1860," *Southwestern Historical Quarterly* 28 (1925): 223–34, 259–86; 29 (1925): 19–35, 98–127; *Austin State Gazette*, Sept. 8, 1849.

37. *Victoria Texian-Advocate*, Feb. 14, 1852; David G. Burnet, "Letter to Robert Neighbors, August 20, 1847," *Communication from the Commissioner of*

Indian Affairs, and Other Documents in Relation to the Indians of Texas, pp. 7–8; *Corpus Christi Star*, June 2, 1849.

38. See Catlett to Medill, May 12, 1849, Stemm to Lea, Feb. 20, 1852, Howard to Lea, Mar. 31, 1852, Capron to Lea, May 24, 1852 in the LROIA, Texas Agency; P. M. Butler and H. G. Lewis, "Report on the Indians of Texas, August 8, 1846," in *Communication from the Commissioner of Indian Affairs, and Other Documents in Relation to the Indians of Texas*, pp. 29–37.

39. See Roemer, *Texas*, pp. 191–263; Paul C. Phillips, *The Fur Trade, Volume II*, pp. 468–76.

40. *Victoria Texian-Advocate*, Oct. 15, 1853; See Michael H. Erskine, "A Cattle Drive from Texas to California: The Diary of M. H. Erskine, 1854," *Southwestern Historical Quarterly* 67 (1964): 397–412; Jane McManus Cazenau (Cora Montgomery), *Eagle Pass, or Life on the Border*, p. 47.

41. Julius Froebel, *Seven Years Travel in Central America, Northern Mexico, and the Far West of the United States*, p. 453. See Oo-chee-cah, "The Story of Seqouyah's Last Days," *Chronicles of Oklahoma* 12 (1934): 25–41, for insight into the dangers Indians faced on the Texas frontier. Also at least two travelers to Texas during the 1840s remarked on the fact that Lipans refused offers of drink due to the fear of being poisoned; see Houstoun, *Texas and the Gulf of Mexico*, pp. 227–28; Francis R. Latham, *Travels in the Republic of Texas: 1842*, pp. 30–31.

42. W. G. Freeman, "Report of Brevet Col. W. G. Freeman, August 15, 1853," *Southwestern Historical Quarterly* 53 (1949): 202–208.

43. R. B. Marcy, *Thirty Years of Army Life on the Border*, pp. 173–74. Marcy was unclear as to when he met the Tonkawas. I found no mention of the Tonkawas from his expeditions to west-central Texas in 1851, to the headwaters of the Red River in 1852, or to the headwaters of the Wichita and Brazos Rivers in 1854. Most likely, he either met some Tonkawas while surveying the Clear Fork and Brazos Reservations with Neighbors in August of 1854, or he formed his observations from the opinions of others. However, Tonkawas did wander north to the Red River country while Marcy was at Fort Arbuckle and Fort Washita; see Foreman, *Advancing the Frontier*, pp. 254–55.

44. See Francis Paul Prucha, *The Great Father: The United States Government and the American Indians, Volume I*, pp. 319–23.

45. *Austin State Gazette*, Jan. 3, 1854.

46. Neighbors to Mix, Oct. 30, 1854, LROIA, Texas Agency; Howard to Neighbors, Mar. 2, 1855, LROIA, Texas Agency; Neighbours, *Indian Exodus*, pp. 104–106.

47. Neighbors to Manypenny, Apr. 17, 1855, LROIA, Texas Agency.

48. Census Roll, Brazos Reservation, June 30, 1855, LROIA, Texas Agency.

49. Amendment to the Treaty of May 15, 1846, Aug. 30, 1855, LROIA, Texas Agency; Virginia P. Noël, *The United States Indian Reservations in Texas, 1854–1859*, pp. 75–79.

50. Olmsted, *Journey through Texas*, pp. 288–92, 349–52.

51. Ibid., pp. 289–90.

52. Ibid., pp. 350–51.

53. For example, see Schilz, *Lipan Indians in Texas*, p. 57; Wilbarger, *Indian Depredations in Texas*, pp. 127–29; Neighbours, *Indian Exodus*, p. 109; *Austin State Gazette*, Aug. 25 and Oct. 6, 1855.

54. Ford, *Rip Ford's Texas*, pp. 400, 236–37.

55. See Berta Hart Nance, "D. A. Nance and the Tonkawa Indians," *Yearbook of the West Texas Historical Association* 28 (1952): 87–95.

56. Vynola Beaver Newkumet and Howard L. Meredith, *Hasinai: A Traditional History of the Caddo Confederacy*, p. 76; Webb, *Great Plains*, pp. 1–9.

57. *Dallas Herald*, Aug. 15 and Oct. 4, 1856; Murl L. Webb, "Religious and Educational Efforts Among Texas Indians in the 1850's," *Southwestern Historical Quarterly* 69 (1965): 22–37.

58. Neighbours, *Indian Exodus*, pp. 118–19; *Dallas Herald*, Aug. 21, 1858; George Klos, "'Our People Could Not Distinguish One Tribe from Another': The 1859 Expulsion of the Reserve Indians from Texas," *Southwestern Historical Quarterly* 97 (1994): 598–619.

59. *Dallas Herald*, May 25, 1859, and Sept. 1, 1858; United States Bureau of Indian Affairs, *Report of the Commissioner of Indian Affairs Accompanying the Annual Report of the Secretary of Interior*, pp. 297–303.

60. Ford, *Rip Ford's Texas*, pp. 231–32, 229–40. See Klos, "The 1859 Expulsion of the Reserve Indians from Texas"; Joseph Carroll McConnell, *The West Texas Frontier or a Descriptive History of Early Times in Western Texas*, pp. 286–313; Neighbours, *Indian Exodus*, pp. 118–39.

61. *Dallas Herald*, July 24, 1858.

62. Reprinted in *Dallas Herald*, July 24, 1858.

63. J. J. Sturm to S. P. Ross, Dec. 30, 1858, U.S. Bureau of Indian Affairs, *Report of the Commissioner*, pp. 221–22.

64. U.S. Bureau of Indian Affairs, *Report of the Commissioner*, pp. 250–52.

65. Zachariah E. Coombes, *The Diary of a Frontiersman, 1858–1859*, pp. 11–12.

66. Compare to Raymond Evans, "'The Nigger Shall Disappear': Aborigines and Europeans in Colonial Queensland," in *Exclusion, Exploitation, and Extermination: Race Relations in Colonial Queensland*, pp. 25–146.

67. See Klos, "The 1859 Expulsion of the Reserve Indians from Texas"; Neighbours, *Indian Exodus*, p. 132.

68. See Klos, "The 1859 Expulsion of the Reserve Indians from Texas"; Neighbours, *Indian Exodus*, pp. 134–35.

69. Neighbors to Greenwood, June 10, 1859, in U.S. Bureau of Indian Affairs, *Report of the Commissioner*, pp. 260–62.

70. Winfrey and Day, *Indian Papers, Volume III*, pp. 331–33; U.S. Bureau of Indian Affairs, *Report of the Commissioner*, pp. 301–302; Klos, "The 1859 Expulsion of the Reserve Indians from Texas"; Neighbours, *Indian Exodus*, p. 136.

71. U.S. Bureau of Indian Affairs, *Report of the Commissioner*, pp. 274–75.

72. "Extra" to the *Frontier News*, June 24, 1859, in U.S. Bureau of Indian Affairs, *Report of the Commissioner*, pp. 316–18.

73. See Klos, "The 1859 Expulsion of the Reserve Indians from Texas"; Neighbours, *Indian Exodus*, pp. 133, 132; *Dallas Herald*, July 3 and July 17, 1858, Jan. 19 and Feb. 9, 1859.

74. Statement of Provisions Issued by S.P. Ross, LROIA, Texas Agency; Noël, *United States Indian Reservations in Texas*, pp. 157–80; Neighbours, *Indian Exodus*, p. 128.

75. *Dallas Herald*, Feb. 9, 1859.

76. Ibid., May 25, 1859.

77. See Winfrey and Day, *Indian Papers, Volume III*, pp. 333–41.

78. Neighbours, *Indian Exodus*, p. 139.

79. On his return to Texas, Ed Cornett, or Carnett, murdered Neighbors on the streets of Fort Belknap on September 14, 1859, as Neighbors spoke to Cornett's brother-in-law, Patrick Murphy. Neighbours, *Indian Exodus*, pp. 138–39, felt that the most plausible motive behind Neighbor's assassination was the fear that Neighbors would attempt to bring the men involved in the violence leading to the removal of the reserve Indians to trial in the federal courts. For a slightly different version of the death of Neighbors and the breakup of the Brazos and Clear Fork reserves, partially based on interviews in the 1920s with settlers from the area, see McConnell, *West Texas Frontier*, pp. 314–34.

80. See Mooney, "Our Last Cannibal Tribe"; Wilbur Sturtevant Nye, *Carbine and Lance: The Story of Old Fort Sill by Lt. Col. W. S. Nye*, pp. 37–40.

81. James Buckner Barry, *A Texas Ranger and Frontiersman; the Days of Buck Berry in Texas, 1848–1906*, pp. 157–68; Nance, "D. A. Nance and the Tonkawa Indians"; Newlin, *The Tonkawa People*, pp. 70–91.

82. Newlin, *The Tonkawa People*, pp. 70–91; Gary Taylor, "Tribe is Holding Texas to Promise: Tonkawas Want Land Payback for Help Years Ago." *National Law Journal* 16:31 (1994): A8.

Chapter 5. Conclusions

1. See Hall, "Incorporation in the World System"; Chase-Dunn and Hall, *Comparing World-Systems*, pp. 59–77.

2. Ibid.

3. For example, see Richard Slotkin, *Regeneration through Violence: The Myth of the American Frontier, 1600–1800*, pp. 551–57.

4. For example, see Wolf, *Europe and the People without History*, pp. 193–94. Compare to Hall, "World-System Perspective"; Chase-Dunn and Hall, *Comparing World-Systems*, pp. 73–74

5. Compare to Wolf, *Europe and the People without History*, pp. 278–85, 158–94.

6. For example, see Taussig, "Culture of Terror."

7. Austin's constructions of the Karankawas and Tonkawas not only set the tone for Anglo-Texan attitudes toward the two groups in Mexican Texas, but they have guided Texas historians' representations of the two groups for over a

century. If one compares the treatment of the Karankawas and the Tonkawas in the 1990 textbook of Robert Calvert and Arnoldo De Leon, *The History of Texas*, with the 1943 textbook of Rupert N. Richardson, *Texas, the Lone Star State*, with Austin's words, one will find a remarkable continuity.

Appendix 1. Sociology and Conquest

1. See Irving L. Horowitz, "Preface," *The Ward-Gumplowicz Correspondence: 1897–1909*, pp. vii–ix.
2. See Sarah E. Simons, "Social Assimilation," *American Journal of Sociology* 6 (1901): 790–822; 7 (1902): 53–79, 234–48, 386–404, 539–56. Compare to Stanford M. Lyman, *Militarism, Imperialism, and Racial Accommodation: An Analysis of the Writings of Robert E. Park*, pp. 24–26; James B. McKee, *Sociology and the Race Problem: The Failure of a Perspective*, p. 122.
3. Frederick Jackson Turner, *The Frontier in American History*, p. 269.
4. Hobson, *Imperialism, a Study*, p. 360; Phillip Siegelman, "Introduction," *Imperialism, a Study*, pp. v-xvi.
5. Joseph A. Schumpeter, "The Sociology of Imperialisms," *Imperialism and Social Classes*, pp. 3–130, 7.
6. See W. E. B. DuBois, *Color and Democracy: Colonies and Peace*.
7. See Ralf Dahrendorf, *Class and Class Conflict in Industrial Society;* Randall Collins, "Some Principles of Long-Term Social Change: The Territorial Power of States," *Research in Social Movements, Conflict and Change*, pp. 1–34; Johnathan Turner, *The Structure of Social Theory;* Randall Collins, *Conflict Sociology: Toward an Explanatory Science*.
8. See Daniel Chirot and Thomas Hall, "World-System Theory," *Annual Review of Sociology* 8 (1982): 81–106.
9. See Hechter, *Internal Colonialism;* Rodolfo Acuña, *Occupied America: The Chicano Struggle Toward Liberation;* Mario Barrera, *Race and Class in the Southwest: A Theory of Racial Inequality;* Robert Blauner, *Racial Oppression in America*.
10. See Stanley Diamond, *In Search of the Primitive: A Critique of Civilization;* Patricia N. Limerick, *The Legacy of Conquest: The Unbroken Past of the American West;* Edward Holland Spicer, *Cycles of Conquest; the Impact of Spain, Mexico and the United States on the Indians of the Southwest, 1533–1960;* White, *History of the American West;* Drinnan, *Facing West;* Benjamin Ringer, *"We the People" and Others: Duality and America's Treatment of its Racial Minorities;* William Appleman Williams, *The Contours of American History;* Hall, "World-System Perspective"; Phillip L. Kohl, "Ethnic Strife: A Necessary Amendment to a Consideration of Class Struggles in Antiquity," *Civilization in Crisis*, pp. 167–79.

Appendix 2. Methodological Issues

1. See Tilly, *Big Structures*.

2. See John H. Goldthorpe, "The Uses of History in Sociology: Reflections on Some Recent Tendencies," *British Journal of Sociology* 42 (1991): 211–30.

3. Compare to Norma Williams and Andrée Sjoberg, "Ethnicity and Gender: The View from Above versus the View from Below," *A Critique of Contemporary American Sociology*, pp. 160–202.

4. Ibid., p. 190.

5. James Axtell, *After Columbus: Essays in the Ethnohistory of North America*, pp. 9–44, 29–36; Gideon Sjoberg and Roger Nett, *A Methodology for Social Research*, pp. 84–90.

Bibliography

Manuscripts

Bexar Archives. Center for American History, University of Texas at Austin.
Letters Received by the Office of Indian Affairs, Texas Agency (LROIA, Texas).
   Center for American History, University of Texas at Austin.

Published Works

Acuña, Rodolfo. *Occupied America: The Chicano Struggle Toward Liberation.* San
   Francisco, Calif.: Canfield, 1972.
Albers, Patricia C. "Symbiosis, Merger, and War: Contrasting Forms of Inter-
   tribal Relationship among Plains Indians." In *The Political Economy of North
   American Indians,* ed. John H. Moore, 94–132. Norman: University of Okla-
   homa Press, 1993.
Allen, Henry Easton. "The Parilla Expedition to the Red River." *Southwestern
   Historical Quarterly* 43 (1939): 53–71.
Allen, W. Y. "Extracts from a Diary of W. Y. Allen, 1838–1839." Edited by
   William S. Red. *Southwestern Historical Quarterly* 17 (1913): 43–60.
Anderson, Gary Clayton. *Kinsmen of Another Kind: Dakota-White Relations in the
   Upper Mississippi Valley, 1650–1862.* Lincoln: University of Nebraska Press,
   1984.
Anonymous. *A Visit to Texas.* Austin: Steck, 1925. Facsimile of New York:
   Goodrich and Wiley, 1834.
———. "A Visit Up the Colorado River: Extracts from an Anonymous Diary,
   17–25 July 1838." Published in *Telegraph and Texas Register,* Houston, Tex.,
   May 1, 1839. Typescript in the Center for American History at the Univer-
   sity of Texas at Austin, 1930.
———. *Texas in 1840, or The Emigrants Guide to the New Republic.* New York:
   Arno, 1974. Facsimile of New York: William W. Allen, 1840.
Arens, W. *The Man-eating Myth: Anthropology and Anthropophagy.* New York:
   Oxford, 1979.

Arredondo, Joaquin. "Joaquin Arredondo's Report of the Battle of the Medina, August 18, 1813." Translated by Mattie Austin Hatcher. *Quarterly of the Texas State Historical Association* 11 (1908): 220–32.

Asad, Talal. "Conscripts of Western Civilization." In *Civilization in Crisis: Anthropological Perspectives, Volume 1 of Dialectical Anthropology: Essays in Honor of Stanley Diamond*, ed. by Christine Ward Gailey, 332–52. Gainesville: University of Florida Press, 1992.

Aten, Lawrence E. *Indians of the Upper Texas Coast*. New York: Academic, 1983.

Austin, Stephen F. "Journal of Stephen F. Austin on His First Trip to Texas, 1821." Edited by Eugene C. Barker. *Quarterly of the Texas State Historical Association* 7 (1904): 287–307.

Axtell, James. *After Columbus: Essays in the Ethnohistory of North America*. New York: Oxford, 1988.

Axtell, James and William Sturtevant. "The Unkindest Cut of All, or Who Invented Scalping." *William and Mary Quarterly* Series 3, 37 (1980): 451–72.

Barker, Eugene C. "A Glimpse of Texas Fur Trade in 1832." *Southwestern Historical Quarterly* 19 (1916): 279–82.

———. *Mexico and Texas, 1821–1835*. Dallas: P. L. Turner, 1928.

———. *The Life of Stephen F. Austin: Founder of Texas 1793–1836: A Chapter of the Westward Movement of the American People*. New York: DaCapo, 1968. Facsimile of Nashville, Tenn.: Cokesbury, 1925.

———, ed. *The Austin Papers, Volumes I & II*. Washington, D.C.: U.S. Government Printing Office, 1924.

———, ed. *The Austin Papers, Volume III*. Austin: University of Texas Press, 1927.

Barrera, Mario. *Race and Class in the Southwest: A Theory of Racial Inequality*. Notre Dame: University of Notre Dame Press, 1979.

Barry, James Buckner. *A Texas Ranger and Frontiersman; the Days of Buck Barry in Texas, 1848–1906*. Dallas: Southwest, 1932.

Berkhofer, Robert F., Jr. *The White Man's Indian: Images of the American Indian from Columbus to the Present*. New York: Alfred Knopf, 1978.

Benavides, Adan. *The Bexar Archives, 1717–1836: A Name Guide*. Austin: University of Texas Press, 1989.

Berlandier, Jean Louis. *The Indians of Texas in 1830*. Edited and introduced by John C. Ewers. Translated by Patricia Reading Leclercq. Washington, D.C.: Smithsonian Institution, 1969.

Biesele, Rudolph L. "Early Times in New Braunfels and Comal County." *Southwestern Historical Quarterly* 50 (1946): 75–92.

Blauner, Robert. *Racial Oppression in America*. New York: Harper and Row, 1972.

Bollaert, William. *William Bollaert's Texas*. Edited by W. Eugene Hollon and Ruth Lapham Butler. Norman: University of Oklahoma Press, 1956.

Bolton, Herbert E. "Ranchería Grande." In *Handbook of American Indians North of Mexico*, Bureau of American Ethnology, Bulletin 30, Part 2, ed. Frederick W. Hodge, 354. Washington, D.C.: U.S. Government Printing Office, 1910.

———. "San Xavier de Horcasitas." In *Handbook of American Indians North of*

Mexico, Bureau of American Ethnology, Bulletin 30, Part 2, ed. Frederick W. Hodge, 437–38. Washington, D.C.: U.S. Government Printing Office, 1910.

———. "San Xavier de Náxera." In *Handbook of American Indians North of Mexico*, Bureau of American Ethnology, Bulletin 30, Part 2, ed. Frederick W. Hodge, 438. Washington, D.C.: U.S. Government Printing Office, 1910.

———. "Tonkawa." In *Handbook of American Indians North of Mexico*, Bureau of American Ethnology, Bulletin 30, Part 2, ed. Frederick W. Hodge, 778–83. Washington, D.C.: U.S. Government Printing Office, 1910.

———. "The Founding of the Missions on the San Gabriel River." *Southwestern Historical Quarterly* 17 (1914): 323–78.

———. *Athanase de Mézières and the Louisiana-Texas Frontier, 1768–1780*. Cleveland, Ohio: Arthur H. Clark, 1914.

———. *Texas in the Middle Eighteenth Century*. Berkeley: University of California Press, 1915.

Bonnell, George W. "Report of G.W. Bonnell, Commissioner of Indian Affairs, Third Congress of the Republic of Texas, First Session, November 3, 1838." In *Communication from the Commissioner of Indian Affairs, and Other Documents in Relation to the Indians of Texas*, United States Congress, Senate Report, Thirtieth Congress, First Session, No. 171, comp. U.S. Bureau of Indian Affairs, 38–50. Washington, D.C.: n.p., 1849.

———. *Topographical Description of Texas to Which Is Added an Account of the Indian Tribes*. Waco, Tex.: Texian, 1964. Facsimile of Austin: Clark, Wing, and Brown, 1840.

Boucher, Phillip P. *Cannibal Encounters: European and Island Caribs, 1492–1763*. Baltimore, Md.: Johns Hopkins University Press, 1992.

Brown, John Henry. *Indian Wars and Pioneers of Texas*. Austin: Statehouse, 1988. Reprint of Austin: L. E. Daniell, 1890.

Burnam, Jesse. "Reminiscences of Capt. Jesse Burnam." Collected by Julia Lee Sinks. Edited by Julia Lee Sinks and George P. Garrison. *Quarterly of the Texas State Historical Association* 5 (1901): 12–18.

Burnet, David G. "Letter to Robert Neighbors, August 20, 1847." In *Communication from the Commissioner of Indian Affairs, and Other Documents in Relation to the Indians of Texas*, United States Congress, Senate Report, Thirtieth Congress, First Session, No. 171, comp. U.S. Bureau of Indian Affairs, 7–8. Washington, D.C.: n.p., 1849.

Butler, P. M. and H. G. Lewis. "Report on the Indians of Texas, August 8, 1846." In *Communication from the Commissioner of Indian Affairs, and Other Documents in Relation to the Indians of Texas*, United States Congress, Senate Report, Thirtieth Congress, First Session, No. 171, comp. U.S. Bureau of Indian Affairs, 29–37. Washington, D.C.: n.p., 1849.

Cabeza de Vaca, Alvar Nuñez. *The Journey of Alvar Nuñez Cabeza de Vaca and His Companions from Florida to the Pacific, 1528–1536*. Translated by Fannie Bandelier. Edited by Adolph F. Bandelier. Chicago: Rio Grande, 1964. Facsimile of New York: A. S. Barnes, 1905.

Calvert, Robert and Arnoldo de Leon. *The History of Texas.* Arlington Heights, Ill.: Harlan and Davidson, 1990.

Campbell, T. N. "Pakawa Indians." In *Handbook of Texas*, vol. 3. ed. Eldon Stephen Branda, 690–91. Austin: Texas State Historical Association, 1976.

———. "Tampaqua Indians." In *Handbook of Texas*, vol. 3. ed. Eldon Stephen Branda, 950. Austin: Texas State Historical Association, 1976.

Campbell, T. N. and T. J. Campbell. *Indian Groups Associated with the Spanish Missions of the San Antonio National Historical Park.* Special Report, #6. San Antonio: Center for Archeological Research at the University of Texas–San Antonio, 1985.

Castañeda, Carlos E. *Transition Period: The Fight for Freedom, 1810–1836. Volume VI, Our Catholic Heritage in Texas, 1519–1836.* Austin: Von Boeckmann–Jones, 1950.

Cazenau, Jane McManus (Cora Montgomery). *Eagle Pass, or Life on the Border.* Edited by Robert Crawford Cotner. Austin: Pemberton, 1966. Facsimile of New York: George Putnam, 1852.

Chamberlain, Samuel E. *My Confession: Recollections of a Rogue.* New York: Harper and Brothers, 1956.

Champagne, Duane. *American Indian Societies: Strategies of Political and Cultural Survival.* Cambridge, Mass.: Cultural Survival, 1989.

Chase-Dunn, Christopher and Thomas D. Hall. "Comparing World-Systems: Concepts and Working Hypotheses." *Social Forces* 71 (1993): 851–86.

———. *Rise and Demise: Comparing World-Systems.* Boulder, Colo.: Westview, 1997.

———, eds. *Core/Periphery Relations in Pre-Capitalist Worlds.* Boulder, Colo.: Westview, 1991.

Chipman, Donald. *Spanish Texas, 1519–1821.* Austin: University of Texas Press, 1992.

Chirot, Daniel and Thomas D. Hall. "World-System Theory." *Annual Review of Sociology* 8 (1982): 81–106.

Chriesman, Horatio. "Recollections of Capt. Horatio Chriesman." Collected by J. H. Kuykendall. Edited by George P. Garrison. *Quarterly of the Texas State Historical Association* 6 (1903): 236–41.

Collins, Randall. *Conflict Sociology: Toward an Explanatory Science.* New York: Academic, 1975.

———. "Some Principles of Long-Term Social Change: The Territorial Power of States." In *Research in Social Movements, Conflict and Change*, ed. Louis Kriesberg, 1–34. Greenwich, Conn.: Jai, 1978.

———. "On the Micro-Foundations of Macro-Sociology." *American Journal of Sociology* 86 (1981): 984–1014.

Collinson, Frank. "The Tonkawas." *Ranch Romances*, July 8, 1938, pp. 128–30.

Comisión Pesquisidora de la Frontera. *Reports of the Committee of Investigation Sent in 1873 by the Mexican Government to the Frontier of Texas.* Official translation. New York: Baker and Godwin, 1873.

Conger, Roger. "Torrey's Trading House." In *Handbook of Texas*, vol. 2. ed. Walter P. Webb, 790–91. Austin: Texas State Historical Association, 1952.

Coombes, Zachariah E. *The Diary of a Frontiersman, 1858–1859.* Edited by Barbara Neal Ledbetter. Newcastle, Tex.: n.p., 1962.

Cravens, Johnathan Nathan. *James Harper Starr: Financier of the Republic of Texas.* Austin: Daughters of the Republic of Texas, 1950.

Dahrendorf, Ralf. *Class and Class Conflict in Industrial Society.* Stanford: Stanford University Press, 1959.

Davidson, Col. Wilson T. "A Comanche Prisoner in 1841." *Southwestern Historical Quarterly* 45 (1942): 335–42.

De Solís, Fray Gaspar José. "Diary of a Visit of Inspection of the Texas Missions Made by Fray Gaspar José de Solís in the Year 1767–1768." Translated by Margaret Kenney Kress. *Southwestern Historical Quarterly* 35 (1931): 28–76.

DeWees, William B. *Letters from an Early Settler of Texas.* Waco, Tex.: Texian, 1968. Facsimile of Cincinnati, Ohio: Hull & Co., 1853.

Diamond, Stanley. *In Search of the Primitive: A Critique of Civilization.* New Brunswick, N.J.: Transaction, 1974.

Dickens, Charles. "The Noble Savage." *Household Words* 7 (1853): 337–39.

Dobyns, Henry F. *Their Number Became Thinned: Native American Population Dynamics in Eastern North America.* Knoxville: University of Tennessee Press, 1983.

Domenech, Emmanuel. *Missionary Adventures in Texas and Mexico. A Personal Narrative of Six Years' Sojourn in Those Regions.* Translated under his own supervision. London: Longman, Brown, Green, Longmans, and Roberts, 1858.

Dresel, Gustav. *Gustav Dresel's Houston Journal: Adventures in North America and Texas, 1837–1841.* Translated and edited by Max Freund. Austin: University of Texas Press, 1954.

Drinnan, Richard. *White Savage: The Case of John Dunn Hunter.* New York: Shocken, 1972.

———. *Facing West: The Metaphysics of Indian-Hating and Empire-Building.* Minneapolis: University of Minnesota Press, 1980.

DuBois, W. E. B. *Color and Democracy: Colonies and Peace.* New York: Harcourt, Brace, and Company, 1945.

Dunaway, Wilma. *The First American Frontier: Transition to Capitalism in Southern Appalachia, 1700–1860.* Chapel Hill: University of North Carolina Press, 1996.

———. "Incorporation as an Interactive Process: Cherokee Resistance to Expansion of the Capitalist World-System." *Sociological Inquiry* 66 (1996): 455–70.

Dunn, William Edward. "The Apache Mission on the San Sabá River: Its Founding and Failure." *Southwestern Historical Quarterly* 17 (1914): 379–414.

Dyer, J. O. *The Lake Charles Atakapas (Cannibals), 1817–1820.* Galveston, Tex.: n.p., 1917.

Erath, George B. "The Memoirs of George Bernard Erath, III." Edited by Lucy A. Erath. *Southwestern Historical Quarterly* 27 (1923): 27–51.

Erskine, Michael H. "A Cattle Drive from Texas to California: The Diary of M. H. Erskine, 1854." Edited by Walter S. Sanderlin. *Southwestern Historical Quarterly* 67 (1964): 397–412.

Evans, Raymond. "'The Nigger Shall Disappear': Aborigines and Europeans in Colonial Queensland." In *Exclusion, Exploitation, and Extermination: Race Relations in Colonial Queensland*, eds. Raymond Evans, Kathryn Cronin, and Kay Saunders, 24–146. Sydney: Australia and New Zealand Book, 1975.

Everett, Dianna. *The Texas Cherokees: A People Between Two Fires*. Norman: University of Oklahoma Press, 1990.

Ewers, John C. "The Influence of Epidemics on the Indian Population and Cultures of Texas." *Plains Anthropologist* 18 (1973): 104–15.

Faiman-Silva, Sandra. *Choctaw at the Crossroads: The Political Economy of Class and Culture in the Oklahoma Timber Region*. Lincoln: University of Nebraska Press, 1997.

Faulk, Odie. *The Last Years of Spanish Texas, 1778–1821*. The Hague: Mouton, 1964.

———. "The Comanche Invasion of Texas, 1743–1836." *Great Plains Journal* 9 (1969): 10–50.

Fehrenbach, T. R. *Lone Star: A History of Texas and Texans*. New York: MacMillan, 1968.

Ferguson, R. Brian and Neil L. Whitehead. "The Violent Edge of Empire." In *War in the Tribal Zone: Expanding States and Indigenous Warfare*, eds. R. Brian Ferguson and Neil L. Whitehead, 1–30. Santa Fe, N.Mex.: School of American Research Press, 1992.

Fletcher, Alice C. and Herbert E. Bolton. "Mayeye." In *Handbook of American Indians North of Mexico*, Bureau of American Ethnology, Bulletin 30, Part 1, ed. Frederick W. Hodge, 824–25. Washington, D.C.: U.S. Government Printing Office. 1907.

Flores, Dan. *Journal of an Indian Trader: Anthony Glass and the Texas Trading Frontier, 1790–1810*. College Station: Texas A&M University Press, 1985.

———. "Bison Ecology and Bison Diplomacy." *Journal of American History* 78 (1991): 465–85.

Folmer, Henri. "De Bellisle on the Texas Coast." *Southwestern Historical Quarterly* 44 (1940): 204–31.

Ford, John Salmon (Rip). *Rip Ford's Texas*. Edited by Stephen B. Oates. Austin: University of Texas Press, 1963.

Foreman, Grant. "Early Trails through Oklahoma." *Chronicles of Oklahoma* 3 (1925): 99–119.

———. *Indians and Pioneers: The Story of the American Southwest before 1830*. Norman: University of Oklahoma Press, 1936.

———. *Advancing the Frontier, 1830–1860*. Norman: University of Oklahoma Press, 1968.

Freeman, W. G. "Report of Brevet Col. W. G. Freeman, August 15, 1853."

Edited by M. L. Crimmins. *Southwestern Historical Quarterly* 53 (1949): 202–208.

Froebel, Julius. *Seven Years Travel in Central America, Northern Mexico, and the Far West of the United States.* London: Richard Bentley, 1859.

Gammel, Hans P. M. N. *The Laws of Texas, 1822–1904,* 10 vols. Austin: Gammel, 1904.

Garrett, Julia Kathryn. *Green Flag over Texas: The Last Years of Spain in Texas.* New York: Cordova, 1939.

Gatschet, Albert S. *The Karankawa Indians. The Coast People of Texas.* Archeological and Ethnological Papers of the Peabody Museum, Volume 1, Number 2. Cambridge: Harvard University Press. 1891.

Gilmore, Kathleen. *The Keeran Site: The Probable Site of La Salle's Ft. St. Louis in Texas.* Office of the State Archeologist, Report Number 24. Austin: Texas State Historical Commission, 1973.

———. "The Indians of the Mission Rosario: From the Books and from the Ground." In *Columbian Consequences, Volume I,* ed. David H. Thomas, 231–44. Washington, D.C.: Smithsonian Institution, 1989.

Glover, William B. "A History of the Caddo Indians." *Louisiana Historical Quarterly* 18 (1935): 872–946.

Goldberg, Johnathan. *Sodometries: Renaissance Texts,Modern Sexualities.* Stanford: Stanford University Press, 1992.

Goldthorpe, John H. "The Uses of History in Sociology: Reflections on Some Recent Tendencies." *British Journal of Sociology* 42 (1991): 211–30.

Gómez-Quiñones, Juan. *Roots of Chicano Politics, 1600–1940.* Albuquerque: University of New Mexico Press, 1994.

Gracey, David B., II. "Jean LaFitte and the Karankawa Indians." *East Texas Historical Journal* 2 (1964): 40–44.

Green, Thomas J. *Journal of the Texian Expedition Against Mier: Subsequent Imprisonment of the Author, His Suffering, and Final Escape from the Castle of Perote.* Austin: Steck, 1935. Facsimile of New York: Harper and Brothers, 1845.

Grinnell, George Bird. *The Cheyenne Indians: Their History and Way of Life,* Two Volumes. New York: Cooper Square, 1962.

Griswold del Castillo, Richard. *The Treaty of Guadalupe Hidalgo: A Legacy of Conflict.* Norman: University of Oklahoma Press, 1990.

Gulick, Charles Adam and Katherine Elliot, eds. *The Papers of Mirabeau Buonaparte Lamar,* Six Volumes. Austin: A. C. Baldwin and Sons, 1922.

Gumplowicz, Ludwig. *The Outlines of Sociology.* Translated by Frank W. Moore. Philadelphia: American Academy of Political Science, 1899.

Haggard, J. Villasana. "The House of Barr and Davenport." *Southwestern Historical Quarterly* 49 (1945): 66–77.

Hall, Thomas D. "Incorporation into the World-System: Toward a Critique." *American Sociological Review* 51 (1986): 390–402.

———. *Social Change in the Southwest: 1350–1880.* Lawrence: University Press of Kansas, 1989.

———. "Historical Sociology and Native Americans." *American Indian Quarterly* 13 (1989): 223–38.

———. "The World-System Perspective: A Small Sample from a Large Universe." *Sociological Inquiry* 66 (1996): 440–54.

Harris, Annie P. "Memoirs of Mrs. Annie P. Harris." Edited by Ethel Mary Franklin. *Southwestern Historical Quarterly* 40 (1937): 231–46.

Haskaarl, Robert. "The Culture and History of the Tonkawa Indians." *Plains Anthropologist* 7 (1962): 217–31.

Hatcher, Mattie Austin. *The Opening of Texas to Foreign Settlement, 1801–1821.* Bulletin Number 2714. Austin: University of Texas, 1927.

Haynes, Sam W. *Soldiers of Misfortune: The Somervell and Mier Expeditions.* Austin: University of Texas Press, 1990.

Hechter, Michael. *Internal Colonialism: The Celtic Fringe in British National Development, 1536–1966.* Berkeley: University of California Press, 1975.

Helms, Mary S. *Scraps of Early Texas History.* Austin: B. R. Warner, 1884.

Henry, William Seaton. *Campaign Sketches of the War with Mexico.* New York: Arno, 1971. Reprint of New York: Harper and Burleson, 1847.

Hickerson, Nancy Parrott. *The Jumanos: Hunters and Traders of the South Plains.* Austin: University of Texas Press, 1994.

Hicks, Elijah. "Journal of Elijah Hicks." Edited by Grant Foreman. *Chronicles of Oklahoma* 13 (1935): 68–99.

Hobson, John A. *Imperialism, a Study.* Ann Arbor: University of Michigan Press, 1965. Reprint of London: n.p., 1938.

Hogan, William R. *The Texas Republic: A Social and Economic History.* Norman: University of Oklahoma Press, 1946.

Holley, Mary Austin. *Texas.* Austin: Steck, 1935. Facsimile of Lexington, Ky.: J. Clarke, 1836.

Hopkins, Terence K. and Immanuel Wallerstein. "Structural Transformation of the World-Economy." In *World System Analysis: Theory and Methodology,* eds. Terence K. Hopkins and Immanuel Wallerstein, 121–43. Beverly Hills, Calif.: Sage, 1982.

Horowitz, Irving L. "Preface." In *The Ward-Gumplowicz Correspondence: 1897–1909,* ed. and trans. Aleksander Gella, vii-ix. New York: Essay, 1971.

Horsman, Reginald. *The Frontier in the Formative Years, 1783–1815.* New York: Holt, Rinehart, and Winston, 1970.

———. *Race and Manifest Destiny: The Origins of American Racial Anglo-Saxonism.* Cambridge: Harvard University Press, 1981.

Houston, Sam. *The Autobiography of Sam Houston.* Edited by Donald Day. Norman: University of Oklahoma Press, 1954.

———. *The Writings of Sam Houston,* Eight Volumes. Edited by Amelia W. Williams and Eugene C. Barker. Austin: University of Texas Press, 1941.

Houstoun, Matilda. *Texas and the Gulf of Mexico, Yachting in the New World.* Philadelphia: G. B. Zeiber and Co., 1845.

Huson, Hobart. *Refugio: A Comprehensive History from Aboriginal Times to 1953,* Two Volumes. Woodsboro, Tex.: Rooke Foundation, 1953.

———. *Captain Phillip Dimmitt's Commandancy of Goliad: An Episode of the Mexican Federalist War in Texas Usually Referred to as the Texian Revolution.* Austin: Von Boekman-Jones, 1974.

Jefferson, Thomas. *The Complete Jefferson.* Assembled and arranged by Saul K. Padover. Freeport, N.Y.: Books for Libraries Press, 1943.

Jenkins, John Holland. *Recollections of Early Texas: The Memoirs of John Holland Jenkins.* Edited by John Holmes Jenkins. Austin: University of Texas Press, 1958.

Jenkins, John Holmes and Kenneth Kesselus. *Edward Burleson: Texas Frontier Leader.* Austin: Jenkins, 1990.

Jennings, Francis. *The Invasion of America: Indians, Colonialism, and the Cant of Conquest.* Chapel Hill: University of North Carolina Press, 1975.

John, Elizabeth A. *Storms Brewed in Other Men's Worlds: The Confrontation of Indians, Spanish and French in the Southwest, 1540–1795.* College Station: Texas A&M University Press, 1975.

Johnson, LeRoy. "The Reconstructed Crow Terminology of the Titskanwatits, or Tonkawas, with Inferred Social Correlates." *Plains Anthropologist* 39 (1994): 377–414.

Johnson, LeRoy and T. N. Campbell. "Sanan: Traces of a Previously Unknown Language in Colonial Coahuila and Texas." *Plains Anthropologist* 37 (1992): 185–212.

Jones, William K. *Notes on the History and Material Culture of the Tonkawa Indians.* Smithsonian Contributions to Anthropology, Volume 2, Number 5. Washington, D.C.: Smithsonian Institution, 1969.

Jordan, Terence. *North American Cattle Ranching Frontiers: Origins, Diffusion, and Differentiation.* Albuquerque: University of New Mexico Press, 1993.

Kavanagh, Thomas W. *Comanche Political History: An Ethnohistorical Perspective, 1706–1875.* Lincoln: University of Nebraska Press, 1996.

Kenner, Charles L. *A History of New Mexico–Plains Indian Relations.* Norman: University of Oklahoma Press, 1969.

Kenrick, Donald and Gratton Puxon. *The Destiny of Europe's Gypsies.* London: Chatto, 1972.

Kesselus, Kenneth. *History of Bastrop County, Texas, before Statehood.* Austin: Jenkins, 1986.

Kilman, Ed. *Cannibal Coast.* San Antonio: Naylor, 1959.

Klein, Alan M. "Political Economy of the Buffalo Hide Trade: Race and Class on the Plains." In *The Political Economy of North American Indians*, ed. John H. Moore, 133–60. Norman: University of Oklahoma Press, 1993.

Klos, George. "'Our People Could Not Distinguish One Tribe from Another': The 1859 Expulsion of the Reserve Indians from Texas." *Southwestern Historical Quarterly* 97 (1994): 598–619.

Koch, Lena Clara. "The Federal Indian Policy in Texas, 1845–1860." *Southwestern Historical Quarterly* 28 (1925): 223–234, 259–286; 29 (1925): 19–35, 98–127.

Kohl, Phillip L. "Ethnic Strife: A Necessary Amendment to a Consideration of

Class Struggles in Antiquity." In *Civilization in Crisis: Anthropological Perspectives, Volume 1 of Dialectical Anthropology: Essays in Honor of Stanley Diamond*, ed. Christine Ward Gailey, 167–79. Gainesville: University of Florida Press, 1992.

Krieger, Alex D. *Culture Complexes and Chronology in Northern Texas with Extension of Puebloan Datings to the Mississippi Valley*. Publication Number 4640. Austin: University of Texas, 1946.

Kuykendall, Gibson. "Recollections of Capt. Gibson Kuykendall." Collected by J. H. Kuykendall. Edited by George P. Garrison. *Quarterly of the Texas State Historical Association* 7 (1903): 29–40

Kuykendall, J. H. "Reminiscences of Early Texans, A Collection from the Austin Papers, I." Edited by George P. Garrison. *Quarterly of the Texas State Historical Association* 6 (1903): 236–53.

Lamar, Howard R. *The Trader on the American Frontier: Myth's Victim*. College Station: Texas A&M University Press, 1977.

Latham, Francis R. *Travels in the Republic of Texas: 1842*. Edited by Gerald S. Pierce. Austin: Encino, 1971.

Lehmann, Herman. *The Last Captive*. Edited by A. C. Greene. Austin: Encino, 1972.

Limerick, Patricia N. *The Legacy of Conquest: The Unbroken Past of the American West*. New York: W. W. Norton, 1987.

Linn, James. *Reminiscences of Fifty Years in Texas*. Austin: Steck, 1935. Facsimile of New York: D. & J. Sadlier, 1883.

Lyman, Stanford M. *Militarism, Imperialism, and Racial Accommodation: An Analysis and Interpretation of the Early Writings of Robert E. Park*. Fayetteville: University of Arkansas Press, 1992.

Lyons, Oren R. "The American Indian in the Past." In *Exiled in the Land of the Free: Democracy, Indian Nations, and the United States Constitution*, ed. Oren R. Lyons and John C. Mohawk, 13–42. Santa Fe, N.Mex.: Clear Light, 1992.

Marcy, R. B. *Thirty Years of Army Life on the Border*. New York: Harper and Brothers, 1866.

Marr, John C. *History of Matagorda County*. Ph.D. diss., University of Texas at Austin, 1928.

Matlock, William A. 1930. "Journal of a Trip through Texas and Northern Mexico in 1846 and 1847." Edited by Eugene C. Barker. *Southwestern Historical Quarterly* 34 (1930): 20–37.

Maverick, Mary A. *Memoirs of Mary A. Maverick*. Edited by Rena Maverick Green. San Antonio: Alamo Printing, 1921.

Mayhall, Mildred P. *The Indians of Texas: The Atákapa, the Karankawa, and the Tonkawa*. Ph.D. diss., University of Texas at Austin, 1939.

McConnell, Joseph Carroll. *The West Texas Frontier or a Descriptive History of Early Times in Western Texas, Containing an Accurate Account of Much Hitherto Unpublished History, Presenting for the First Time in Historic Form a Detailed Description of Old Forts, Indian Fights, Depredations, Indian Reservations, French and Spanish Activities, and Many Other Interesting Things, and Written from*

Data, No Less Than Seventy-Five Per Cent of Which Was Personally Obtained by the Author Directly from Dusty Old Departmental Files and Archives in Washington, D.C., Austin, Texas, and Various County Seats and from Several Hundred Surviving Old Settlers Found All the Way from the Red River to the Rio Grande, and in Other States. Jacksboro, Tex.: Gazette Print, 1933.

McElhannon, Joseph Carl. "Imperial Mexico and Texas." *Southwestern Historical Quarterly* 53 (1949): 117–50.

McKee, James B. *Sociology and the Race Problem: The Failure of a Perspective.* Urbana: University of Illinois Press, 1993.

McMahon, John K. *History of the Second Seminole War, 1835–1842.* Gainesville: University of Florida Press, 1967.

McNitt, Frank. *The Indian Traders.* Norman: University of Oklahoma Press, 1962.

Mead, George H. *Mind, Self and Society.* Chicago: University of Chicago Press, 1934.

Meinig, D. W. *Imperial Texas: An Interpretive Essay in Cultural Geography.* Austin: University of Texas Press, 1969.

Melville, Herman. *The Confidence-Man: His Masquerade.* Edited with introduction and notes by Stephen Matterson. New York: Penguin, 1990. Reprint of New York: Dix, Edwards, 1857.

Miller, Robert L. *The Life of Robert Hall: Indian Fighter and Veteran of Three Great Wars.* Austin: Ben C. Jones, 1898.

Montaigne, Sanford H. *Blood over Texas.* New Rochelle, N.Y.: Arlington House, 1976.

Montejano, David. *Anglos and Mexicans in the Making of Texas, 1836–1986.* Austin: University of Texas Press, 1987.

Mooney, James. "Our Last Cannibal Tribe." *Harper's Monthly Magazine* 103 (1901): 550–55.

Moore, John H. *The Cheyenne Nation: A Social and Demographic History.* Lincoln: University of Nebraska Press, 1987.

Morgan, George R. and Omer C. Stewart. "Peyote Trade in South Texas." *Southwestern Historical Quarterly* 87 (1984): 269–96.

Muckleroy, Anna. "The Indian Policy of the Republic of Texas." *Southwestern Historical Quarterly* 25 (1922): 229–60; 26 (1922): 1–29, 128–48, 184–206.

Nance, Berta Hart. "D. A. Nance and the Tonkawa Indians." *Yearbook of the West Texas Historical Association* 28 (1952): 87–95.

Nance, John Milton. *After San Jacinto: The Texas-Mexican Frontier, 1836–1841.* Austin: University of Texas Press, 1963.

———. *Attack and Counterattack: The Texas Mexican Frontier, 1842.* Austin: University of Texas Press, 1964.

———. "Was There a Mier Expedition Flag?" *Southwestern Historical Quarterly* 92 (1989): 543–57.

Nathan, Paul D., trans., and Leslie Byrd Simpson, ed. *The San Sabá Papers: A Documentary Account of the Founding and Destruction of the San Sabá Mission.* San Francisco: J. Howell, 1959.

Neale, William and William A. Neale. *Century of Conflict, 1821–1913.* Edited by John C. Rayburn and Virgina Kemp Rayburn. New York: Arno, 1976. Reprint of Waco, Tex.: Texian, 1966.

Neighbours, Kenneth F. *Indian Exodus: Texas Indian Affairs, 1835–1859.* N.p.: Nortex, 1973.

Newcomb, William W., Jr. "A Reappraisal of the 'Cultural Sink' of Texas." *Southwestern Journal of Anthropology* 12 (1956): 145–53.

———. *The Indians of Texas: From Prehistoric to Modern Times.* Austin: University of Texas Press, 1961.

———. "The Ethnohistorical Investigation." In *A Lipan Apache Mission: San Lorenzo de Santa Cruz, 1762–1771,* Bulletin Number 14, eds. Curtis Tunnell and W. W. Newcomb, Jr., 141–80. Austin: Texas Memorial Museum, 1969.

———. "The Karankawa." In *Handbook of North American Indians, Volume 10, Southwest,* eds. Alfonso Ortiz and William C. Sturtevant, 359–67. Washington, D.C.: Smithsonian Institution, 1983.

———. "Historic Indians of Central Texas." *Bulletin of the Texas Archeological Society* 64 (1993): 1–63.

Newcomb, William W. and T. N. Campbell. "Southern Plains Ethnohistory: A Re-Examination of the Escanajaques, Ahijados, and Cuitoas." In *Pathways to Plains Prehistory: Anthropological Perspectives on Plains Natives,* eds. Don Wyckoff and Jack Hoffman, 29–43. N.p.: Oklahoma Anthropological Society, 1982.

Newkumet, Vynola Beaver and Howard L. Meredith. *Hasinai: A Traditional History of the Caddo Confederacy.* College Station: Texas A&M University Press, 1988.

Newlin, Debra Lamont. *The Tonkawa People from Earliest Times to 1893.* Journal Number 21. Lubbock: West Texas Museum Association, 1982.

Noël, Virginia P. *The United States Indian Reservations in Texas, 1854–1859.* M.A. thesis, University of Texas at Austin, 1924.

North, Douglass Cecil. *The Economic Growth of the United States, 1790–1860.* Englewood Cliffs, N.J.: Prentice-Hall, 1961.

Nye, Wilbur Sturtevant. *Carbine and Lance: The Story of Old Ft. Sill by Lt. Col. W. S. Nye.* Norman: University of Oklahoma Press, 1942.

Oberste, William H. *History of Mission Refugio.* Refugio, Tex.: Refugio Timely Remarks, 1942.

———. *Texas Irish Empresarios and Their Colonies: Power and Hewetson, McMullen and McGloin, Refugio and San Patricio.* Austin: Von Boekman–Jones, 1953.

Olmsted, Frederick Law. *A Journey through Texas, or a Saddle-Trip on the Southwestern Frontier.* Austin: University of Texas Press, 1978. Reprint of New York: Dix, Edwards, 1857.

Oo-chee-cah. "The Story of Sequoyah's Last Days." Edited by Grant Foreman. *Chronicles of Oklahoma* 12 (1934): 25–41. First published in *Cherokee Advocate,* June 26, 1845.

Owens, Elizabeth McAnulty. *Elizabeth McAnulty Owens: The Story of Her Life.* San Antonio: Naylor, 1936.

Padilla, Juan Antonio. "Texas in 1820." Translated by Mattie Austin Hatcher. *Southwestern Historical Quarterly* 23 (1919): 47–68.

Pearce, Roy H. *Savagism and Civilization: A Study of the Indian and the American Mind.* Baltimore: Johns Hopkins University Press, 1965.

Peterson, John H., Jr. "The Indian in the Old South." In *Red, White, and Black: Symposium on the Indians in the Old South,* 116–33. Proceedings of the Southern Anthropological Society, Number 5. Athens: University of Georgia, 1971.

Phillips, Paul C. *The Fur Trade,* Two Volumes. Norman: University of Oklahoma Press, 1961.

Pichardo, Jose Antonio. *Pichardo's Treatises on the Limits of Louisiana and Texas, Volume I.* Translated and edited by Charles W. Hackett. Austin: University of Texas Press, 1931.

Pike, Zebulon M. *An Account of Expeditions to the Sources of the Mississippi, And Through the Western Parts of Louisiana, . . . And a Tour Through the Interior Parts of New Spain.* Ann Arbor: University Microfilms, 1966. Facsimile of Philadelphia: C.A. Conrad, 1810.

Prucha, Francis Paul. *The Great Father: The United States Government and American Indians,* Two Volumes. Lincoln: University of Nebraska Press, 1984.

Rawls, James J. *The Indians of California: The Changing Image.* Norman: University of Oklahoma Press, 1984.

Reichstein, Andreas. *Rise of the Lone Star: The Making of Texas.* Translated by Jeanne R. Wilson. College Station: Texas A&M University Press, 1989.

Reid, Samuel Chester. *The Scouting Expeditions of McCulloch's Texas Rangers or, The Summer and Fall Campaign of the Army of the United States in Mexico– 1846: Including Skirmishes with the Mexicans, and the Storming of Monterrey; Also the Daring Scouts at Buena Vista; Together with Anecdotes, Incidents, Descriptions of Country, and Sketches of the Lives of Hays, McCulloch, and Walker.* Freeport, N.Y.: Books for Libraries, 1970. Reprint of Philadelphia: G. B. Zeiber, 1847.

Ribeiro, Darcy. *The Americas and Civilization.* Translated by L. L. Barrett and M. M. Barrett. New York: Dutton, 1971.

Richardson, Rupert N. *The Comanche Barrier to South Plains Settlement: A Century and a Half of Savage Resistance to the Advancing White Frontier.* Glendale, Calif.: Arthur H. Clark, 1933.

———. *Texas, the Lone Star State.* New York: Prentice-Hall, 1943.

Ricklis, Robert Arthur. *Aboriginal Life and Culture on the Upper Texas Coast: Archaeology at the Mitchell Ridge Site, 41GV66, Galveston Island.* Corpus Christi, Tex.: Coastal Archeological Research, 1994.

———. *The Karankawa Indians of Texas: An Ecological Study of Cultural Tradition and Change.* Austin: University of Texas Press, 1996.

Ringer, Benjamin. *"We the People" and Others: Duality and America's Treatment of its Racial Minorities.* New York: Tavistock, 1983.

Roemer, Ferdinand. *Texas.* Translated by Oswald Mueller. San Marcos, Tex.: German Texas Heritage Society, 1983. Facsimile of San Antonio: Standard Printing, 1935.

Rogin, Michael Paul. *Fathers and Children: Andrew Jackson and the Subjugation of the American Indians.* New York: Alfred Knopf, 1975.

Roseberry, William. "Political Economy." *Annual Review of Anthropology* 39 (1988): 161–85.

———. "La Falta de Brazos: Land and Labor in the Coffee Economies of Nineteenth Century Latin America." *Theory and Society* 20 (1991): 351–82.

Salinas, Martin. *Indians of the Rio Grande Delta: Their Role in the History of Southern Texas and Northeastern Mexico.* Austin: University of Texas Press, 1990.

Sánchez, José María. "A Trip to Texas in 1828." Translated by Carlos E. Castañeda. *Southwestern Historical Quarterly* 29 (1926): 249–88.

Sanday, Peggy Reeves. *Divine Hunger: Cannibalism as a Cultural System.* Cambridge: Cambridge University Press, 1986.

Schaedel, Richard P. "The Karankawa of the Texas Gulf Coast." *Southwestern Journal of Anthropology* 5 (1949): 117–37.

Schilz, Thomas F. *People of the Cross Timbers: A History of the Tonkawa Indians.* Ph.D. diss., Texas Christian University, 1983.

———. *The Lipan Indians in Texas.* El Paso: Texas Western, 1987.

Schlesier, Karl H. "Commentary: A History of Ethnic Groups in the Great Plains, AD 150–1500." In *Plains Indians, AD 500–1500: The Archeological Past of Historical Groups,* ed. Karl H. Schlesier, 308–81. Norman: University of Oklahoma Press, 1994.

Schumpeter, Joseph A. "The Sociology of Imperialisms." In *Imperialism and Social Classes,* ed. Paul M. Sweezy, trans. Heinz Norden, 3–130. New York: Augustus M. Kelley, 1951.

Sheehan, Bernard W. *Seeds of Extinction: Jeffersonian Philanthropy and the American Indian.* Chapel Hill: University of North Carolina Press, 1973.

Sheridan, Francis C. *Galveston Island or, A Few Months Off the Coast of Texas.* Edited by Willis W. Pratt. Austin: University of Texas Press, 1954.

Sibley, John. "Historical Sketches of the Several Indian Tribes in Louisiana South of the Arkansas River and Between the Mississippi and River Grand." In *Travels in the Interior Parts of America Communicating Discoveries Made in Exploring the Missouri River, Red River, and Washita as Laid before the Senate by the President of the United States, in February of 1806 . . . ,* comp. Thomas Jefferson, 40–53. London: Richard Phillips, 1807.

———. *A Report from Natchitoches in 1807.* Edited by Annie Heloise Abel. New York: Museum of the American Indian, Heye Foundation, 1922.

Sibley, Marilyn McAdams. *Travelers in Texas, 1761–1860.* Austin: University of Texas Press, 1967.

Siegelman, Phillip. "Introduction." In *Imperialism, a Study,* by John A. Hobson, v–xvi. Ann Arbor: University of Michigan Press, 1965.

Simons, Sarah E. "Social Assimilation." *American Journal of Sociology* 6 (1901): 790–822; 7 (1902): 53–79, 234–48, 386–404, 539–56.

Sjoberg, Andrée F. *The Bidai Indians of Southeastern Texas.* M.A. thesis, University of Texas at Austin, 1951.

————. "The Culture of the Tonkawa, A Texas Indian Tribe." *Texas Journal of Science* 5 (1953): 280–304.

————. "Lipan Apache Culture in the Historical Perspective." *Southwestern Journal of Anthropology* 9 (1953):76–98.

Sjoberg, Gideon and Roger Nett. *A Methodology for Social Research.* Prospect Heights, Ill.: Waveland, 1997.

Sjoberg, Gideon and Ted R. Vaughan. "The Bureaucratization of Sociology: Its Impact on Theory and Research." In *A Critique of Contemporary American Sociology,* eds. Ted R. Vaughan, Gideon Sjoberg, and Larry T. Reynolds, 54–113. Dix Hills, N.Y.: General Hall, 1993.

Slatta, Richard W. *Comparing Cowboys and Frontiers.* Norman: University of Oklahoma Press, 1997.

Slotkin, Richard. *Regeneration through Violence: The Myth of the American Frontier, 1600–1860.* Middletown, Conn.: Wesleyan University Press, 1973.

Smith, F. Todd. *The Caddo Indians: Tribes at the Convergence of Empires.* College Station: Texas A&M University Press, 1995.

Smith, Herman. "Origins and Spatial/Temporal Distribution of the Rockport Archeological Complex, Central and Lower Texas Coast." *Midcontinental Journal of Archeology* 9 (1984): 27–42.

Smith, Thomas T. "Fort Inge and Texas Frontier Military Operations, 1846–1869." *Southwestern Historical Quarterly* 96 (1992): 1–25.

Smithwick, Noah. *The Evolution of a State or Recollections of Old Texas Days.* Austin: Steck, 1935. Facsimile of Austin: Gammel, 1900.

Sowell, Andrew Jackson. *A History of Ft. Bend County.* Richmond: Fort Bend County Historical Museum, 1974. Facsimile of Houston: Coyle, 1904.

Spicer, Edward Holland. *Cycles of Conquest; the Impact of Spain, Mexico and the United States on the Indians of the Southwest, 1533–1960.* Tucson: University of Arizona Press, 1962.

Spurlin, Charles. "Mobilization of Texas Militia for the Mexican War." *Military History of Texas and the Southwest* 15:3 (n.d.): 21–44.

Stapp, William Preston. *The Prisoner of Perote Containing a Journal Kept by the Author Who Was Captured by the Mexicans at Mier, Dec. 25, 1842, and Released from Perote, May 16, 1844.* Austin: Steck, 1935. Facsimile of Philadelphia: G. & B. Zeiber, 1845.

Stenberg, Richard Rollin. *American Imperialism in the Southwest, 1800–1837.* Ph.D. diss., University of Texas at Austin, 1932.

Surrey, N. M. Miller. *The Commerce of Louisiana during the French Regime, 1699–1763.* Columbia University Studies in History, Economics, and Public Law, Number 167. New York: Columbia University, 1916.

Svaldi, David. *Sand Creek and the Rhetoric of Extermination: A Case Study in Indian–White Relations.* New York: University Press of America, 1989.

Swanton, John. "Remarks." *Proceedings of the International Congress of Americanists* 20 (1922): 53–59.

Takaki, Ronald. *Iron Cages: Race and Culture in Nineteenth-Century America.* New York: Alfred A. Knopf, 1979.

Taussig, Michael. "Culture of Terror—Space of Death, Roger Casement's Putumayo Report and Explanation of Torture." *Comparative Studies in Society and History* 26 (1984): 467–97.

Taylor, Gary. "Tribe is Holding Texas to Promise: Tonkawas Want Land Payback for Help Years Ago." *National Law Journal* 16 (31) (1994): A8.

Teal, Annie Fagan. "Reminiscences of Mrs. Annie Fagan Teal." Contributed by Mrs. Thomas O'Connor. Collected by Mrs. T. C. Allan. *Southwestern Historical Quarterly* 34 (1930): 317–28.

Texas Almanac and State Industrial Guide, 1966–1967. Dallas: Belo, 1965.

Thornton, Russell. *American Indian Holocaust and Survival: A Population History since 1492.* Norman: University of Oklahoma Press, 1987.

Tilly, Charles. *Big Structures, Large Processes, and Huge Comparisons.* New York: Russell Sage Foundation, 1984.

Todorov, Tzvetan. *The Conquest of America: The Question of the Other.* Translated by Richard Howard. New York: Harper and Row, 1984.

Turner, Frederick Jackson. *The Frontier in American History.* Foreword by Ray Allen Billington. New York: Holt, Rinehart, and Winston, 1962. Reprint of New York: H. Holt, 1920.

Turner, Johnathan. *The Structure of Social Theory,* Third Edition. Homewood, Ill.: Dorsey, 1982.

United States Bureau of Indian Affairs. *Report of the Commissioner of Indian Affairs Accompanying the Annual Report of the Secretary of Interior.* Washington, D.C.: George W. Brown, 1860.

Wallace, Ernest and David M. Vigness. *Documents of Texas History.* Austin: Steck, 1963.

Waller, Edwin. "Reminiscences of Judge Edwin Waller." Edited by R. E. Pearson. *Quarterly of the Texas State Historical Association* 4 (1900): 33–53.

Wallerstein, Immanuel. *The Modern World-System: Capitalist Agriculture and the Origins of the European World-Economy in the Sixteenth Century.* New York: Academic, 1974.

———. *The Modern World System, II: Mercantilism and the Consolidation of the European World Economy, 1600–1750.* New York: Academic, 1980.

Webb, Murl L. "Religious and Educational Efforts Among Texas Indians in the 1850's." *Southwestern Historical Quarterly* 69 (1965): 22–37.

Webb, Walter Prescott. *The Great Plains: A Study in Institutions and Environment.* New York: Houghton-Mifflin, 1936.

———. *The Texas Rangers: A Century of Frontier Defense,* Second Edition. Austin: University of Texas Press, 1965.

Weber, David J. *The Mexican Frontier, 1821–1846: The American Southwest under Mexico.* Albuquerque: University of New Mexico Press, 1982.

———. *The Spanish Frontier in North America.* New Haven: Yale University Press, 1993.

Weddle, Robert S. *The San Sabá Mission, A Spanish Pivot in Texas.* Austin: University of Texas Press, 1964.

———. *Wilderness Manhunt: The Spanish Search for LaSalle.* Austin: University of Texas Press, 1973.

Weniger, Del. *The Explorer's Texas: The Lands and Waters.* Austin: Eakin, 1984.

Weston, Kathy. "Lesbian/Gay Studies in the House of Anthropology." *Annual Review of Anthropology* 23 (1993): 339–67.

White, Beth. *Goliad Remembered, 1836–1940: The Raucous, Cultured Century.* Austin: Nortex, 1987.

White, Richard. *The Roots of Dependency: Subsistence, Environment and Social Change among the Choctaws, Pawnees, and Navajos.* Lincoln: University of Nebraska Press, 1983.

———. *"It's Your Misfortune and None of My Own": A History of the American West.* Norman: University of Oklahoma Press, 1991.

———. *The Middle Ground: Indians, Empires, and Republics in the Great Lakes Region, 1650–1815.* Cambridge: Cambridge University Press, 1991.

Wilbarger, J. W. *Indian Depredations in Texas. Reliable Accounts of Battles, Wars, Adventures, Forays, Murders, Massacres, Etc., Etc., together with Biographical Sketches of Many of the Most Noted Indian Fighters and Frontiersmen of Texas.* Austin: Pemberton, 1967. Reprint of Austin: Hutchings, 1889.

Williams, Norma and Andrée F. Sjoberg. "Ethnicity and Gender: The View from Above versus the View from Below." In *A Critique of Contemporary American Sociology*, eds. Ted R. Vaughan, Gideon Sjoberg, and Larry T. Reynolds, 160–202. Dix Hills, N.Y.: General Hall, 1993.

Williams, Walter L. *The Spirit and the Flesh: Sexual Diversity in American Indian Culture.* Boston: Beacon, 1986.

Williams, William Appleman. *The Contours of American History.* New York: New Viewpoint, 1973.

Winfrey, Dorman H. and James M. Day, eds. *The Indian Papers of Texas and the Southwest, 1825–1916, Volume II, 1844–1845 and Volume III, 1846–1859.* Austin: Pemberton, 1966.

Winfrey, Dorman H.; James M. Day; George Nielsen; and Albert D. Patillo, eds. *The Indian Papers of Texas and the Southwest, 1825–1916; Volume I, 1825–1843.* Austin: Texas State Library, 1959.

Wishart, David J. *An Unspeakable Sadness: The Dispossession of the Nebraska Indians.* Lincoln: University of Nebraska Press, 1994.

Wolf, Eric. *Europe and the People Without History.* Berkeley: University of California Press, 1982.

Wolff, Thomas. "The Karankawa Indians: Their Conflict With the White Man in Texas." *Ethnohistory* 16 (1969): 1–32.

Index

cannibalism: (*continued*)
by Anglo-Texan settlers, 84, 159;
anthropological perspectives on,
152; as cultural construction,
130–31; as response to colonial-
ism, 159
Capoques, 14
Caritas, 55, 132
Carrizos, 102–103
Cavas, 23
Cazorla, Luis, 17, 27
Cha-pa-ton, 111
Cherokees, 29, 39, 41, 62–63, 66,
68–69, 82
Choctaws, 7, 28, 39, 66, 84
Choctaw Tom, 118
Clay, Henry, 94
Coapites, 14
Cocos, 14, 16–17, 25–27, 46, 60
Coke, Richard, 118
Collinson, Frank, 74
colonization projects: description,
37–39, 70; impact on Karankawas
and Tonkawas, 40, 42, 60, 61
Comancheros, 42–43
Comanches: location in 1821, 6–7;
location in 1836, 63; relations
with Anglo-American settlers, 42,
44, 57–58, 61, 66–67, 82, 97; 116;
relations with other Texas Indians,
16–17, 25–26, 28–30, 55–56, 59–
61, 74, 82, 84, 88, 90; relations
with United States, 106, 116;
trade relations, 25, 43
conquest: influence of cultural constructions on, 130–32; influence
of geopolitics on, 124–27;
influence of human agency on,
132–33; influence of participation
in world-economy on, 127–30; sociological approaches to understanding, x–xv, 135–38
conquest hypothesis, 135
Coombes, Zachariah, 117
Copanos, 14

Cornett, Ed, 165
Cortina, Juan, 104
cotton production, 41–42, 70–71,
91, 96
Courbière, Andres de, 27
Coushattas, 7, 66, 68, 71, 156–57.
See "Trinity" Indians
"Cow-Boys" (mixed ethnicity, but
mostly Anglo-Texan, bandit
gangs), 71–73, 76
Creeks, 39, 66
Croix, Teodoro de, 27
Cujanes, 14
cultural constructions by Anglo-
Americans: of Karankawas, 36,
46–47, 52–54, 80–82, 165–66;
of Tonkawas, 36, 77, 85–86, 115–
16, 165–66. *See also* cannibalism;
conquest
cultural sink hypothesis, xi
Cummings, Miss, 57

Delawares, 39, 41, 66
de Leon, Martín, 38, 51, 53, 63, 75–
76
DeWees, William, 44, 48–49
DeWitt, Green, 38, 51, 58–59, 61,
63, 75
Diamond, Stanley, 138
Dickens, Charles, 99
Dimmitt, Phillip, 75
Domenech, Abbe, 102–103
Douglas, Kelsey, 66, 82
Dresel, Gustav, 67
DuBois, W. E. B., 137
Duwali, 62, 66

Eaton, John H., 68
Edwards, Haden, 62
Egg, 66
El Mocho, 27, 125, 127–29
Emets, 23
Erath, George B., 118, 119
Ervipiames, 23–24, 35
Ewing, W. G., 73

Fields, Richard, 62
Ford, R. S. (Rip), 85, 115–16
Francisco, 19
Fredonian Rebellion, 62, 156
Freeman, W. G., 109
Frenzel, Frank, 103
Froebel, Julius, 109
fur trade in Texas, 41, 108

Garland, Peter, 116, 118
Gilleland, Daniel, 54
Goldthorpe, John H., 139
Gosata, 77
Green, Cambridge, 88
Guerrero, Vicente, 38
Gumplowicz, Ludwig, ix–x, 135
Gurley, E. J., 118

Hall, Robert, 84
Harris, Annie, 18–19
Harrison, William Henry, 12
Hasinai Confederacy, 7, 23, 25–29,
    63, 97
Hechter, Michael, 138
Henderson, James Pinckney, 94,
    105
Hispanos, 42, 97
historical sociology, 139–43
Hobson, John, x, 136
Holley, Mary Austin, 54
Hord, R. H., 103
Houston, Sam, 12, 63–65, 68–69, 74,
    82, 94, 99
Howard, George, 111
human agency, theory of, xiv
Hunter, John Dunn, 62
Hynes, John 101

immigration into Texas: American
    Indian, 7–8, 39, 60; Anglo-
    American, 38–39, 96, 59–60;
    German, 96; Irish, 39; Mexican, 38
imperialism, x, 136
Indian fear of settler violence, 109,
    163

Indian-hating, 99, 161
Indian hunting, 51
Indian policy: of Mexico, 39–40; of
    Republic of Texas, 63–69, 90–91;
    of United States in Texas from
    1846 to 1859, 96–98, 107, 113
Indian Tom, 105
internal colonialism, x, 138
Ionis, 97, 106

Jackson, Andrew, 12, 68
Jefferson, Thomas, 9–11, 14
Jenkins, 141
Jimson, 111
Johnson, Middleton T., 119
Jones, Anson, 65, 68, 88, 93–94
José Maria (Anadarko), 118
José Maria (Karankawa), 16, 128
Joyoso, 58, 132

Karankawas: berdache, 18, 20; can-
    nibalism, 16, 21–22, 51–52, 83;
    centralization process, 34–35; cer-
    emonial life, 18–19; cultural sur-
    vival in the Rio Grande Delta,
    101–105; epidemics, 53, 155; loca-
    tion in 1528, 14; location in 1821,
    7; location in 1836, 63, 74; mate-
    rial culture, 20–21; physical ap-
    pearance, 20; process of conquest,
    124–34; relations with Anglo-
    American settlers, 45–54, 76, 79–
    82, 91–92, 100–103, 122; rela-
    tions with French, 15; relations
    with Jean Lafitte's settlement, 18;
    relations with Mexican authori-
    ties, 51; relations with Tejano set-
    tlers, 53, 60, 104; relations with
    Republic of Texas, 64; relations
    with Spanish, 16, 26; Spanish mis-
    sions for, 15–17, 25; social con-
    ditions, 80–82; social organiza-
    tion, 14, 18; subsistence activities,
    18, 20, 53–54, 60, 74, 77–78,
    80; survival as individuals, 105;

Prudencia, 50, 53, 60, 132
Puckshunnubbee, 84
Pueblos, 42

Quapaws, 39

Rabb, William, 56–57
raiding as an economic activity, 42–
    45, 56–59, 71–73, 78, 97
Ranchería Grande, 24, 26
ranching, 42, 71, 91, 96
Randall, Lt., 98
rape of American Indian women, 51
Ripperdá, Baron de, 26
Rodriquez, Juan, 24, 128
Ross, James J., 57
Ross, Shapley S., 121
Ross, Sul, 116
Runnels, Hardin, 118

Sanas, 23
Sánchez, José María, 58
Santa Anna, Antonio López de, 63
Savariego, Manuel, 76
Scalping, 48
Schumpeter, Joseph, 136
Seminoles, 66, 97, 113
Shawnee Prophet, 12
Shawnees, 39, 41, 66
Sheridan, Francis, 67
Sibley, John, 18, 22, 29
Sibley, Marilyn, 140
Simon, 111
Simons, Sarah, 135
Sjoberg, Andrée, xi, 142
Smith, Frances, 41
Smith, J. M., 118
Smith, Persifor, 98
Smithwick, Noah, 47, 83, 141
Snyder, Gabriel, 56, 133
Solís, Gaspar José de, 19, 21–22
Somervell, Alexander, 65
Starr, James, 72
Steiner, J. M., 118

Stephens, Sam, 116
Sturm, J. J., 116
Swanton, John, xi

taking on the role of the other, 142–
    43
Tampaquas, 102–105
Tawakonis, 43–44, 97, 106
Taylor, Zachary, 95, 107
Teal, Annie, 53
Tecumseh, 12
Tejanos, 42, 44, 53, 60, 63, 67, 69,
    71, 75, 78, 90–91, 96, 97
Texas: in 1821, 4–5; geographic fea-
    tures, 3–4; incorporation into
    United States, 93–95; incorpora-
    tion into world-system, ix–x, 91
Texas independence, origins of,
    62–63
Texas Rangers, American Indian in-
    fluence (Comanche, Lipan, and
    Tonkawa) on organization of, 83
Thomas, George, 120
Tohahas, 23
Tohos, 23
Tonkawas: at Brazos Reservation,
    114–15, 119; cannibalism, 33, 77,
    83–86, 114, 121, 159–60; census
    at Brazos Reservation, 111; cen-
    tralization process, 30, 34–35;
    ceremonial life, 31–32; destruc-
    tion of the western Tonkawas,
    75–77; epidemics, 27, 89; at Fort
    Griffin, 121; in Indian Territory,
    121–22; location in 1601, 23; lo-
    cation in 1700, 22–23; location in
    1821, 7, 29; location in 1836, 63,
    74; location in 1838, 82; material
    culture, 32–33; origins, 23–24;
    physical appearance, 33; process
    of conquest, 124–34; relations
    with Anglo-American settlers,
    45, 54–61, 75–77, 82, 86–88, 91–
    92, 97, 107, 111, 113; relations